PROBABLE OUTCOMES

Secular Stock Market Insights

ED EASTERLING

Cypress House

PROBABLE OUTCOMES
Secular Stock Market Insights

Cypress House
155 Cypress Street
Fort Bragg, CA 95437
(800) 773-7782
www.cypresshouse.com

This publication is designed to provide accurate and authoritative
information in regard to the subject matter covered. It is sold with
the understanding that the publisher is not engaged in rendering
professional services. If professional advice or other expert assistance
is required, the services of a competent professional person should
be sought.

Book design and production: Mike Brechner / Cypress House
Cover Design: Elizabeth Peterson
Cover photo *Lightning!*: © iStockphoto.com / Soubrette
Cover photo *Dramatic Sky*: © iStockphoto.com / Charles Schug

Library of Congress Cataloging-.in-Publication Data

Easterling, Ed, 1959-
  Probable outcomes : secular stock market insights / Ed Easterling.
-- 1st ed.
      p. cm.
  Includes index.
  ISBN 978-1-879384-82-8 (casebound : alk. paper)
  1. Stock exchanges. 2. Business cycles. 3. Investments. I. Title.
  HG4551.E367 2010
  332.64'2--dc22

                          2010047271

Printed in Canada
1 3 5 7 9 8 6 4 2

Contents

FIGURES

Acknowledgments

Probable Outcomes: Secular Stock Market Insights is dedicated to the readers of *Unexpected Returns* and the visitors to CrestmontResearch.com, who have repeatedly expressed interest in further understanding secular stock market cycles and investment approaches to successfully navigate them. Your challenging questions and penetrating inquiries have driven deeper analyses, enhanced understandings, and fuller insights. Thank you.

Many bright minds, through their writings and presentations, have indirectly contributed to the development of the Crestmont Research concepts as presented in *Probable Outcomes* and *Unexpected Returns*. Although there are too many to name individually, many are included in the bibliography.

Throughout the process, my loving wife, Kelly, has been an encouraging partner, strong supporter, and very detailed reviewer. Her thrice reading went beyond her interest, yet each time yielded significant contributions.

Toward achieving the final result, I would like to express special appreciation to a series of people who diligently critiqued drafts of the manuscript. All of them tackled the book and provided comments that enhanced the content, presentation, organization, and message. The first one to respond also had the most extensive comments: maverick investor Dr. Jerry Lancourt and his insightful wife, Jinna, rendered an immediate impact to both the tone and content. Academic experts and pragmatic practitioners Dr. John Peavy and Dr. Jeff Hart provided numerous perspectives and verifications. Sage Paul Marriott peppered the text with incisive points and emphasis, while all-star financial advisors Lori Bensing and Greg Krpalek ensured relevance for investors. Economists and economic historians Dr. Richard Sylla and Dr. Mark Dotzour delivered detailed insights about economic issues and history. Isaac Presley and Charlie Poznek, with diverse backgrounds in the financial industry as well as being students of financial markets, offered keen comments that further enhanced the text and messages. For Yohn Baldwin, the manuscript represented new ground into an unfamiliar topic, which led to edits that enhanced the book for a broader audience. Returning from *Unexpected Returns* were great friends and challenging critics Andrew Thorby, Phil McKee, and Brent Haggard.

Finally, high accolades to Cynthia Frank and the staff at Cypress House for their extraordinary efforts, creativity, and penetrating detail, which were invaluable in producing *Probable Outcomes*.

INTRODUCTION

Unexpected Returns: Understanding Secular Stock Market Cycles was written in 2004 based upon data from 1900 through 2003. The course of the markets over the past seven years has confirmed the timeless reality of the principles related to stock market returns. Over that time, in the current secular bear market, investors experienced a strong cyclical bull market with low volatility, followed by a dramatic and highly volatile cyclical bear market. It is commonplace for long-term secular bear markets of below-average returns to be punctuated by interim short-term periods that generally trend upward or downward for a few years or less.

Unexpected Returns addressed the concepts and characteristics of secular stock market cycles, periods that often extend a decade or longer. It identified that a secular bear market was underway, and provided the legend to understand its likely course and to recognize when it might end. The book concluded with the suggestion that investment strategy should shift as the market climate changes. Investors, to use a boatman's analogy, should "Row, Not Sail," with more active and diversified investment strategies during secular bear market periods. Sailing, which uses the buy-and-hold approach with traditional asset classes, should be limited to secular bull market periods.

As a new decade begins, investors are asking whether a secular bull market might be on the horizon. Secular bear periods have ranged in duration from four to twenty years, while secular bulls have extended from four to twenty-four years. Now that ten years have passed for this secular bear, especially since the average bear cycle is thirteen years, investors want to know if the next bull market is three years away. Optimistic analysts are offering hopeful data, while wishful pundits have many scenarios for double-digit returns.

Probable Outcomes: Secular Stock Market Insights addresses these questions not only with some of the tools from *Unexpected Returns* but also with an expanded array of charts and insights. Over the past seven years, Crestmont Research has developed new graphics to highlight secular stock market cycles, their cause, and their components. The analyses provide greater details about the earnings cycle, the price/earnings ratio, volatility, and the implications for investors. *Probable Outcomes* is not an update of *Unexpected Returns;* it is an expansion of the concepts, and an application of the information toward a view of this decade, 2010–2019.

During the past decade, several key issues have arisen that impact this secular bear cycle and create significant implications for its future. First, though a decade has passed, the secular bear is not close to being over. The desire for a near-term conclusion reflects a false sense of hope, contradicting the principles that drive stock market returns. Second, two shifts in economic conditions have created significant risks for this secular bear cycle. The inflation rate, which is the driver of the secular cycles, is near zero as the decade starts. It is precariously perched on the fence between deflation and inflation; a significant movement in either direction will have serious implications. In addition, economic growth that once was a stable constant may be poised for a surge or may have downshifted to lower growth. Both conditions have serious implications for the stock market. Third, a significant number of investors have yet to acknowledge the realities of the current secular bear market. For individuals, especially those near or in retirement, this delayed recognition will reduce their flexibility to take appropriate action. For institutions, especially those with underfunded obligations, the delay in making a downward adjustment of assumptions for investment returns will lead to heightened shortfalls and inevitable crisis.

Probable Outcomes does not present a magic investment approach or a new investment strategy; neither does it make recommendations about particular investments, investment managers, nor asset classes. Its objective, as with *Unexpected Returns,* is to foster an understanding of secular stock market cycles, and to prepare investors to successfully address the current secular bear market. In addition, this book does not deliver a singular opinion about the future; rather, *Probable Outcomes* focuses on delivering a sufficiently detailed understanding of the underlying issues and principles. This will enable the reader to make his or her own assessments about the decade of the 2010s. Major uncertainties exist about the inflation rate and economic growth. In addition, many individual and institutional investors hold a persisting outlook of unrealistic expectations. Therefore it's time to revisit and extend the understanding of secular stock market cycles.

SECTION I

PAST AND FUTURE

Those who cannot remember the past
are condemned to repeat it.

— *George Santayana*

Chapter 1

What's Ahead

On January 1, 2000, at the start of the new millennium, hopeful investors expected another decade to complement the one that had just ended. Just before the opening bell, investors and traders alike took note as the baton of a former year, decade, and millennium passed to the next one. The S&P 500 Index (S&P 500) crossed the threshold at 1,469, and the Dow Jones Industrial Average (DJIA) stood at 11,497.

Not everyone expected another doubling of the stock market within five years, as had occurred on average over the previous two decades. Some were more optimistic, while others said a reversion to more historically average returns was due. Of course, there were the naysayers and perma-bears who always spew doom and gloom. The correction is near! Few imagined, however, that January 1 was also the start of the current secular bear market.

Advance ten years to January 1, 2010. A decade has passed, and we are already 10% of the way into the next century. The S&P 500 is lagging significantly at 1,115, while the DJIA has trimmed down to 10,428.

This is a story about secular stock market cycles, the long-term periods in the stock market that deliver wonderful surges followed by wealth-taking falls. The plot is not about the long-term averages across these periods, but rather the details about and within the cycles.

The upcoming chapters explore and highlight the range of probable outcomes for this decade. There are major uncertainties that could either end the current secular bear market or defer it into the next decade. One objective is to help investors solve the puzzle about stock market returns over the 2010s and to assist them through the maze toward investment success.

Investors and market analysts are realizing that the market losses and relatively short-term cyclical bear markets in the 2000s were not aberrations. The emotional roller coaster of market hope and fear that continued through that decade increased the acceptance among investors that the stock market is in a secular bear period.

As a new decade starts, following a lost decade of returns from the stock market, there are three general outlooks for this decade. Many investors and market analysts are hopeful that the next ten years will deliver returns closer to the historical average. Others, however, are concerned that the economy and financial markets will confront stiff headwinds or possibly even further crises. Then, of course, there are optimists who hope that this decade (the 2010s) might make up for the last one by delivering solid, double-digit returns.

Investors who are hoping for average returns or pondering whether the market has reached fair value have yet to recognize that the stock market is not a machine that generates historically average returns over the long term. The reality for all investors is that hope should not be a strategy. The beginning of a new decade is an appropriate time to peer into the future through the secular stock market lens. Despite the dismal performance of the 2000s decade, the current secular bear market is far from over. This secular bear started at a historically high valuation level as measured by the price/earnings ratio (P/E), well into the stratosphere of market valuations due to the bubble of the late 1990s. Ten years later, the stock market is near where it started. The prior decade only served to lower valuations to a more reasonable level of market valuation, albeit still high.

The inflation rate is the driver of secular stock market cycles. Inflation indicates a positive inflation rate; deflation indicates a negative inflation rate. The inflation rate currently remains relatively low, but the tectonic forces of inflation and deflation are causing pressure that may erupt before the end of this decade. In this book, the term "inflation rate" refers to both inflation (the positive state) and deflation (the negative state). The outlook for the inflation rate is a major uncertainty for the current secular bear cycle.

Likewise, economic growth over the past century and the previous several decades had been a steady engine for relatively consistent corporate earnings growth over full business cycles. Trends over the past decade, however, cast a significant veil of uncertainty over this decade and beyond.

The assumption for future stock market gains by individual and institutional investors has slowly declined over the past ten years. Many investors, even those who have started to accept the current environment, still hold hope for returns that, in reality, are out of reach from traditional stock and bond market exposure. Most alarming, defined pension plans and retirement accounts with long-term obligations have yet to recognize the substantial magnitude of the pending shortfalls that will occur as this secular bear continues its course. Depending upon the outcomes of the two major uncertainties, inflation rate and economic growth, those shortfalls could be devastating.

Before getting into the details, the first step is to address the desire held by hopeful investors: long-term average returns.

Aspiring Average

When the stock market reaches its fair value, does it deliver average returns? Many of the reports from analysts about the overall state of the stock market speak of its being this much undervalued or that much overvalued. Investors long for the time when the stock market is fairly valued, as though they could finally receive average returns. After the prior decade, many investors feel like the mouse that has just discovered his misstep: forget the cheese, just let me out of the trap! In droves, investors are ready to forgo the hope of supercharged returns like those of the 1990s for the common average of the past century.

The well-known and most-respected long-term average return from the stock market is the one provided in the annual compendium published by Morningstar—the often-called Ibbotson Series. Consultants, financial analysts, advisors, and investors seeking a benchmark for long-term stock market returns reach for this annually revised testament of historical financial market data.

Toward the back of that book, following miles of data columns and mostly upward-sloping charts, the number that everyone seeks is included in a chapter titled "Using Historical Data in Forecasting and Optimization." It shows that the long-term average return from the stock market is near 10%. Conventional wisdom believes that any number representing more than eighty years of history must be a valid indication for the next decade or two. Everyone knows that the stock market has ups and downs, yet eighty years is certainly enough time to produce a valid measure for the average condition, right? Well, actually not.

The three components of stock market returns are dividend yield, earnings growth, and the change in the price/earnings ratio (P/E); any other elements will fall within one of those three. The discussion of the Ibbotson Series in the Morningstar publication provides the details for all three components and the insights needed to fully appreciate the Average (capitalized to acknowledge its aura as a presumed market truism).

**Figure 1.1. Components of Long-Term Average
Stock Market Return: 1926–2009**

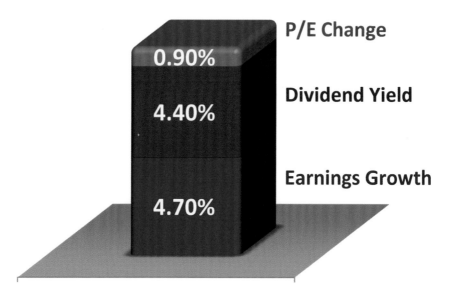

Morningstar updates their *Classic Yearbook* annually to include another year's data into the long-term series. To reduce the distortions from any single set of data, figure 1.1 reflects the average of multiple series for greater consistency. From each of the three yearbooks preceding 2010, the long-term total return from the stock market according to the Ibbotson Series is near 10%. The components vary slightly across the three publications, yet the total return is fairly consistent. Earnings growth contributed 4.1%–5.3% toward the total return, dividend yield provided 4.3%–4.4%, and P/E change added 0.8%–1.1%. Simplifying the ranges, the average values are 4.7% + 4.4% + 0.9%, for a total of 10%, as presented in figure 1.1.

According to the trite expression, however, the devil is in the details.

Most noteworthy, the series begins in 1926. This is critically important because the series starts during a period when P/E was fairly low. Ibbotson's P/E for 1926 is 10.2. Since the level of P/E is such a major driver of stock market returns, the starting level of P/E for this most recognized series is an under-appreciated footnote. If the series had started with P/E closer to the average for the recent decade near 25 (or even at recent levels near 20), then the accepted historical average return would be closer to 7%!

When assessing the contributions of the components to the long-term average, it is worth noting that a starting P/E near 20 contributes a dividend yield closer to 2.5%. The level of P/E is a major driver of the dividend yield investors receive. When P/E is near 10, the dividend yield is twice as high as it is when P/E is 20. That element alone strikes almost 2% from the long-term average.

Further, the long-term average includes a near doubling of P/E. From current levels, virtually everyone accepts that a doubling is unlikely, and many are concerned that P/E may decline from current levels. For this assessment, assume that P/E remains unchanged at currently high levels. By excluding the effect of an increase in P/E, the long-term average is reduced by another 1%.

Taken together, the two issues of dividend yield and P/E change explain the difference between a long-term average of 10% and 7%. Had Ibbotson started the long-term series years earlier or later, when P/E was closer to 20, all of us would carry quite different expectations for long-term returns.

Therefore the long-term return of almost 10% represents the return for an investor who enters the market when P/E is 10.2, stays for more than eighty years when the inflation rate averages just over 3% (to boost nominal earnings growth), and exits after inflation subsides and the market P/E has just about doubled from where it started.

Just like the favorite shirt or outfit that you hope to keep long enough to come back in style, the long-term average return of 10% will be a relic in the back of the closet for any period that does not start from a low P/E. When starting from a relatively high P/E, two of the stock market return components cannot contribute as they did from 1926.

Moreover, fair value is not the precursor to average returns—whether the average is 10% or 7%. The concept of fair value relates to the appropriate value for the stock market given existing economic and market conditions. For example, when the inflation rate is in the mid-range, then bond yields should be in the mid-range to compensate for that level of inflation. Likewise, since stocks are financial assets, the stock market's valuation level should reflect the conditions of inflation. As a result, fair value is a relative concept, not an absolute one. Valuation is relative to the inflation rate; it is not a level that is arbitrarily anchored to a long-term average.

For some analysts, the reference point for fair value is the historical long-term average for P/E. This group of analysts could be called the "reversion-to-the-meanists." They believe that an average P/E near 15 is the magnetic center of the stock market universe. Regardless of conditions, they believe that when P/E diverges from its average, it is either overvalued or undervalued. Though this position may implicitly assume that the inflation rate cycle will be average over time, thereby creating average P/Es over time, it overlooks the granularity that investors should expect for fair value during periods that are not specifically average.

To illustrate, the average temperature in Chicago is fairly mild across the year, despite wide swings from summer to winter. The reversion-to-the-meanists' view of Chicago weather is accurate and valid for full climate cycles, but the mean temperature is not a good proxy for individual interim seasons or vacation planning. Condition-adjusted, or normalized, measures make for a more accurate and valid perspective. Though your mid-weight clothing is appropriate on average in Chicago, you will be much more successful and comfortable by packing to address the city's sweltering summers or frigid winters.

Likewise with stock market portfolios: Investors can invest with a sense of blind hope for the long-term average return, thereby receiving great surprises in secular bull markets and seemingly endless frustration during secular bears. Alternatively, investors can recognize the significance of market conditions and the secular environment to adjust expectations and investment strategy. The reversion-to-the-meanists will be right sometimes, but there is an opportunity to be more accurate and relevant more often by understanding the current level of valuation and its impact on subsequent returns.

A Few Details

This story is one of interdependencies and circular references. That may sound like a cross between a shrink and a spreadsheet, but it means that the material ties together in ways that do not follow a progression in the building of concepts.

For example, condensation on the window of a car or home is the result of warm, moist air meeting cooler temperatures on the opposing surface of the glass. This poses the conundrum: Is the condensation caused by moisture, temperature change, or both? Some say that moist air causes the condensation, while others advocate that it wouldn't happen without the influence of cooling. Before long, the argument will sound like a circular reference.

Should a book about condensation start with a description of humidity or of temperature? Obviously, that depends on what is assumed to be first in order. Secular stock market cycles are caused by several interactions across economics and finance. As a result, the concepts will weave together as the causes and dynamics of secular cycles are explored. Throughout the journey into economics and finance, one goal is to keep the equations to a minimum.

This means that at times the material will be simplified for illustration or explanation, while at other times, the discussions will delve into more detail. The intention is to provide a deeper exploration of the concepts and issues, and to avoid some of the major

misunderstandings about stock market returns that have evolved
from generalization or erroneous logic.

This book is written in five sections. The first revisits some of the
primary elements and charts from *Unexpected Returns.* This provides
the backdrop and context for subsequent discussions about the principles of economics and finance that drive secular stock market cycles. Further, the review will confirm that the stock market is deep
in the throes of a secular bear cycle with significant implications for
this decade.

The second section explores the key measures and drivers of the
economy and economic growth. This provides the background that
economic growth is a fundamental driver of earnings growth, which is
a primary driver of the stock market over the long term. In addition,
the analysis highlights the major downshift in economic growth during the 2000s, which represents Major Uncertainty #1. The discussion
continues into the dynamic of the inflation rate and its role as Major
Uncertainty #2. The section concludes with a review of the relationship between economic growth and earnings growth and the ability
to assess the expected future for the stock market based upon conclusions about the probable outcomes for the Major Uncertainty Duo.

The third section considers how and why the financial side of the
stock market reacts to its economics side. The discussion shows how
the interaction of the two sides drives the price/earnings ratio (P/E),
the measure of valuation that is the primary cause of variability in
stock market returns over longer-term periods. After exploring details
about P/E, the section concludes with a discussion about the myths
and misunderstandings associated with some of the great theories
of the financial markets.

The fourth section begins to apply the knowledge from the earlier
sections to assess secular stock market cycles from several perspectives: a century-long view as well as bite-sized decades. This will dem-
onstrate not only how the machine operates but also what drives its
component parts. In addition to looking at the end result of returns,
the discussion explores the interim course of the stock market and its
turbulence of volatility. Taken together, returns and volatility in secular bear markets have practical implications for investors that are too
often ignored. There are, however, many alternatives for developing

a successful investment strategy. Though this book concentrates on developing an understanding of the market environment, chapter 10 offers a few key points related to investment principles that will assist investors in evaluating approaches for investment strategy.

The concluding section explores the practical implications for various groups of investors, and identifies the probable outcomes for this decade based upon the most likely direction for economic growth and the inflation rate. Though the alternate endings to the story of the 2010s might be disappointing, the script closely follows the typical course of a secular bear market. Investors and advisors who recognize secular stock market cycles can greatly benefit over this decade from understanding and investing accordingly.

As you proceed through the chapters, note that duplication of a concept is done to enable certain sections or chapters to be used independently. In other instances, the goal of reiteration is to promote understanding through shifts in perspective. Further, when the same chart repeats, either it is placed again for convenience or it conveys a second message.

By the end, this book will meet its objectives if it helps you to develop: (1) a deeper and richer understanding of secular stock market cycles; (2) a more realistic and objective outlook for stock market returns over the decade of the 2010s; and (3) a confident recognition that the traditional investment approach of buy-and-hold for the long term should give way to a more active, skill-based, and diversified way of investing.

Chapter 2

Unexpected Returns Revisited

The past ten years have provided a dramatic course for the stock market and financial markets. Before diving into the details that will develop the probable outcomes for the next ten years, this chapter will briefly discuss selected material from *Unexpected Returns: Understanding Secular Stock Market Cycles.* The intention is not to summarize the book; rather it collects key points as background for upcoming topics. For those who have read *Unexpected Returns,* this chapter can serve as a refresher for select concepts and an update of some materials. For those who have not read the book, this chapter provides a few of the major principles that serve as a foundation for chapters that follow. Appendix A presents a complete listing and annotated comments about the ten key concepts enumerated throughout *Unexpected Returns.*

Secular Stock Market Cycles

Well-recognized and published statistics tell us that the long-term return from the stock market has been 10%. The reality is that the 10% average reflects the combination of periods with above-average returns and those with below-average returns. These periods, however, are not random sets of over and under. Rather, the stock market experiences these periods based upon fundamental conditions in the economy and the financial markets.

Further, the conditions are recognizable, and therefore stock market returns are relatively predictable over extended periods of time. These periods are known as secular stock market cycles. The term "secular" is derived from a Latin word that means an era, age, or extended period. Actually, an original Latin variation of the word has been closer to hand than most people realize.

On the back of the American one-dollar bill is the Great Seal of the United States. One part of the seal is the circle on the left-hand side bearing a pyramid topped with an eye. Look closely under the pyramid: there is a banner with the phrase "novus ordo seclorum."

In 1782, Charles Thomson, a Founding Father of the United States, and secretary of the Continental Congress, worked as the principal designer of the Great Seal. There is extensive symbolism included in the seal. When Thomson proposed the seal to Congress, he described the meaning of *novus ordo seclorum* as "the beginning of the new American Era."

When the word "secular" is used to describe stock market cycles, it expresses that the cycle is an extended period with something in common throughout. Secular bull markets are extended periods that cumulatively deliver above-average returns. These periods are driven by generally rising multiples of valuation as measured by the price/earnings ratio (P/E). Secular bear markets are the opposite: extended periods with cumulative below-average returns driven by a generally declining P/E for the market. Thus the secular aspect of these periods relates to the generally rising or falling trend in P/E over an extended period of time.

P/E is the price of the market divided by the earnings of the market. Investors and analysts often apply to individual stocks the same formula used for the market. This valuation multiple essentially represents the number of years' worth of earnings that investors will pay for the investment. During certain conditions, typically when the inflation rate is low and interest rates are low, investors are willing to pay higher prices measured as a multiple of earnings for the market and for stocks in general. When inflation and interest rates are high, or when deflation (negative inflation) occurs, investors are driven to pay lower prices and multiples for the market. In section 3, "Finance for Financial Physics," the discussion goes deeper into the financial reason for those decisions. At this point, it is important to remember that the stock market moves through periods of above- and below-average returns—known as secular stock market cycles.

The secular cycles are graphically visualized in figure 2.1, reflecting the secular bull market periods (green bars) and secular bear market periods (red bars). The blue line below the bars reflects the cycle of the P/E ratio that drives the green-bar and red-bar periods.

The most significant aspects to note in this chart include the variability in time over which secular cycles occur. Some cycles were relatively short, while others lasted close to two decades. This graph also begins to gives us a sense that returns come in spurts rather than a more consistent uphill grind around an average that some people incorrectly believe is normal. Figure 2.1 serves to introduce the concept of long-term secular stock market cycles and to whet appetites for more details and insights.

Figure 2.2 organizes the historical data into rolling ten-year periods. The concept of rolling periods is that each successive period starts one year later than the previous set. The first period is 1900–1909, the second is 1901–1910, etc. The hills in the figure represent periods of above-average returns driven by a rising P/E ratio, and the valleys are below-average return periods driven by a decline in the P/E ratio from the beginning to the end of the ten-year period. The hills generally correspond to the green-bar periods from figure 2.1, and the valleys to the red-bar periods.

This chart presents the effect of secular stock market cycles on decade-long investment horizons. Though a decade is the primary horizon of this book, a decade is also a period long enough that many people accept it as long term. It is also long enough to smooth the effects of the annual ups and downs in the market so the patterns of secular stock market cycles can be seen more clearly.

Additionally, figure 2.2 highlights the significant swings in the average annual compounded return over periods as long as a decade. It demonstrates how the effects of secular stock market periods can be dramatic to portfolio returns. This graph introduces the impact of long-term secular stock market cycles on investment portfolios by showing the high degree of variability in stock market returns over ten-year periods and longer.

Figure 2.1 Secular Stock Markets Explained

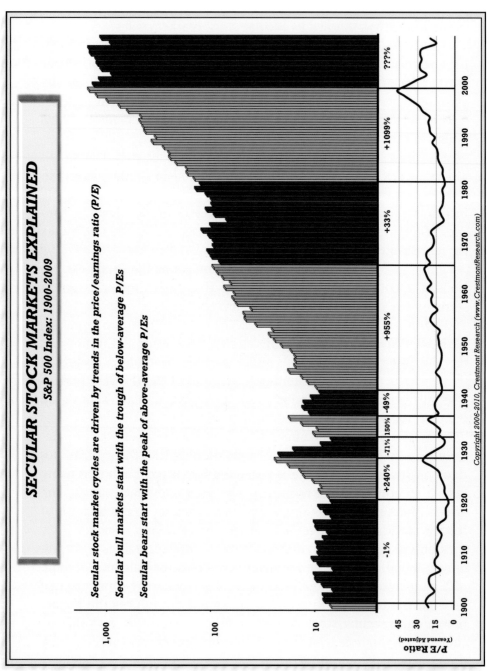

Figure 2.2. Rolling 10-Year Stock Market Return

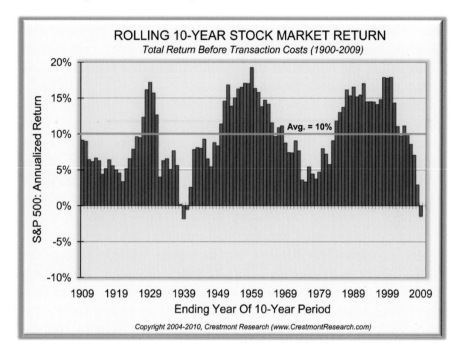

ROLLING 10-YEAR STOCK MARKET RETURN
Total Return Before Transaction Costs (1900-2009)

Copyright 2004-2010, Crestmont Research (www.CrestmontResearch.com)

Current Secular Bear Market

The current secular bear market started in 2000. Its characteristics have been relatively typical of a secular bear market, except for its starting P/E. This secular bear started at an extreme level of valuation that was attained over the last three years of the 1990s. As early as 1996, the stock market actually had reached levels of valuation that are indicative of secular bull ends and secular bear starts. The momentum of the market and dreams of a new economy fueled a bubble that extended stocks to a point 50% higher than a typical secular bull market top.

The first year of the new secular bear was more of a stall. By the end of the year, the stock market had fallen modestly—less than 10%. The following year acted similarly, as though investors were accepting a cooling-off period from the roaring '90s. From the unrealistic heights it had reached, the stock market should have corrected much more quickly. It held up fairly well despite negative economic news and a recession. Though the market generally sustained its level, volatility in the market began to increase further from a slightly elevated level. By the end of 2002, a year of relatively dramatic declines and high volatility, investors were starting to hope that the correction was complete and that portfolios could return to double-digit production.

After three years that clipped almost 30% off of the market, however, valuations had just returned to typical secular bull peaks. Three years on one side of the millennium had simply offset the three-year bubble from the other side. Over the next few years, the stock market rallied. The unsustainable gains reinforced investors' longings, despite high valuations that were getting even higher. Rationality slowly and reluctantly reentered the market. Before long, the climb sputtered despite record reported earnings and relatively low interest rates.

The story from this distance may look clear, while in reality there were—as there always are—lots of conflicting signs and hopeful paradigms. There were times over the past decade when the inflation rate appeared to be rising, but not by all measures. On the contrary, globalization, decoupling, and record profit margins provided enough fodder for the bulls to reign a few years. There were many more factors, all of which enabled any perspective to appear plausible. Nonetheless, all along, the market could not overcome its fundamental principles. The secular bear was grinding ahead with surges and falls that kept the market from getting much above the secular bull high, while it tantalized with hope the notion that another bull run in the market might be just around the corner.

By 2007, market volatility had reached extremely low levels, and risk complacency was pervasive. Hope was at its pinnacle that the long correction after the bubble of the late '90s might be over, but there's nothing like another bursting bubble to get in the way. The housing market and related securities ran out of steam, and before long the financial markets seized into worldwide crises. Stocks plunged again, and then began to recover relatively quickly and dramatically.

Each of the major events over the prior decade was unique—they always are. The exact course of the market and the catalyzing events could not have been predicted. The overall picture, however, is somewhat like a coloring book: the outline is in place, waiting for the details to be filled in.

What is the outline for a secular bear market? This is relevant not only for the past ten years but also for the next ten. To invest successfully over this decade, it is important to understand the market environment. The principles that drive secular cycles form the outline and explain how it is likely to progress over the remainder of this secular bear period.

Secular bear markets are typically flat and choppy periods that generate limited returns. If this secular bear continues for another ten years, then the result will likely be a flat line or one with a slight upward tilt. Either way, investors will not have gained even one doubling from the market in twenty years. This contrasts with a typical secular bull, where each doubling of the market index averages about five years or so. The mental picture for secular bear markets is a choppy ocean with dramatic swells.

Inside these secular stock market periods are the cyclical periods. These are the short-term, interim bull and bear swings that are driven by current news and market psychology. In secular bear markets, the short-term cycles typically run upward for a few years before falling for a year or two. In secular bull markets, the short-term cycles have an upward bias.

Finally, secular cycles are volatile. Even casual observers know that the stock market swings up and down from day to day. Many expect, however, that the daily movements meld into a more stable annual pattern. Yet the swings in the market from year to year are much more dramatic that most people realize. Further, volatility has a cycle, and it too is more dramatic than expected. Though some years have very few days or months that gain or lose very much, there are other times when it will feel like a hurricane. Keep in mind that some periods will be calm and others will have rough seas.

In summary, as the secular bear market continues, expect a decade that looks as flat as the ocean, with waves that last a couple to a few years on each side of the crest. Half of the years will be very dramatic, and there will be periods of quarters or years when the ocean is nearly still or in rough seas. Though this describes the decade of the 2000s, it also reflects the characteristics of past secular bear markets.

Still Not Halfway

Secular stock market cycles are driven by distance, not by time. Though an average number of years can be calculated, the true measure of the position in the cycle is the level of P/E. Once P/E peaks and begins to decline, a secular bear market has started. If P/E stays at or near its highs, then a secular bull market cannot start no matter how long the market stays at that level. A secular bull market requires a doubling or tripling of P/E over an extended period. If P/E starts high, it cannot experience the multiplier effect that drives above-average returns.

There are four indicators confirming that the stock market remains early in the secular bear cycle: high P/E, low dividend yield, low inflation, and low interest rates.

Figure 2.3 displays the historical P/E ratio at year-end for the S&P 500 index from 1900 through 2009. The historical average is 15.5, adjusted for the extreme values of the bubble years. Though the market

Figure 2.3. Historical P/E Ratio: 1900–2009

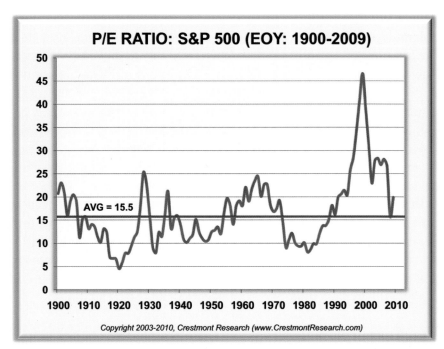

Copyright 2003-2010, Crestmont Research (www.CrestmontResearch.com)

plunge in 2008 drove P/E to 15.4, the surge during 2009 left P/E at year-end standing near 20—well above average, yet below the typical peak in the mid-20s. P/E is the primary measure of valuation, as it reflects the multiple of annual earnings that investors are using to value the stock market. At the start of this decade, the normalized P/E remains relatively high, and is the first, and primary, indicator of high market valuation.

Figure 2.4 presents the historical dividend yield for the S&P 500 index from 1900 through 2009. Dividend yield measures the annual return from dividends based upon the price of the investment. For the S&P 500, dividend yield reflects the aggregate dividends per share of all companies in the index, divided by the price per share of the index.

Dividends tend to be fairly consistent over time, with a growth rate that generally reflects the long-term growth rate in earnings. As a result, dividend yield is driven by changes in the price level much more than by changes in dividend amounts. Most companies recognize that investors desire relatively consistent growth for dividends. During

Figure 2.4 Historical Dividend Yield: 1900–2009

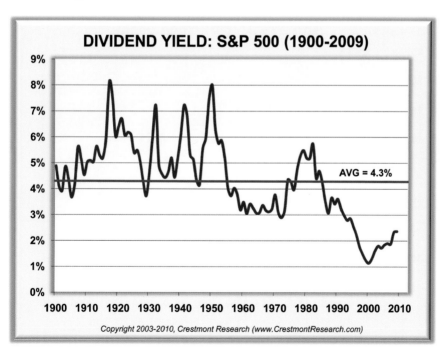

periods of accelerated earnings growth, companies tend to limit dividend growth, thereby improving the chances that they will not reduce dividends when earnings invariably cycle. At the end of 2009, dividend yield for the S&P 500 index was slightly over 2%—still below the historical average of approximately 4%, and far away from levels that would be indicative of a secular bear market end. Keep in mind that the low dividend yield is the second indicator of high price valuation.

Figure 2.5 depicts the historical inflation rate as measured by the consumer price index from 1900 through 2009. The inflation rate is the main driver of price levels for financial assets. Further, the price level of a financial asset is the main driver of subsequent returns. As a result, the inflation rate is the main determinant of return expectations for financial assets.

Investors adjust prices according to their demands for lower or higher returns in response to changes in the inflation rate. Rising inflation increases the level of return required by investors, thereby

Figure 2.5. Historical CPI Inflation: 1900–2009

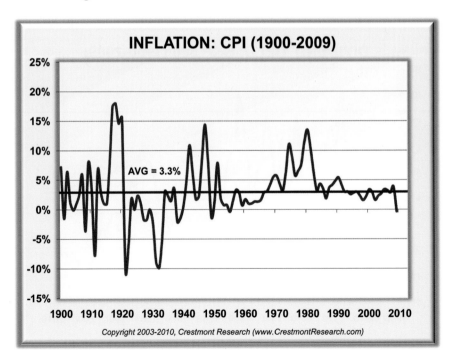

Copyright 2003-2010, Crestmont Research (www.CrestmontResearch.com)

causing prices to decline. When significant deflation occurs, the future growth rate for nominal earnings and dividends turns negative. Consequently, the valuation level of stocks falls. Both higher inflation and significant deflation cause the stock market P/E to decline.

These principles convey that the inflation rate is a primary driver of stock market valuation over the long term. The inflation rate at the end of 2009 was near zero, well below the average of 3.3%. The current level is near the threshold of deflation, and probably a bit below the level of price stability, generally near 1%. Nonetheless, the current relatively low level of inflation is the third indicator for a relatively high level of stock market valuation.

Figure 2.6 presents the historical market interest rate for a U.S. Treasury bond with a maturity of 20 years or the equivalent, from 1900 through 2009. Interest rates reflect the price that investors are willing to accept when they lend money. Since investors want to be compensated for their investment, including the expected effects of

Figure 2.6. 20-Year Treasury Bond Yield: 1900–2009

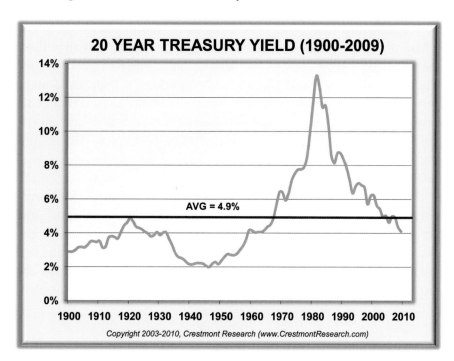

inflation, interest rates provide a barometer of the relative level of return expected by the financial markets. After debt has been issued, and when it is actively traded in the financial markets, the price of the debt constantly adjusts upward or downward to reflect the then current expected return. For longer-term debt securities, including bonds, the market interest rate is known as the yield. The 20-year U.S. Treasury bond yield at the end of 2009 was near 4%, below the average of 4.9%. The relatively low yield on bonds is the fourth indicator of the relatively high valuation for financial assets.

Distance, Not Time

At this point, despite having been in a secular bear for a decade, the stock market has not made much progress, and remains on the front end of this cycle. There are no rules or restrictions about how quickly economic conditions, particularly the inflation rate, can change. This secular bear will end when the inflation rate rises significantly and peaks, or when deflation overtakes us, and then troughs. Note that it is not enough for bad conditions to arise; they must then be controlled and start to reverse before the next secular phase can begin.

The reason to hope it does not happen too quickly is that there are only two courses out of this secular bear. The first is a slow, extended deterioration of inflation rate conditions, which could mean either high inflation or deflation. That allows the underlying economy to grow and build companies' earnings. Under the slow course, the P/E decline offsets rising earnings. The result is a flat, choppy end to the secular bear market over another decade or longer, with few or no gains in the market.

The second course is a rapid deterioration of inflation-rate conditions. Earnings growth will not be able to offer much support, and the market will likely lose one-third or more of its value over a period of five years or so. Yet, unlike 2008, when the decline was due to a financial crisis and not the result of inflation-rate problems, the recovery takes many years—often a decade or longer as inflation or deflation is battled into submission.

What To Do About It

Secular bear markets are not hopeless periods suited only for investor hibernation. These periods, much like winter for the farmer, provide characteristics and challenges that investors can address. Recognition is the first step.

For farmers, the cold, dark months of winter do not provide the rich, vibrant conditions of summer. Crops that thrive in summer barely germinate in winter. Adept and productive farmers know that different crops or different approaches are required as the seasons change. Crops that nearly grow themselves in summer require a much more active approach of selection, greenhouses, and other supplements during winter.

Likewise, adept and successful investors recognize that the stock market has long seasons of secular bull markets and secular bear markets. When the conditions provide the tailwinds of a rising P/E, investors can be successful using more passive portfolios that virtually invest themselves in the rising tide of the market. Then, when the storms of a secular bear market arrive, investment strategy needs to shift to a more active and diversified approach.

Chapter 10 of *Unexpected Returns* is titled "Row, Not Sail" to emphasize the difference in the strategies that are appropriate for secular bear and secular bull markets. When the book was written in 2004, the stock market had already entered a secular bear market cycle. Secular bear markets are storms of upside and downside volatility that leave the market with little progress by their end. The chapter title highlighted the need for investors to adapt to the conditions by taking out an oar to row their portfolios through the choppy waters. The more passive and concentrated sailing approach that had been so successful during the previous secular bull market of the 1980s and '90s would no longer provide the forward progress that investors want and need.

Over the past ten years, the current secular bear market has continued to be a fairly typical secular bear period. It has also shown us that there are likely to be quite a few more years to go. Though passive sailing-based portfolios have lost purchasing power to inflation, many active rowing-based portfolios not only have navigated past inflation but also have delivered real returns. The outlook remains firmly in secular bear territory, and rowing should remain the investor's tool of choice.

Financial Physics

Unexpected Returns introduced a model titled "Financial Physics," which explains the interaction among principles of economics and finance as drivers of secular stock market periods. Financial Physics serves as the framework for the next two sections, and provides the basis to assess the probable outcomes for the stock market over this decade. The model reflects the relationship of three elements of economics, on the left, with three factors of finance, on the right. The relationships among the variables drive longer-term stock market returns and secular stock market cycles.

Financial Physics is best read upward from the bottom. As leadership authority Stephen Covey recommends, begin with the end in mind. On the lower right-hand side of figure 2.7, you will find the first, or actually final, part of the model—the stock market.

In the model, the stock market variable represents the level of the stock market at some point in the future. One of the objectives of *Probable Outcomes* is to assess the level of the stock market in 2019. Conventional wisdom, of course, would say that the market is too random to have even a vague perspective about the next few years, much less about the year 2019. Conventional wisdom is right about the next few years, but wrong about this decade.

For an estimate of the level of the stock market in 2019, only two variables are needed: earnings per share (EPS) and the price/earnings ratio (P/E) for 2019. When EPS is multiplied by the P/E, the result is the index value for the stock market. For example, if EPS for the S&P 500 index is $60 and the P/E is 20, then the value of the S&P 500 index would be 1,200. To forecast the level of the stock market in 2019 therefore requires a reasonable estimate for EPS and P/E for that year.

The interactions of the Financial Physics model provide the framework to develop the assumptions. Three elements of economics drive the two financial components of the stock market.

Figure 2.7. Financial Physics Model

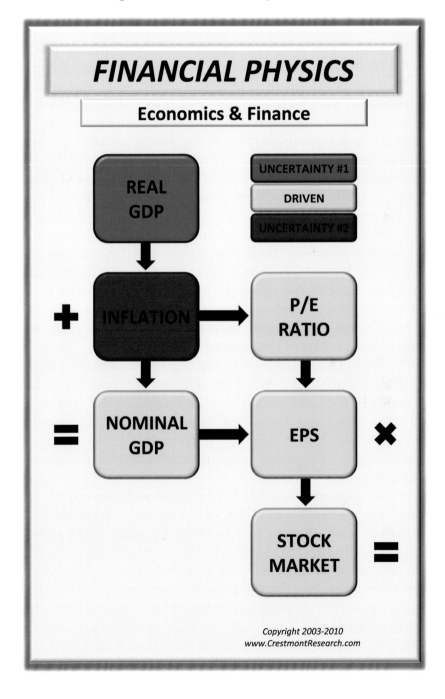

Copyright 2003-2010
www.CrestmontResearch.com

The first variable, EPS, represents profits from companies. For a stock market index, EPS is the net profits of all companies in the index, divided by the related number of shares.

Historically, profit margins have fluctuated across the business cycle. The forces of capitalism cause a cycle of high margins that attract new competitors, only to be followed by lower margins under the pressure of excess capacity. The cycle continues around a baseline level of profitability. Profit margins over the long term are relatively consistent; therefore the growth rate in earnings generally tracks the growth rate of sales. For a diversified group of companies in a broad stock index, for example, the aggregate rate of growth for sales is similar to the overall growth rate of the economy. Since sales and profits are reported in nominal terms, including the effects of the inflation rate, nominal gross domestic product (GDP-N) is the appropriate measure for the economy to use as a surrogate for sales.

Hence the first link between finance and economics in the Financial Physics model is the relationship between EPS and GDP-N. The relative consistency of economic growth provides a more stable variable to drive the EPS estimate than simply extrapolating EPS from highly variable points in the business cycle.

EPS and GDP-N are reported in nominal terms, including the impact of the inflation rate. When the inflation rate is excluded from nominal GDP, the result is real gross domestic product (real GDP). Real GDP has been fairly consistent historically, and is driven by economic factors that lead to its relative consistency. Therefore, long-term forecasts of real GDP growth in recent decades have been reasonably predictable.

In addition to being the link between real and nominal GDP, the inflation rate is the driver of P/E over long-term cycles. Section 3 discusses in detail this second link in the Financial Physics model. Through the two links, the economic and financial components of the model are interconnected, with some of the parts driven by other parts. Historically, the primary driver of Financial Physics was inflation. Due to recent uncertainties about real economic growth, there are now two drivers.

The next chapter explores in detail the economy as a way to assess which of the possible outlooks for the economic growth and the inflation rate are most likely over this decade and longer. There are reasons why economics is known as the dismal science. The objective of the chapter is to demystify economic growth and the inflation rate without grand theories or multifactor formulas.

POINTS OF EMPHASIS

- Secular stock market cycles are driven by changes in P/E, which is determined by the cycle of inflation and deflation.

- Secular stock market cycles are not defined by time, but rather they are driven by the level of and change in P/E.

- Various measures and indicators confirm that the current period represents a secular bear market that started in 2000 and remains on the front end of the cycle.

- Financial Physics is Crestmont Research's model to explain the interconnected relationships between economics and finance that drive stock market returns over time.

SECTION II

ECONOMICS FOR FINANCIAL PHYSICS

Quandary [kwan-dre]: A perplexing circumstance requiring a choice between equally uncertain options.

CHAPTER 3

IT'S THE ECONOMY

Secular stock market cycles are driven by relatively few economic principles. This chapter will concentrate on a broad view of the economy and will employ a few examples for illustration and emphasis. The intention is to be accurate, but not complete — completeness requires finer elements that could complicate the message.

The objective of providing the concepts and details is to demystify the economy and convey that the system is interconnected. The discussion will explore the ways in which the various components and drivers of the economy relate to each other. This is important in order to understand how one issue or action impacts others, sometimes with unintended consequences.

This is not a discussion of economic policy, only of economic principles. Friedman, Krugman, and others can debate policy. Milton Friedman and his wife, Rose, wrote *Free to Choose,* a solid treatise about conservative economic policy. Paul Krugman penned *The Conscience of a Liberal,* a thoughtful, liberal view of economic policy. Both are provocative works, but neither would change the following principles of economics.

This chapter starts with an exploration of several scenarios for future economic growth and thereby future earnings growth — a significant driver of stock market returns over time. The details and examples that follow are intended to help you decide which of the economic scenarios is most likely.

Pop Quiz

Before venturing into a discussion of economics and the economy, pause a moment for a pop quiz to amplify interest in the subject. Beyond the insights from the question and its answer, this will start the journey toward the potential scenarios for the economy over this decade and the implications for stock market returns.

Over the past century in the United States, real economic growth before inflation has averaged near 3% per year. Over the decades of the 1970s, 1980s, and 1990s, the compounded average annual growth rate was 3.2%, 3.0%, and 3.2% respectively. So during the decade of the 2000s (2000–2009), when consumers were loading up their credit cards, homeowners were said to be using home equity like an ATM, unemployment averaged 5.5% and fell below 4% at times, and leverage was being added to leverage, what was the compounded annual growth rate before inflation rounded to the nearest percent?

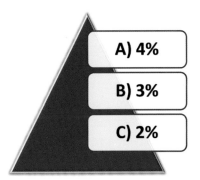

The first choice, 4%, is the most logical response. It reflects the perception that much of the consumption and leverage artificially accelerated economic growth. People that choose 4% expect that the factors in the question boosted economic growth above the historical and recent average growth rate.

Following such a strong period of economic growth, most people answering "A" expect a period of below-average growth over the 2010s to make up for the excesses of the prior decade. They expect that periods during which growth was fueled by debt will be followed by offsetting moderation as the vestiges of leverage and excess consumption are addressed.

The second choice, 3%, is the contrarian response. It reflects a belief that this time was not different. Though some of the factors included in the question may have impacted economic growth, people who choose 3% either don't believe that those factors had much effect, or presume that there may have been similarly unique factors during prior decades. Nonetheless, economic growth of 3% has endured for more than one hundred years and has been very consistent in recent decades. Some people in this group believe that 3% is likely for this decade, while others have begun to adopt the notion of a New Normal with slowing growth due to recent trends in demographics, government policy, taxes, etc.

The third choice, 2%, is the correct response, despite being least selected. Many investors are surprised that the decade of the 2000s experienced compounded annual growth of only 1.9%. Some economists say that it was a decade sandwiched by two recessions, while others blame it on the severe recession of 2008 and the related financial crisis. Yet excluding the recession of 2008 from the decade, the growth rate for the first eight years of the 2000s was still only 2.6%. Further, cumulative economic growth throughout the decade of the 2000s did not exceed 2.7%. It would have required an unusual surge—near 4.5% annually—in the final two years for the full decade to reach the historical average annual growth rate of near 3%.

This sets the stage for a dilemma. Will the decade of the 2010s restore the long-term average by growing at 4%, thereby defying the predominant belief of a slow-growth decade? Was the prior decade of the 2000s an anomaly, with future economic growth simply returning again to its long-term trend of 3%? Did something change ten years ago, and has economic growth downshifted to a level near 2%, or as some might contend, could the rate be even lower due to the economic, financial, and/or policy headwinds in front of us? All three scenarios are plausible, which makes economic growth Major Uncertainty #1.

The answer to the dilemma has very significant implications for stock market returns over this decade and longer. To fully appreciate the implications of economic growth, and to help you develop a perspective about the scenarios, this discussion first explores the left side of Financial Physics—economic principles.

The field of economics is much like the field of medicine: there are many specialties and a range of generalists. Since Financial Physics focuses on key macroeconomic measures and principles, this chapter will not cover supply and demand, price mechanisms, or other microeconomic principles that drive resource allocations or decision-making within the economy. Instead, the focus is on the major factors that drive overall economic activity, and a historical perspective about the overall U.S. economy over the past century.

Why Economics Is Relevant

Why does a book about long-term stock market returns and cycles delve into economics? The stock market is a collection of many companies across a wide variety of industries throughout the economy. Shares of stock represent the ownership of companies that have chosen to register their stock with the Securities and Exchange Commission so that the public may freely trade them. As a result, the price of the stock changes constantly as investors buy and sell it. Thus, the term "stock market" represents the active trading and constant revaluation of the stock of companies.

A fundamental driver of the price of a stock is the profits that the related company generates and is expected to generate into the future. The economy represents the engine that ultimately drives profits, so the story about economics will start with a few examples about the components of the engine and how it operates. Economic growth is Major Uncertainty #1 because of the close relationships between economic growth and earnings growth, and then between earnings growth and stock market returns over longer-term periods.

For this illustration about the economy, imagine an island inhabited by a small group of people. At first, each lives alone and is completely self-sustaining. Each person farms and fishes for food, builds and maintains a hut, and stitches clothing. At this point, the island's economy is extremely limited and provides the people only the bare essentials.

To quantify this example, assume that each individual over the same period of time can farm three units of food, make or repair two units of clothing, and build or maintain one unit of shelter. Obviously, some people will be good at producing food and can finish that task in an hour before spending half a day threading the needle or patching the roof. Others will toil all day in the garden and then quickly mend shirt or shelter.

One day, three of the people decide to barter, trading food, clothing, and shelter. One of the islanders has a penchant for sewing, and is able to create or mend clothing for three in half a day. Another islander lives on productive soil with ample fresh water and sunlight. This farmer can produce three times the daily ration with half a day's work. The third person is fast with a hammer, and can build three units of shelter by noon. These three realize that if they concentrate on their respective specialties and trade with each other, then they can free up more time for leisure or for production. Before long, they start using their extra time to make other products or deliver new services.

Soon thereafter, the islanders decide to specialize in their most productive talents or resources. The result is that the amount of food, clothing, shelter, and other goods increases significantly as each finds his or her highest and best use. In addition, barter becomes complicated and limiting. Food is needed daily, clothing occasionally, and housing sporadically. Barter is more difficult when there are gaps in time between the exchanges of goods or services. To simplify the transactions, the islanders therefore carve shells into coins and establish a system of money.

Before continuing with the illustration, it may be helpful to highlight the basic principles of the economy. First, almost all of an economy is the conversion of labor into goods or services. A fairly small portion of the final goods is basic materials. Even these require labor to extract them, relocate them to the first place of use, and process them into usable form. At the heart of the economy is the function of people working toward producing goods and services.

Second, if more goods and services can be produced, then there will be more products for everyone. On the island, each inhabitant previously worked all day just to have the essentials. Once production increased, then everyone had more goods or leisure time or both.

Third, an economy reflects the transactions among people who work at one task to use the results of their work to acquire all the other things they want. Modern economies use a system of money, rather than barter, to facilitate the exchanges. This concept of money will arise again when the inflation rate is explored in detail.

Returning to the island, ultimately some people start businesses that employ other people to make goods or provide services that groups can do more efficiently than individuals working alone. Some companies are small entrepreneurial firms, while others grow to be big business conglomerates. Regardless of size, companies are simply organizations of people working to produce goods and services. The workers receive wages, and the business owners seek profits to support growing the business and providing an attractive return on the invested capital. At this point, the basic framework has been outlined and can relate to a variety of relevant concepts.

Key Economic Measures

In the island scenario, a complex web of companies, workers, and owners developed through which the residents interacted to produce and consume goods and services. A primary concept within an economy is production. Economists have various ways to measure the quantity of overall production; one of the most common is known as gross domestic product (GDP).

GDP is the value of all final goods and services produced within a country in a year. The measure of final goods and services includes all of the value that was added at each stage of production. For example, a chair that is made from wood includes not only the value of the carpenter's work but also the time and costs of growing the timber that was transported to the mill to be sawn into planks and then shipped to the supplier who delivered the parts for the carpenter to craft into a chair. For 2009, GDP in the United States was approximately $14.6 trillion.

Historically, economic growth has progressed through a cycle of expansion and recession. Expansions are periods of positive economic growth, when the overall GDP increases from one year to the next. Recessions generally are periods of economic decline, when the overall GDP decreases. In the United States, the National Bureau of Economic Research (NBER) is the official organization that designates periods of recession through the review of a variety of economic measures.

Though GDP is one factor, NBER considers others when dating the start and end of a recession.

For this discussion, the concept of economic cycles can be simplified to mean that expansion reflects GDP growth, and recession reflects GDP decline. The expansion periods over the past century have become generally longer, and recessions have become less frequent. On average, the economy experiences approximately three recessions every two decades. There were two in the 2000s, one in the 1990s, two (arguably, one) in the 1980s, one in the 1970s, and two in both the 1960s and the 1950s. In the early 1980s, the two recessions were twelve months apart; the first lasted six months, and the second lasted sixteen months.

When the economic cycle is averaged over time, as reflected in figure 3.1, the U.S. has experienced approximately 3% growth in real GDP, which excludes the effect of the inflation rate. The growth rate has been relatively consistent over time. Note in figure 3.1 that real economic growth for the entire period from 1900–2009 compounded at 3.3%. Further, the growth rate for the previous three decades before the 2000s (the 1970s, '80s, and '90s) all reflect real growth near 3%.

The decade of the 2000s, however, delivered economic growth of only 1.9%. In the past, slower growth decades were offset by above-average growth decades. History could portend a strong decade of growth, averaging 4% or more annually over this decade. Equally possible, the economic engine could have downshifted last decade to a future of 2% annual growth. If the 2000s was an anomaly, then the 2010s may simply bounce back to a 3% rate. The implications for stock market returns are significant, which is why economic growth is the Major Uncertainty #1 for the current secular bear market cycle. The drivers of economic growth, in the next discussion, should provide perspectives about the past and insights for the future.

Key Economic Drivers

There are several ways to assess GDP and break it into component parts. One is to view the economy based upon its essential elements: labor and productivity. Since an economy represents the conversion of labor to value, the quantity of labor is a major driver of economic

Figure 3.1. Real GDP Growth: 1900–2009

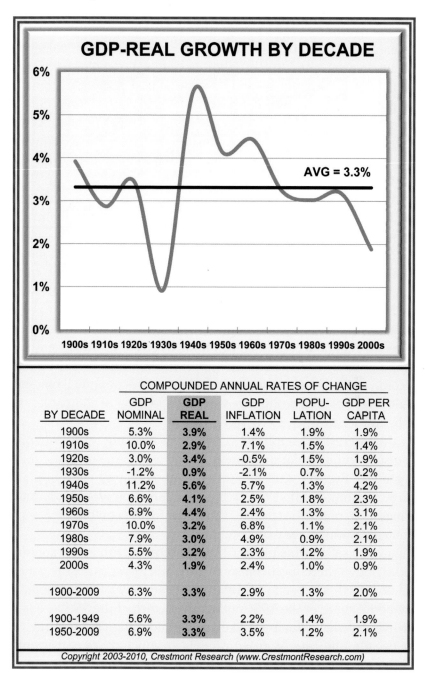

GDP-REAL GROWTH BY DECADE

AVG = 3.3%

1900s 1910s 1920s 1930s 1940s 1950s 1960s 1970s 1980s 1990s 2000s

	COMPOUNDED ANNUAL RATES OF CHANGE				
BY DECADE	GDP NOMINAL	GDP REAL	GDP INFLATION	POPU-LATION	GDP PER CAPITA
1900s	5.3%	3.9%	1.4%	1.9%	1.9%
1910s	10.0%	2.9%	7.1%	1.5%	1.4%
1920s	3.0%	3.4%	-0.5%	1.5%	1.9%
1930s	-1.2%	0.9%	-2.1%	0.7%	0.2%
1940s	11.2%	5.6%	5.7%	1.3%	4.2%
1950s	6.6%	4.1%	2.5%	1.8%	2.3%
1960s	6.9%	4.4%	2.4%	1.3%	3.1%
1970s	10.0%	3.2%	6.8%	1.1%	2.1%
1980s	7.9%	3.0%	4.9%	0.9%	2.1%
1990s	5.5%	3.2%	2.3%	1.2%	1.9%
2000s	4.3%	1.9%	2.4%	1.0%	0.9%
1900-2009	6.3%	3.3%	2.9%	1.3%	2.0%
1900-1949	5.6%	3.3%	2.2%	1.4%	1.9%
1950-2009	6.9%	3.3%	3.5%	1.2%	2.1%

output and growth. Back on the island, if the number of working people doubled from one year to the next, without any improvement in tools or techniques (but with a doubling of existing tools), the quantity of output could double if everyone produced something of value. In the United States, labor growth has contributed an average of about 1% annually—and by some measures slightly more—to GDP growth over the past century.

There are a number of ways to assess the quantity of labor. Within the overall population, there are measures to isolate the working-age population, workforce participation, actual employment, and even average labor hours.

All of these measures have elements of inconsistency at times, and thus do not necessarily provide a completely accurate assessment of economic labor. For example, the working-age population grew as baby boomers entered the workforce. The surge of young and inexperienced workers may not have initially contributed the full economic effect of the average, more experienced worker. If so, the result would have been an increase in economic labor that was slightly less than the increase in working-age population growth. Over time, as boomers gained experience, their contribution as economic labor may have become greater than the simple impact of their numbers. Adding to the complexity of seeking a precise measure of economic labor, more people have pursued productive work independent of companies, and can be harder to track using some measures.

In the interest of simplicity, considering the long-term horizon of this discussion, population growth can be used as a surrogate for labor growth. Even if other measures of labor growth were used, the change of a few decimal points in either direction would not distort the messages of this discussion. When the focus is on principles, precision can be the enemy of insight.

Figure 3.2 reflects the history of population growth by decade since 1900. Though there has been some variability over time, the general level of growth has been slightly over 1% annually. For example, the baby-boom surge of the 1950s offset the dearth of the 1930s. For the past five decades, which are likely to be more indicative of the current decade, the rate of growth has been much more consistent at slightly over 1%. As a rule of thumb for this discussion, the rate of growth attributable to labor for economic growth will be 1%.

Figure 3.2. Population Growth: 1900-2009

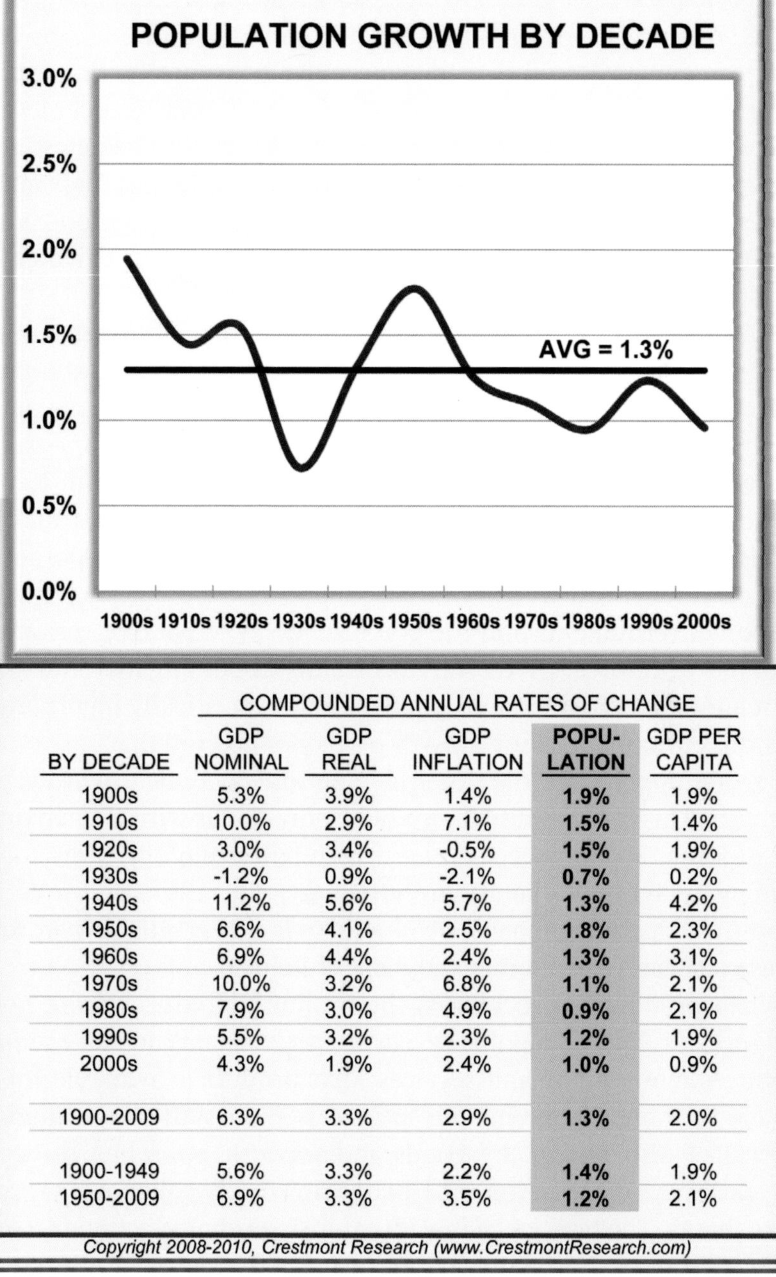

POPULATION GROWTH BY DECADE

COMPOUNDED ANNUAL RATES OF CHANGE					
BY DECADE	GDP NOMINAL	GDP REAL	GDP INFLATION	POPU- LATION	GDP PER CAPITA
1900s	5.3%	3.9%	1.4%	1.9%	1.9%
1910s	10.0%	2.9%	7.1%	1.5%	1.4%
1920s	3.0%	3.4%	-0.5%	1.5%	1.9%
1930s	-1.2%	0.9%	-2.1%	0.7%	0.2%
1940s	11.2%	5.6%	5.7%	1.3%	4.2%
1950s	6.6%	4.1%	2.5%	1.8%	2.3%
1960s	6.9%	4.4%	2.4%	1.3%	3.1%
1970s	10.0%	3.2%	6.8%	1.1%	2.1%
1980s	7.9%	3.0%	4.9%	0.9%	2.1%
1990s	5.5%	3.2%	2.3%	1.2%	1.9%
2000s	4.3%	1.9%	2.4%	1.0%	0.9%
1900-2009	6.3%	3.3%	2.9%	1.3%	2.0%
1900-1949	5.6%	3.3%	2.2%	1.4%	1.9%
1950-2009	6.9%	3.3%	3.5%	1.2%	2.1%

As a final thought on population growth over this decade and beyond, consider the effect of baby boomers entering retirement. This much-discussed topic generally suggests a slowing of economic growth. Some boomers, however, may not retire from the workforce as early as previously projected due to the secular bear market that started in 2000. They may choose to stay employed to supplement savings. Likewise, because investment returns are expected to be below average over this decade, boomers may want to supplement their investment income by working. For others, who rely upon pensions, lower investment returns and underfunded plans have already driven some pensions to contemplate reductions to benefits.

How might this impact economic growth? Some boomers will rely upon supplemental income beyond Social Security during retirement. These boomers often contribute economic production that is generally higher than the average worker's, assuming that compensation is a reasonable reflection of their contribution to production. As a result, one of these retirees potentially provides economic productivity that is significantly greater than the statistically average hypothetical worker. Further research may be needed to assess the expected effect of boomer retirements and the potential delay in boomer retirement from the workforce. Given the uncertainty about any material effect from boomer retirements, that factor is not specifically incorporated into the outlook for labor growth or economic growth.

Beyond population, the other element of economic growth is productivity. This is the ability to produce more goods with a given quantity of labor. Productivity can be driven by technology (new tools), training (making workers more efficient), education, and a variety of output-enhancing means. Productivity is an essential driver to increase a society's economic standard of living.

When productivity increases, the economy produces more goods and services. There's a point herein to emphasize: When an economy produces more goods and services, that product is available for everyone to share. Economic and political policies affect the market's process of distributing the goods and services, but when the economy produces more output, the people in society collectively receive more things. The basic principle is that increased production increases society's standard of living by producing more output to distribute.

Microeconomics, politics, and social policies determine how markets distribute the production.

Economists generally associate the economic standard of living with the amount of goods and services that a population owns or consumes. The standard of living in the U.S. has increased significantly over the past century, with gains during each decade. For example, consider the lifestyle and possessions of today's families compared to those of the 1950s. More families now have multiple cars, larger houses, many more appliances, and numerous technological trinkets. These have resulted from the progressive and compounding effects of increased productivity. As reflected in figure 3.3, productivity in the U.S. has contributed an average of about 2% annually to GDP growth over the past century. Figure 3.3 reflects productivity as measured by GDP per capita. Since this analysis is using population growth as a surrogate for labor growth, the percentages in the graph also reflect labor-productivity increases for the periods presented.

The Bureau of Economic Analysis (BEA) generates GDP data about the entire economy, while Bureau of Labor Statistics (BLS) develops measures of labor productivity for a subset of the economy. At times, the two measures diverge as a result of the different methodologies used by the two agencies. They have already begun to evaluate methods to integrate GDP-productivity data. According to "Integrated GDP-Productivity Accounts," a December 2008 paper prepared jointly by BEA and BLS:

> Two of the most important statistical tools for analysis of macroeconomics and growth are the national accounts (encompassing gross domestic product, or GDP) and the multifactor productivity (MFP) statistics, which measure output per unit of combined inputs. Although they share a common accounting framework, in the United States these statistics are compiled by separate agencies — the national accounts by the Bureau of Economic Analysis (BEA) and the productivity statistics by the Bureau of Labor Statistics (BLS). Dale W. Jorgenson and J. Steven Landefeld (2006) identified the expansion and improved integration of the nation's national accounts and productivity statistics as a high priority of their 'new architecture' for the U.S. national accounts.[1]

Though the BLS measures of labor productivity are often quoted, the advantage of using GDP-related data in figure 3.3 is its consistency with the remainder of this economic analysis. In addition, the GDP-related measure of productivity relates to the entire economy, rather than to selected sectors. Finally, it is more likely that the labor productivity data will ultimately conform to the more comprehensive GDP data. Therefore, though there is value to following both measures of productivity, the GDP-related productivity measure is more appropriate for this analysis.

Under this approach, all increases in the economic output as measured by GDP can be attributed to labor growth or to productivity—an economy has either more people producing, the same people producing more, or a combination of more people and proportionately greater production. Population growth is fairly stable and predictable over the next few decades. Productivity growth as measured by GDP, however, declined significantly last decade. These two components contribute to production in the economy. The recent divergence of the economy from the long-term trend emphasizes economic growth as Major Uncertainty #1.

On the opposite side of production in the economy is consumption. To measure a country's economic standard of living, economists use the measure of GDP per capita (per person). As a single measure, this adjusts for population growth and enables us to see how much more product is being used, and thus produced, across the economy.

Fallacy of Consumption

The press and economic analyses often report that consumption drives the economy. There are many verses to this song. They include: the typical consumer has too much debt and won't be able to spend in the future; tax refunds or stimulus payments will enable the consumer to spend money and improve the economy; or reductions of government spending will hurt the economy.

Herein lies a fallacy created through the misuse of economic logic. Essentially, everything that an economy produces is (a) consumed by people, (b) saved and invested, or (c) used by the government to provide services. If the economy produced nothing, then there would

Figure 3.3. Economic Productivity: 1900–2009

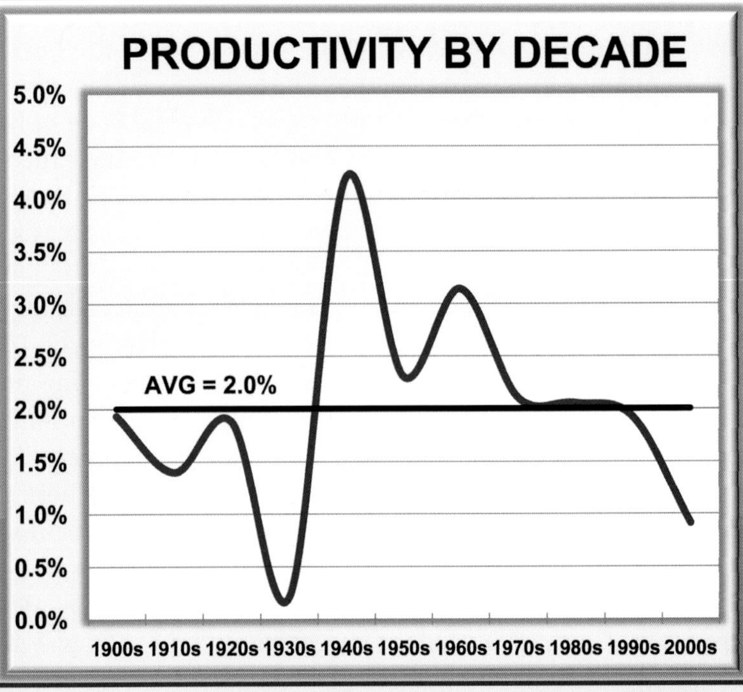

PRODUCTIVITY BY DECADE

BY DECADE	COMPOUNDED ANNUAL RATES OF CHANGE				
	GDP NOMINAL	GDP REAL	GDP INFLATION	POPU- LATION	GDP PER CAPITA
1900s	5.3%	3.9%	1.4%	1.9%	1.9%
1910s	10.0%	2.9%	7.1%	1.5%	1.4%
1920s	3.0%	3.4%	-0.5%	1.5%	1.9%
1930s	-1.2%	0.9%	-2.1%	0.7%	0.2%
1940s	11.2%	5.6%	5.7%	1.3%	4.2%
1950s	6.6%	4.1%	2.5%	1.8%	2.3%
1960s	6.9%	4.4%	2.4%	1.3%	3.1%
1970s	10.0%	3.2%	6.8%	1.1%	2.1%
1980s	7.9%	3.0%	4.9%	0.9%	2.1%
1990s	5.5%	3.2%	2.3%	1.2%	1.9%
2000s	4.3%	1.9%	2.4%	1.0%	0.9%
1900-2009	6.3%	3.3%	2.9%	1.3%	2.0%
1900-1949	5.6%	3.3%	2.2%	1.4%	1.9%
1950-2009	6.9%	3.3%	3.5%	1.2%	2.1%

be nothing to consume or give to government. Once the economy produces and sells goods or services, the resulting money goes either to workers or to owners.

When companies purchase materials and supplies, the payments by one company are another company's revenues. Ultimately, revenues become someone's wages or an owner's savings. The only part of economic value that is not ultimately wages or profits is the value of the original raw material before applying labor. This simplified example ignores the cost of the original raw material, as it is a relatively small value.

Virtually all of what people make in wages is spent on consumption. If it's not consumed, then it's saved. The savings rate in the United States has ranged from near 10% to almost zero, averaging not far from 5%; therefore, about 95% of wages goes to consumption, after the part that is taken by the third component—government.

At this point, you are probably beginning to anticipate where this is going: exposing the reverse logic that led to the fallacy of consumption. Because most of economic production (GDP) ultimately is consumed, supposedly, increasing consumption should thereby increase the economy. That, however, is not necessarily true, nor is it generally the case. Consumption without production is capital destruction. Instead, economic production facilitates consumption, as workers are able to spend part or all of what they are paid. Consumption is the distribution of production.

Consider an extreme example for illustration. Contrast one economy built on the concept of production-without-consumption and another economy that emphasizes consumption-without-production. In the former, if everyone produced without any consumption, all value and products would accrue to savings. Wealth would grow rapidly for workers and owners alike. Obviously, this assumes that the economy was producing products that consumers outside of the economy purchased. In contrast, consumption without production can last only as long as there are savings, or the ability to amass debt—which generally is a passive draw on savings. Ultimately, if consumption is the driver of the economy, without sufficient production to not only support consumption but also provide capital for growth, then the economy will be unsustainable.

Pundits often call for consumers to spend more to boost the economy. The implicit presumption is that families should either (a) save less, spend more, or borrow to spend; or (b) use some unexplained source of money that is beyond their income. With savings rates at a relatively low level and with debts at relatively high levels, consumption appears to be a fair share of production. Future consumption growth is therefore dependent upon future production increases.

Why is this important? When considering concepts of economics and economic growth, it is important not to be confused by the fallacy of consumption. Consumption is a follow-on result from production; it is not economic growth by itself.

Some people will contend that consumption drives production, which can divert you into a circular logic that has no beginning or end. It may sound as though consumption and production are perpetual motion machines that interrelate for ever-higher gain. The reality is that when the economy is taken as a whole, the starting line is always the first conversion of labor-time into work-product that provides value for subsequent consumption.

An economy cannot drive GDP, much less an increase in GDP, for greater standards of living without having the net result across all three variables increase (consumption, investment, and government). If one variable increases at the expense of another, the net result will not be positive. For example, if consumers spend all of their wages, then there will be no savings for investment. The result would be a loss to economic growth. In addition, when government takes a larger share of production though higher taxes, there remains less consumption and investment to support growth in the economy.

Government Productivity

Certainly the title "Government Productivity" will seem an oxymoron or the beginning of a bad joke, yet there are aspects of government spending that promote productivity. The upcoming discussion of economic principles will not enter into judgments about policy, which would be necessary to quantify the portions of government spending that are productive and counterproductive. Rather, it should be recognized that this third variable in the economic equation is generally regarded as a draw away from consumption and investment, which are the drivers of production and productivity.

Though government draws its share in the form of money, the economic effect is that workers commit a portion of their work hours to government. If a worker pays 20% of income in taxes, it is economically similar to working 50 of 250 workdays for the benefit of the government. If government spending is generally productivity-related, then the effects are minimal, since the same monies left to the private sector would have been generally productivity-related. If government spending is generally counterproductive or neutral, then the effects will be negative.

The purpose of raising issues about the impact of government on the economic equation is to acknowledge that the consideration of potential economic scenarios will be impacted by this third variable to the economic equation. If government, at all levels, continues to increase its share of the economy, the impact of government—whether productive or counterproductive—is likely to increase. Regardless of the social benefits or economic fairness, and irrespective of political leaning, it is important to recognize that the current trend toward increased government participation in the economy may affect the economy over this decade.

Final Thoughts

In conclusion, the optimum mix of economic activity is obviously a combination of production and consumption with sufficient savings to drive future productivity. Further, an allocation from production is always designated to government to provide essential and desirable services. The primary drivers of the economy are labor growth and productivity increases. Labor growth tends to be the more stable of the two; historically, productivity has been the larger contributor and the more variable component in the short term. The previous discussions are intended to help provide or reinforce a working understanding of principles of the economy.

Most surprising and unexpected, real economic growth was less than 2% in the last decade. The lower growth occurred despite the misperception that financial leverage and spendthrift consumers in the 2000s made it much higher. The downshifting of economic growth last decade, well below the historical average, emphasizes economic growth as Major Uncertainty #1. Nonetheless, all three scenarios of economic growth (4%, 3%, 2%) are later incorporated into an assessment of the probable outcomes for the stock market over this decade.

Assessments about future growth of the economy should consider the underlying driver of the economy (production) and whether current trends and conditions are likely to promote productivity. The level of population growth is largely known based upon demographic trends. Uncertainties about the recent rate of growth, as well as likely policies affecting the economy, make real economic growth an important variable for assessing the probable outcomes for stock market returns over this decade.

Friedman and Krugman will argue about whether personal free choice or government oversight and control is the best system to drive an economy of and by humans. Textbooks may address the concepts theoretically, yet in reality, people are driven by strong instincts of human nature and propensity. Friedman will argue in favor of a system that encourages behaviors that are beneficial for society overall by incentivizing people to act in their own self-interest. Krugman will argue that selfish behaviors are less than optimal and that government can play a productive role toward orchestrating economic transactions and rules of the marketplace. Friedman seeks equality of opportunity; Krugman seeks equality of outcome. Neither is all right or all wrong. Maybe economics, in theory, should be an art rather than a science; in reality, it is a combination of both.

POINTS OF EMPHASIS

- Economic growth, as measured by real GDP, historically averaged near 3.3% annually, and 3.2%, 3.0%, and 3.2% in the three decades before the 2000s.

- Economic growth is driven by the production of goods and services, which is based upon increasing the quantity and productivity of labor.

- Economic growth in the decade of the 2000s averaged 1.9%, a significant departure from previous trends. While history offers examples of below-average periods that were followed by above-average periods, the lower level of growth may be a new trend.

- Economic growth has significant implications for the stock market and the current secular bear market. It represents Major Uncertainty #1, which ultimately will be one of the two major factors driving the probable outcomes for this decade.

CHAPTER 4

INFLATION INFATUATION

A significant fear of inflation entered the spotlight during the late 2000s as energy and commodity prices soared to new highs. Pundits preached pessimism about a new era of inflation. Core measures of the inflation rate, however, sent other signals: the isolated price increases of energy, food, and shelter had not permeated overall general conditions.

A year later, the deflation dragons depressed audiences with reminiscences of the Great Depression, yet core measures of the inflation rate plodded along at subdued levels. How did the concepts of price increases and the inflation rate get so convoluted?

The first step is to distinguish between price increases and the inflation rate. Price increases occur when there is an imbalance between the supply and demand for a particular product or service. Prices are a great communicator of market conditions. For example, when corn is abundant in the summer—that is, when supply is high relative to demand—prices fall and consumers can readily find corn on sale. In winter, when supplies are relatively less available, corn becomes more expensive.

In contrast, inflation is the thief of purchasing power. Inflation relates to the overall level of prices across an economy rather than the level of prices for selected items. For example, reflect back upon the cost of things that you bought in 1990. While you're at it, think about everything you purchased during 1990. Now, hypothetically, take that amount of money in cash and place it in an envelope.

Roll the example forward two decades. Though your tastes and preferences have obviously changed over the past twenty years, pretend that you repeat your purchases from 1990 over the next year. Take out the envelope and start spending. The typical measure of the consumer inflation rate indicates that you will run out of money in about seven months. One hundred 1990 dollars buy just under sixty dollars' worth of goods and services today. Some things are higher in price while others are less expensive. The measure for the inflation rate, however, relates to the total basket of purchases.

In other terms, based upon readily accepted measures of the inflation rate, an item that cost $1 in 1990 would cost about $1.75 today. The increase in overall prices from one period to the next is the concept of inflation, which represents an overall loss of purchasing power.

The inflation rate is the major villain and antagonist in this story. It is important to probe a bit into his past and to understand his personality and propensities. Price increases may be high-profile cameos or distractions to the plot, but the inflation rate is a significant determinant of how the story will end. The inflation rate represents Major Uncertainty #2 in the current environment, and will have significant implications for the probable outcomes of the current secular bear cycle and stock market returns over this decade.

Inflation in the Economy

The inflation rate is an economic issue with several financial implications. Milton Friedman, a well-recognized and respected economist, identified that inflation is a monetary phenomenon. To explain the concept of the inflation rate in monetary terms, it may be helpful to return to the island economy.

Near the end of the story, the islanders had fashioned money by carving shells into coins. Before long, the people were exchanging a coin for corn, two coins for a shirt, and many coins for a hut. Money, on the island and in the modern economy, is nothing more than a medium of exchange.

The value of money is limited to the relative value of all items in the economy. In other words, money is just an instrument to facilitate the barter of all goods and services across the economy. Therefore the overall value of money is driven by the quantity of money in relation to the quantity of goods.

For each specific good or service, consumers decide through market transactions whether the hour of a plumber is worth a shirt or an ear of corn. Nonetheless, at any point in time, there are a given number of coins to facilitate a certain amount of trade.

Consider the effect of creating an extra coin for every coin that existed. On January 1, assume that each holder of a coin is given another of equal denomination. Will everyone suddenly be twice as rich? Can everyone suddenly afford twice as many goods? Absolutely not. Businesses will suddenly realize that people have twice as many coins, and the value of money has been reduced by half. The exchange of a plumber's hour for a shirt will remain the same, yet the relative number of coins for the plumber's hour will adjust to the new quantity of coins circulating in the system. If the new coins had created any value, there would be a strong drive to strike an infinite number of coins. In reality, the new coins only serve to dilute the value, or purchasing power, of existing coins. In addition, the uncertainty created by such monetary inflation only further drives bad economic decisions, and escalates compensating actions including price increases, hoarding, leveraging, etc. Once started, inflation is like a wildfire with miles of tinder out front.

The inflation rate is a principal concept toward understanding and anticipating secular stock market cycles. The nuances of the inflation rate are less important than a general, yet accurate, appreciation for the concept. Before selecting a measure of the inflation rate, several of them will be considered and two will be closely compared for validity. Since the future inflation rate is Major Uncertainty #2, it is important to have a reasonably accurate measurement of past and future trends and potential risks.

Measures of Inflation

Economists have their own favorite measures of the inflation rate. Some prefer measuring prices at the wholesale level (e.g., the producer price index and the commodity price index). Others prefer measures at the retail level (e.g., consumer price index [CPI] and personal consumption expenditures [PCE]), and still others assess it on an economy basis (e.g., gross domestic product [GDP] deflator). Within these various series, there are numerous variations that either exclude certain volatile components from the broad index (e.g., core CPI) or exclude extreme values within the broad index (e.g., trimmed mean PCE). There is no need to memorize or decipher the alphabet soup of inflation acronyms. For this analysis, the choices can be quickly narrowed. The purpose of identifying the plethora of measures is to acknowledge that many alternatives exist and to provide exposure to the range of choices.

For this analysis of financial market and economic history, it is desirable to have a measure with a credible reputation and extensive history. The focus is on the general trend over time rather than precision or timely monthly signals. Monetary policymakers may want measures that reduce the month-to-month distortions, yet most of the analyses in this book relate to longer cycles and annual periods.

The primary measure of the inflation rate used in Crestmont Research work is the broadest and most comprehensive measure of the consumer price index, CPI-U (consumer price index, all urban consumers). Throughout these discussions and across the analyses and charts, this measure will be referenced as CPI. The U.S. Bureau of Labor Statistics (BLS) produces the index. It is the most common measure reported by the national media, and is actively used by economists. The BLS provides monthly and annual history starting from 1913, and other comparable series can be used to extend the inflation index history to 1900 or earlier.

Figure 4.1 displays the cumulative index value and annual change for CPI from 1900 through 2009. The cumulative index reflects the compounding effect of the inflation rate over time—the cumulative loss of purchasing power. From inflation alone, a dime in the mid-1940s could buy as much as a dollar today. A nickel in the mid-1910s had the purchasing power of a dollar today. If, for example, your grandparents had buried $100 in a coffee can in 1915, they could buy only half as many items when they unearthed it in 1945. They may have been disenchanted by the loss of purchasing power—not appreciating the concept of inflation—so they buried it for you to find in 2009, hoping that it would have grown back its lost value.

Figure 4.1. Inflation History: Cumulative and Changes

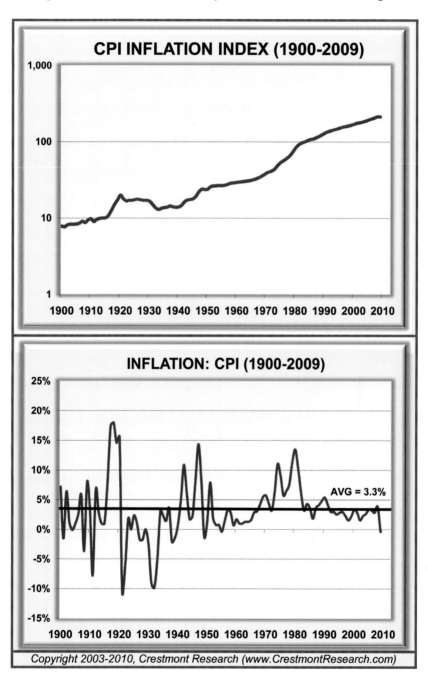

Of course, by the time you spent the money, it would purchase only the equivalent of $5 from 1915. In other words, the mixed bag of goods and services that your grandparents could buy with $100 in 1915 cost about $2,000 in 2009.

Keep in mind that financial assets are simply savings for future purchases or investment. When you later decide to spend your savings or the income from it, if you have not increased your nest egg to cover inflation, you will suffer a decline in lifestyle and purchasing power.

Some people do not consider the risks and effects of the inflation rate when they retire. Upon retiring in their early sixties, almost half of them will live another thirty years or longer. If the cost of your lifestyle continues to increase at the rate of inflation, assuming historically average inflation, you will be able to afford only half as much food, clothing, shelter, and fun over your retirement.

Another reason to extend the discussion on inflation is to emphasize not only that inflation dilutes the spending power of savings over time but also that financial assets aggressively react to changes in the threats from inflation. This is discussed further in chapter 6.

A Second Measure

Components of economic growth provide a second measure of the inflation rate. As discussed earlier, economic growth can be measured in real terms, excluding the effect of the inflation rate, and in nominal terms, which includes the inflation rate. The first measure, real GDP (GDP-R), is the typical value that is reported by government analysts and the press, since it reflects the increase in the quantity and value of goods and services. The second measure, nominal GDP (GDP-N), reflects the actual price of all goods and services including the overall price increases represented by the inflation rate. As a result, the difference between the two measures, real and nominal GDP, is a measure of the inflation rate.

This measure of the inflation rate is known as the GDP deflator (GDP-D). The main difference between GDP-D and CPI is the underlying basket of goods and services used for each index. The GDP deflator represents the inflation rate index for goods and services produced in a particular year based upon a prior base year. For example, the deflator for this year reflects this year's production at last year's prices. The difference is presented as a percentage.

CPI uses a fixed basket of goods and services that is intended to profile consumers' purchases regardless of what they actually purchase in a given year. The basket is changed over time, yet it is intended to provide a measure of price changes for a diverse basket of goods. For example, the basket might include one pound of chicken, one pound of beef, two shirts, cell phone charges, etc. The price of the basket is measured this month and last month, and then the overall price change is reflected as a percentage.

Figure 4.2. Inflation Measures Compared: CPI and GDP Deflator

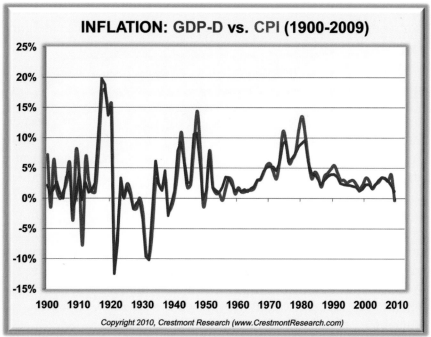

Over time, the two indexes reflect fairly similar levels of inflation, because the inherent difference between the two measures averages out over time. CPI does not reflect consumer substitutions that occur between periods. From the example above, if consumers eat two pounds of chicken rather than a combination of chicken and beef, the GDP deflator adjusts to the actual economy of all chicken while the CPI maintains the mixed basket. Of course, the CPI essentially expects that consumers will later rebalance the beef consumption. In the short run, there are differences, yet as figure 4.2 reflects, the two measures are very similar over time.

The consistency of the measures, given the differences in their approach and methodology, provides reassurance for the validity of both. For short-term policy decisions or for specific applications, one of these measures or one of the many other measures may be a more applicable choice. When assessing the impact of the infla-tion rate on the stock market over secular periods, either of these two overall inflation indexes is appropriate. In general, the analyses that follow will include CPI since it is a more publicly recognized index. This discussion about the GDP deflator serves to confirm CPI as a credible measure and to show that there is at least one good alternative.

Risks of Inflation

For secular stock market cycles and for the outlook over this decade, the primary concern is the general trend in the inflation rate rather than the change over a given month or year. Even during decades when the inflation rate rose or fell, it did not always rise and fall consistently each quarter or year. The financial markets are more concerned with the general direction of the trend rather than the intermediate aberrations. Therefore, looking out to 2019, what are the risks of inflation? The following are just a couple of the many un-predictable issues that make the inflation rate Major Uncertainty #2.

One issue is the dual mandate of the U.S. monetary authority, the Federal Reserve Board and Federal Reserve System — collectively, the Fed, which operates with coequal mandates of stable prices (no/low inflation) and maximum employment (low unemployment). When-ever there are two equal mandates, even when they are only indi-rectly related, performance toward one mandate often compromises the other as the authorities attempt to either fully achieve one or partially achieve both.

If the employment mandate receives even a slight bias over the inflation mandate, then the result for the second mandate will be worse than it could have been otherwise. If the focus is compromised away from inflation control, then the risk of inflation increases. The point of the past few comments is not a judgment about whether the policies are appropriate, only that an approach that includes multiple objectives necessarily increases the risk of underperformance or failure on any single objective.

As this decade begins, unemployment is relatively high. The inflation rate is relatively low. The Fed will be adding new voting members—which adds an element of uncertainty about the balance of future Fed policy between the employment mandate and the inflation mandate. If the policy begins to shift toward the employment mandate considering the current circumstances of high unemployment and low inflation, there is the potential for acquiescence to higher inflation.

Another argument for higher inflation includes the current outlook for substantial ongoing federal government deficits. Federal deficits are not necessarily inflationary, yet the ultimate outcome for perpetual deficits generally results in inflation. A temporary deficit that is subsequently repaid can be managed to avoid monetization and thus would avoid inflation. Permanent or perpetual deficits, however, ultimately lead to inflation. At this point, in 2010, there appears to be a significant risk of ongoing deficits.

But Do Deficits Matter?

There is general concern that deficits ultimately lead to inflation; however, not all deficits are created equal. If, for example, the national economy is $1,000, national debt is $500, and the annual deficit is $5, is a 1% increase in the national debt inflationary? If the economy is growing at 5% (3% real growth plus 2% inflation), then the economy will produce $1,050 in the following year. If the national deficit increases by $5 to $505, then the ratio of national debt to income will fall from 50% to 48%. Over the long term, this would ultimately lead to a very low debt ratio.

If, on the contrary, the annual deficit is 10% of outstanding debt (i.e., $50), then the debt ratio will increase to more than 52% after the first year. If the annual deficit persisted at this level, the debt ratio would ultimately increase to unsustainable levels.

Deficits and debt become a significant inflation issue when they add to the money supply. The term "monetize" refers to the creation of money, often referencing the process by which deficits are permanently funded with government debt. When deficits are monetized, they add to the money supply. If monetization creates money growth that exceeds economic growth, then the result is inflation.

On the contrary, even though deficits that grow slower than the economy create additional money supply, there is a need for even greater monetary growth to support the higher rate of economic growth. As a result, the Fed can recognize fiscal policy's contribution to monetary growth, limit the monetary policy contribution to the growth in aggregate money supply, and thereby control inflation. In other words, when the demand for money growth exceeds the money supply from fiscal deficits, the Fed still has room to control inflation by limiting its contribution to the money supply.

Deficits do matter, but only to the extent that they cause the national debt ratio to increase or to the extent that they compromise the Fed's flexibility toward controlling the growth of the money supply and inflation. As this decade starts, ongoing deficits and excessive debt growth represent significant issues and risks toward future inflation. Excessive debt growth is another major issue impacting the inflation rate as Major Uncertainty #2.

Deflation Gets Its Due

Deflation, which is negative inflation, is a general decline in prices across the economy. Who doesn't want everything to be cheaper?

Unfortunately, the implication of all prices being lower under deflation also generally means that wages are lower. Consider the effects if the prices of all goods fell 10% next year while your wages also fell 10%. If that was all that happened, then you could be indifferent. The purchasing power of your wages would remain the same and you would be able to have the same standard of living.

In reality, the result is not a steady balance of purchasing power, albeit at declining price levels. For example, debt has a price that is set by the terms of the loan document. When the prices of items throughout the economy are declining due to deflation, the stated amount of debt remains fixed. In many instances, debts are collateralized by assets. Almost all of the time, the interest and principal related to debts are serviced by income. When deflation causes both asset prices and nominal income levels to decline, the ultimate result is loan defaults and increasing pressure on asset values as lenders liquidate foreclosed collateral.

Another example relates to corporate and government obligations, including labor contracts and defined benefits under retirement plans. In both instances, the obligations often are stated in contracts that do not permit downward adjustments with deflation. As a result, the obligations remain fixed, or possibly even increasing, under their stated terms. When the funding sources decline under deflation, the result creates shortfalls to the profits of companies and the budgets of governments. There are many other examples throughout the economy in which disruptions occur due to deflation; thus it is a highly destructive and undesirable condition.

Furthermore, an expected trend of declining prices and wages fuels behaviors that exacerbate the condition. Deflation, as well as inflation, tends to trend due to built-in reinforcement mechanisms and people's actions. The inflation rate in either direction, and especially for deflation, is not a condition that can be switched on and off.

To illustrate the drivers in the inflation-rate cycle, the discussion returns to the impact of money supply. It is more than simply the money in banks and wallets. There is another factor that impacts the supply of money, one that has particular effects on deflation. This is known as velocity, which relates to the number of times that the units of money circulate in a year. Over time, velocity is relatively consistent. To achieve $100 of economic activity in a year, it may take only $50 in monetary units. The first person buys from the second who in turn buys from the third and so on. The same money can change hands multiple times during the year, supporting the overall economic activity during that year.

Velocity is important because the effective quantity of money is equal to the units of money multiplied by its velocity. If the previous $50 is circulated twice in a year, then it will support $100 of economic activity.

For example, consider the game of Monopoly, in which players move around the board buying and building properties. A fixed amount of money is available, but the players are able to use it repeatedly to transact business. If each round of the board represents a year, then velocity would be the total value of all transactions during the round, divided by the amount of available money.

In the U.S. economy, the value of transactions during a year, as measured by nominal GDP, is about two times as large as a common measure of money supply. Therefore, from the original example, when $50 supports $100 in annual transactions, the velocity is 2. This is important because the inflation rate relates to the quantity of money in relation to available goods. When $50 circulates twice, the effective quantity of money is twice the counted supply. The inflation rate is driven by the effective quantity of money.

If velocity changes, then there is a change in the effective quantity of money. When the quantity of money changes in relation to the level of economic activity, inflation or deflation ultimately follows. There are few instances that suddenly and significantly accelerate velocity; thus velocity change is generally not a cause of inflation. If velocity recovers after it has declined, especially after a period of significant monetary infusion, rising velocity certainly could be a compounding agent for inflation.

Economic events that spark deflation, however, can drive a destructive process of further deflation. As deflation starts, there is a tendency for borrowers to repay debts. During deflation, assets enter a trend of declining value. Debts represent a fixed amount of money, plus interest. If asset values are falling while debts are constant or rising due to interest, then there is a propensity to sell assets to pay debts. These asset sales can further depress asset values, and the repayment of debts can decrease the available units of money. Further, when prices in the economy are falling, people will tend to delay purchases — expecting goods to be less expensive next month than they are today. The delay in purchases across the economy slows the velocity of money. Deflation reinforces more deflation as money units decline while velocity slows. This combination of fewer units of money and slower turnover reduces the effective money supply and thereby reinforces deflation.

Deflation is an undesirable process because it reflects ever-lower prices in the economy. Lower prices and profits result in declining stock prices. Deflation is a challenge for the Fed to address. Many of the traditional tools of monetary policy are ineffective in deflation. It is not important for this discussion of secular stock market cycles to continue further into aspects of deflation or the ways to address it. The most significant points to understand are that deflation is self-reinforcing and that it has a negative effect on P/E ratios.

In summary, inflation and deflation typically trend toward more of that same condition; they are not temporary disruptions. Systemic inflation and deflation become anticipated, so individuals never have a chance to get in front of the wave. By definition, the wave is in front of everyone, not just the other guy. As a result of its risks and effects, the inflation rate not only is the villain but also is Major Uncertainty #2.

POINTS OF EMPHASIS

- The inflation rate results from changes in the balance between the quantity of goods in an economy and the quantity of money to support the exchange of goods.

- Inflation occurs when money increases faster than the economy; deflation occurs when money increases slower than the economy or declines in relation to the economy.

- The quantity of money is the money supply multiplied by the turnover velocity of money in the economy.

- The inflation rate at the start of 2010 was near zero, precariously positioned for a decline into deflation or a rise to an undesirable level of inflation... or it could stay near price stability. Therefore the inflation rate is Major Uncertainty #2 confronting the stock market and the current secular bear cycle; it will be one of the two major factors ultimately driving the probable outcomes for this decade.

CHAPTER 5

EARNINGS RECYCLED

In the Financial Physics model, earnings represent a primary connection point between economics and finance. Earnings in the aggregate are ultimately driven by economic growth, and in the end provide the annual cash flows that drive stock prices. This discussion starts with a look at the economics side of the relationship and then shifts to the finance side.

When the effects of the inflation rate are added to the real growth in the economy, the result is nominal gross domestic product (GDP-N). If the inflation rate is positive, then GDP-N will be higher than real growth. On the contrary, during deflation, GDP-N is lower than real economic growth and can actually decline in current dollars despite increases in real output.

All prices, wages, revenues, and profits are transacted in nominal terms. As previously discussed, the term "real" reflects hypothetical prices without the effect of the inflation rate, and the term "nominal" means the actual prices. Though GDP is provided in both real and nominal terms to account for increases in the quantity of goods produced as well as their actual value, references to corporate revenues and earnings are generally stated in nominal terms.

One of the most fundamental aspects of investing in the stock market is that investments represent ownership in companies that are expected to deliver returns through the production of earnings. Earnings—also referred to as profits—provide capital to businesses to support growth, as well as cash to shareholders in the form of dividends.

Consider, for example, the value of a hypothetical company with the following assumptions: the stock price is $25 per share, earnings per share is $1.25, and dividends are about $0.50 per share. You are one of many shareholders. This could be a company with $1 billion in revenues, employing thousands of people, paying tens of millions of dollars in taxes, and generating $50 million in profits. Your shares are among more than 40 million shares that are held by all of the company's owners.

Assume for a moment that the company reorganizes as a nonprofit company. It lowers its prices by the amount of the distributed profits — about 2% or so. Though the typical company has after-tax profits greater than 2%, profits that are retained to support growth or to replace assets do not create value if the company will never have distributable profits. Without profits to distribute, assuming that all retained profits are required for growth, the company will essentially be a nonprofit entity. A nonprofit company that becomes ten times its former size still remains a nonprofit. Additionally, the new value for the stock of the nonprofit company will be zero, since an investor will never receive a return on the investment.

This example illustrates the impact of permanently eliminating distributable profits, and has two purposes. The first is to emphasize the notion that big, publicly traded companies are more than impersonal financial assets; they represent organizations of people working to deliver products or services that are sufficiently valuable to customers. Second, the value of the company is highly dependent upon the company's ability to ultimately generate distributable profits. Mature companies often have profits and pay dividends. Early stage companies or unprofitable giants generally have value if they are expected to make profits ultimately. Stocks do not require constant profits and dividends to have value, but they do need to generate, or have the expectation of generating, distributable cash flow at some point in the future. Upcoming chapters address how the price of the stock relates to the amount of earnings. For now, the objective is to identify profits at their point of origin and then extend this discussion to a higher-level consideration of overall profits for companies in the stock market.

Economy and Earnings

Without spending a lot of time reiterating past discussions about the economy, a series of graphical illustrations will help segue from GDP-N to earnings per share (EPS). Figure 5.1 presents nominal GDP, the combination of real GDP from figure 3.1, and the GDP deflator, as a measure of the inflation rate, from figure 4.2. GDP-N is a measure in actual dollars of the economic value produced annually in the United States.

Figure 5.1. Nominal GDP: 1900–2009

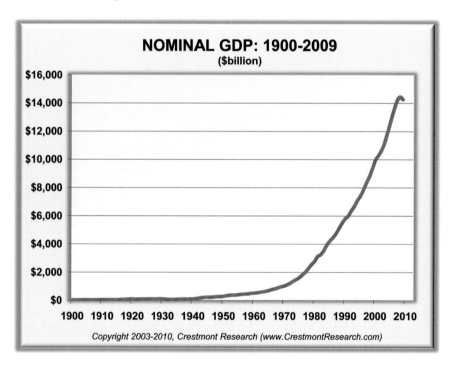

GDP-N, like most other cumulatively increasing series, exponentially arches upward due to the compounding effects of growth. For example, assume that GDP-N starts at $100. Next, assume that GDP-N grows at 3% per year—initially the growth is $3 (3% of $100). Without the powerful effects of compounding, the series would progress as $100, $103, $106, $109, etc., and would be $190 in thirty years.

The reality, however, is that the dynamic of compounding accelerates the growth a little each year to cumulatively deliver vastly higher results. This occurs because the subsequent growth not only is based upon the original amount but also includes the previous additions of growth. As a result, the series is $100, $103, $106.1, $109.3, etc. After thirty years, the cumulative result is $242.7, or 28% more than the simple result of $190. Compounding may not have appeared to add much initially, 0.1 and 0.3, but over time the pennies became dimes and, before long, delivered dollars.

Figure 5.2. Nominal GDP: 1900–2009 (Log Scale)

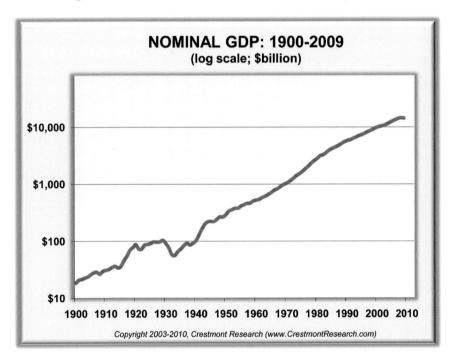

Over longer periods, some people find that the line in figure 5.1 appears to distort the underlying rate of growth because of the exponential curve. One technique used to adjust visually for the effect of compounding is to change the scale on the left axis. Typically, the increments are presented in nominal terms, in which the distance between 100 and 110 on the side axis of the graph is the same as the distance between 200 and 210 (each increment of 10 is equally spaced). Alternatively, the increments can be spaced so that the distances are similar in percentage terms. Thus the 10% distance from 200 to 220 would have the same vertical spacing on the chart's axis as the 10% distance from 100 to 110. As a result, growth that occurs at a steady rate is represented graphically as a line with a relatively consistent slope (without an arching curve). This approach is known as the logarithmic scale, commonly called the log scale.

Figure 5.2 displays GDP-N on a log scale. Though there have been variations in the growth rate of the economy over the period presented, this view more effectively highlights the actual rate of growth with less apparent distortion. Yet the growth rate in nominal terms varies more than economic growth in real terms. This is due to the effect of the inflation rate.

The long, generally straight line indicates that GDP-N has increased at a relatively consistent rate over the long-term. Bite-sized decades, however, provide additional insights and perspective. Figure 5.3 uses a rolling ten-year bar graph to present the nominal growth for all ten-year periods since 1900, separated into the two components of the inflation rate and real growth. This graph highlights the varying effect of the inflation rate on overall economic growth. The core real growth has been relatively consistent in the more recent periods. Recall from earlier discussions about GDP that the Great Depression suppressed economic activity but did not suppress the underlying drivers of the economy. The population grew across that period, and the fundamentals of productivity (education, technology, experience, etc.) progressed as well. Once the economic malaise ended, economic activity responded accordingly with a recovering surge. That effect is reflected as below-average periods when the 1930s are included, and above-average periods that follow. Once the economy caught up with the underlying fundamentals, economic growth settled near the long-term average.

Before overlaying EPS and GDP, it's important to note that the shorter-term business profit cycle differs from the longer-term economic growth cycle. The business cycle of rising and falling profits is not completely dependent upon the economic cycle of expansion and recession. There are many years in which the economy grows, but aggregate company profits decline. Though expansions and re-cessions certainly affect profitability, the variability of earnings occurs more frequently than the nearly decade-long gaps between reces-sions. For this discussion, the terms "business cycle" and "earnings cycle" can be used interchangeably; likewise, the terms "profits" and "earnings" are synonymous.

Figure 5.3. Nominal GDP: Rolling 10 Years (1900–2009)

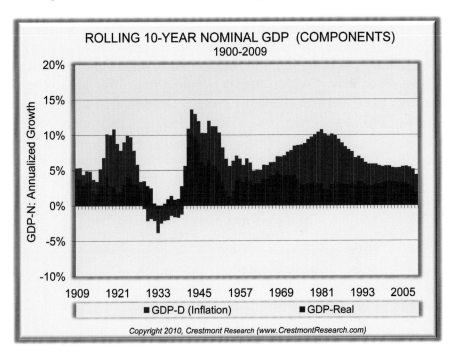

Profits are a necessary result of business operations that facili-tate the continuation and growth of the enterprise. Profits serve as a switching mechanism, directing capital and labor to the commercial activities that are most wanted and needed. They indicate that goods and services have value, and encourage the further production and availability of desired goods and services.

Profits are the ultimate measure of productivity for a business. When two or more businesses in an industry compete, the business with the greater profits percentage is generally more effective in converting capital and labor into goods or services and delivering them to customers. Across industries, profitability is the return that attracts capital. As a result, in a market-based economy, profitability reflects which goods and services consumers most desire, and it drives the allocation of resources needed to provide those goods and services.

Though businesses generally seek ever-greater profits, the reality of competition creates constant downward pressure on profits and constant upward pressure on productivity. On a broad basis, this tug-of-war impacts the overall earnings cycle within the economic cycle.

As companies become more profitable, new competitors are attracted into business. As the production capacity increases, profit margins are compromised, thus driving out weaker competitors and driving productivity within stronger competitors. After weaker competitors close, general economic growth and new demand start the cycle again.

Figure 5.4. EPS Cycle:
Annual Percentage Changes (1950–2009)

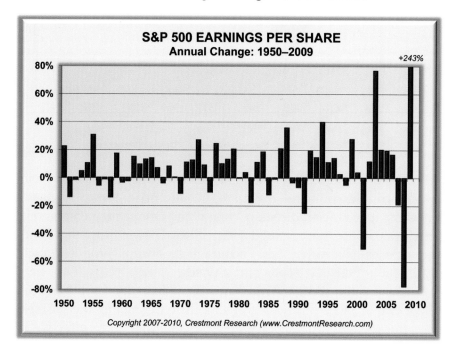

Individual companies have profit cycles that are driven by factors related to the company, its industry, and the overall economy. Some companies generate profits at the same time that others lose money. When a diversified group of companies are aggregated into an index, for example the S&P 500, the composite profitability tends to mute the impact of company and industry factors and tends to highlight overall corporate profitability. Though corporate profits and the economy are closely related, the corporate profit cycle is shorter and more dramatic than the economic cycle.

Figure 5.4 reflects the earnings cycle with streaks of profitability growth punctuated with years or multiple years of profits declines. Over the prior decade, the magnitude of the swings has been more significant than in prior periods, yet the pattern remains similar.

When EPS for a broad stock market index, the S&P 500, is overlaid onto the GDP-N graphs, the historical relationship between economic growth and earnings growth becomes apparent. This relationship can be explained through a logical progression from the economy to earnings.

First, GDP-N can be a surrogate for corporate revenues. Revenues in the aggregate from a large, diversified group of companies tend to reflect the overall economy rather than unique companies or industries. Next, profit margins tend to fluctuate around an average level, an equilibrium of profitability. Thus corporate profitability has a strong relationship to the economy over the long term. Next, EPS of a broad stock market index is a reasonable proxy for overall corporate profitability. A large and diverse group of companies like the S&P 500 generally reflects the overall economy. Thus EPS has a fundamental relationship to GDP.

The fundamental relationship, however, does not mean that the two data series are highly correlated. The significant variability of profit cycle fluctuates around the more stable economic growth cycle. As reflected in figure 5.5, GDP-N increased every year except 2009 during the sixty-year period since 1950, yet more than one-third of the time (35%), EPS declined despite economic growth.

The key takeaways up to this point in the discussion are: first, GDP-N drives EPS; and second, corporate profits can, and often do, decline despite growth in the economy. The second dynamic creates

Figure 5.5. EPS Cycle vs. GDP-N (1950–2009)

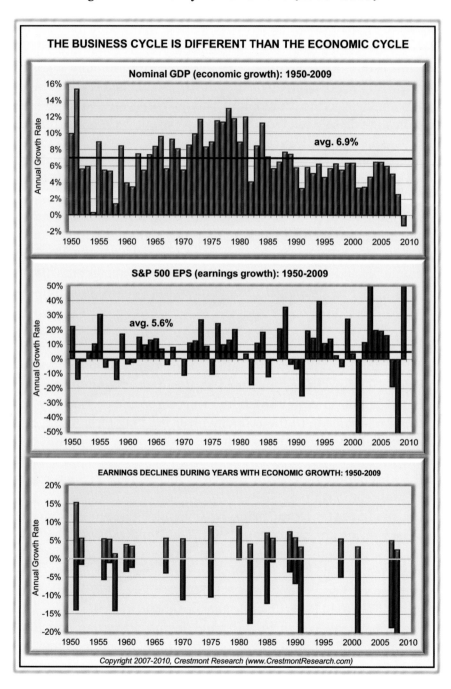

relatively frequent surprises for investors and analysts who are not familiar with and the relative consistency of the profit cycle. They often confuse the profit cycle with the economic cycle of recessions and expansions. This is so important that this discussion will delve further into the history of the profit cycle later in this chapter. Finally, EPS growth for the S&P 500, the proxy for the stock market, increases at a slightly slower rate than overall economic growth. This reflects the additions of new business start-ups that contribute to the economy and the generally more stable and slower-growing nature of mature companies that tend to compose the publicly traded stock market.

The two concepts of GDP-N and EPS can be combined graphically for further perspectives. Figure 5.6 adds EPS to the log-scale graph of cumulative economic growth. This provides the best view of EPS cycling around the steady course of GDP-N. Notwithstanding the significant short-term variability of the earnings cycle, the longer-term relationship reflects a relatively high correlation coefficient at more than 90%.

Figure 5.6. Nominal GDP and EPS:
1900–2009 (Log Scale)

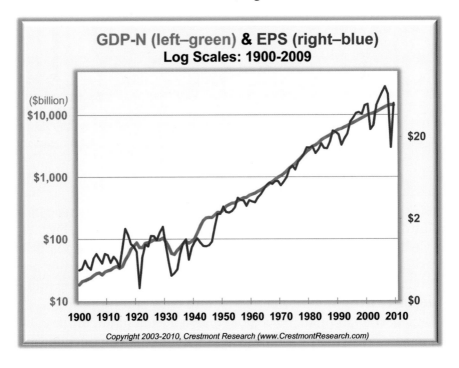

Figure 5.7 overlays GDP-N onto the annual growth rate chart for
EPS. This highlights the magnitude of variability that occurs in EPS,
especially in relation to GDP-N. Though the economy drives EPS over
the long-term, the economic growth cycle does not drive the substantial short-term swings in EPS.

Figure 5.7. Nominal GDP and EPS:
Rolling 10 Years (1900–2009)

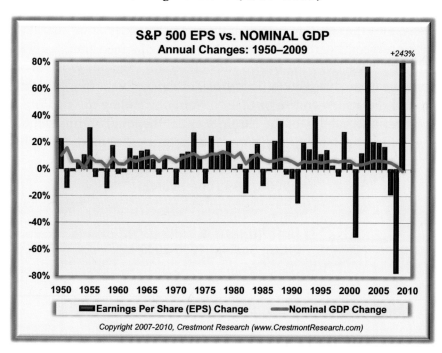

The value of this strong and fundamental relationship for the Financial Physics model is that GDP can be used to predict a normalized level for EPS. This has analytical value not only for developing
a historical series that normalizes distortions created by the business
cycle but also for generating estimates for the future. The relatively
consistent growth rate for GDP, or at least the readily available pre-
dictions for future GDP, enables the use of a methodology to extrapolate the baseline level for EPS given estimates of future GDP.

It is now appropriate for a more detailed exploration of the earnings cycle to reinforce the need to accommodate its distortions. If

the EPS cycle were relatively muted, it would be much less relevant or even unnecessary to seek a baseline level for EPS and its growth trend over time. The magnitude of the EPS cycle, however, has a significant effect not only on determining a normalized level for EPS but also on the related ratios and measures that incorporate EPS as a component or factor. Given that the variability is more than a couple of bumps, normalizing adjustments to the reported series are needed to avoid incorrect or even contradictory conclusions.

Most analyses of stock market valuation and returns include the price/earnings ratio (P/E) as a measure. P/E is highly dependent upon, and leveraged by, its denominator: earnings. The E in P/E is an abbreviation for earnings per share (EPS) since the numerator (price) is generally stated on a per-share basis. Whether EPS relates to an individual stock or an index of stocks, EPS by its definition is presented in per-share or equivalent terms.

The EPS cycle is dramatic, yet in some ways relatively consistent. EPS over the long term is driven by economic growth; therefore it has a core baseline growth rate, and economic growth limits its ultimate growth rate. At times, the wide range of the EPS cycle presents a substantially misleading P/E. The EPS cycle, especially since it often distorts P/E, requires adjustments to avoid distortions that can lead to incorrect or misleading conclusions.

Concepts to Consider

This discussion about the earnings cycle will use the most popular broad-based U.S. stock market index: the S&P 500. The analysis starts with the decade of the 1950s, based upon the consistency and availability of data. In addition, some economists and academics view periods after the Great Depression and World War II as being more representative of the modern economy. This provides sixty years of history over which to assess the cycles of EPS.

Over the past sixty years, through periods of high and low inflation, the average annual growth rate of EPS has been approximately 7.4%. This average is not the compounded growth rate; rather it reflects the average for the middle 90% of the sixty periods. The set excludes 5% of the highest values and 5% of the lowest values to provide a measure that is representative of the vast majority of oc-currences and to avoid distortion from extreme values.

To illustrate, the average of all sixty periods is 10.1%, compared to the middle 90% average of 7.4%. Almost all of the difference be-tween 10.1% and 7.4% relates to the past two years. In 2008, earn-ings fell 78% from $66.18 to $14.88, and in 2009, earnings recovered 243% to $50.97. Before those two years, without any exclusion, the average was 7.6%. But the effect of adding the values 243 and –78 to the series increased the average to 10.1%.

Moreover, the distorted increase in the average does not result from cumulative gains. The increase of 243% was not sufficient to recover from the 78% decline. Substantially larger gains in EPS are required to offset losses due to the mathematical effect of gains and losses. As a result, a simple average will always be larger than the compounded average.

When the series includes values that are as extreme as those of the past two years, the impact can be significant. Keep in mind that it is ironic that the two extreme years occurred just recently; they could have happened anytime in the past. The analysis still would have ex-cluded extreme values, however, since there was still a distortion from the previous most extreme values. By the time that a couple of values on each end are excluded, the average remains fairly constant near 7.4% until the exclusions are almost a third of the extreme values.

In addition, the compounded average is subject to distortion and is not a reliable measure of the average growth rate. The starting and ending values can significantly affect the result. For example, the compounded rate for the sixty years from 1949 through 2009 is 5.3%. By ending just one year earlier, in 2008, the result for fifty-nine years would be 3.2%. The cycle low of 2008 significantly im-pacts the compounded average return. Likewise, at the recent cycle high in 2006 at $81.51, the compounded return for fifty-seven years would be 6.4%. A major point to recognize is that the values for spe-cific beginning and ending points can make a significant difference to the conclusions that are derived from an analysis. As a result, oc-casional adjustments need to be made to develop analyses that are relevant and to reduce distortions caused by issues such as starting and ending points.

Beyond calculating the compounded growth rate, the use of growth rates to extrapolate future values is not reliable. To illustrate, EPS was $2.32 in 1949. Had EPS grown consistently at the most recent cycle low rate of 3.2%, the 2009 value would have been $15.36. On the contrary, at the most recent cycle high rate of 6.4%, EPS for 2009 would have been $95.94. And if anyone dared to suggest using the unadjusted simple average as the compounded rate (10.1%), EPS for 2009 would have been $745.98.

This illustration demonstrates that small changes in the growth rate can have a significant impact on the future value, even without addressing the potential impact of the starting value. When the starting value changes significantly over a few years, the effects from the growth rate are magnified. From today, consider how different a forecast would be depending on whether the series started at $81.51 in 2006 or $14.88 in 2008.

The key points from this discussion about the subtleties of compounded growth and average growth are twofold. First, simple extrapolation is highly sensitive to assumptions. This was highlighted in the previous example. Second, it is important to recognize the potential distortion from simple extrapolation to rationally assess the credibility of forecasts based upon that method.

There are methodologies to normalize the EPS cycle for a more accurate indication of the underlying growth rate. Additionally, there are approaches to generate reliable forecasts of EPS that do not include the distortion from simple extrapolation. These methodologies will be presented after a more detailed exploration of the earnings cycle.

The EPS Cycle

History provides insights into the typical characteristics of the earnings cycle. Though statistics about the average growth rate of earnings are helpful for the long run, the business cycle drives periods of surge and stall for earnings growth over shorter periods of one to five years. Even the drama of the descriptive words "surge" and "stall" understates the significant magnitude and short duration of the EPS cycle.

The recent analysis of average growth rate developed a range of values —most of which were in the mid-single digits (below 10%). As a general rule of thumb, the typical annual growth rate for EPS is generally between 5% and 8%.

Earnings have grown over time, just as the economy has grown. During the sixty years since 1950, earnings grew in nearly twice as many years as it fell. The ups and downs were not completely random; rather, earnings followed a relatively consistent cycle of growing handsomely for three to five years before declining for a year or two. When earnings increase, they surge ahead by 10% or more during nearly three-quarters of the years. During the falls, almost half of the years decline by 10% or more. The magnitude is surprising to people who expect a more consistent growth rate over time.

Figure 5.8 reflects the history of annual changes in actual reported earnings over the past sixty years, 1950–2009. Whereas most of the gains occur in relatively short streaks of three to five years, a few have been shorter, and, only one cycle exceeded five years: a six-year run

Figure 5.8. S&P 500 EPS Growth Annually: 1950–2009

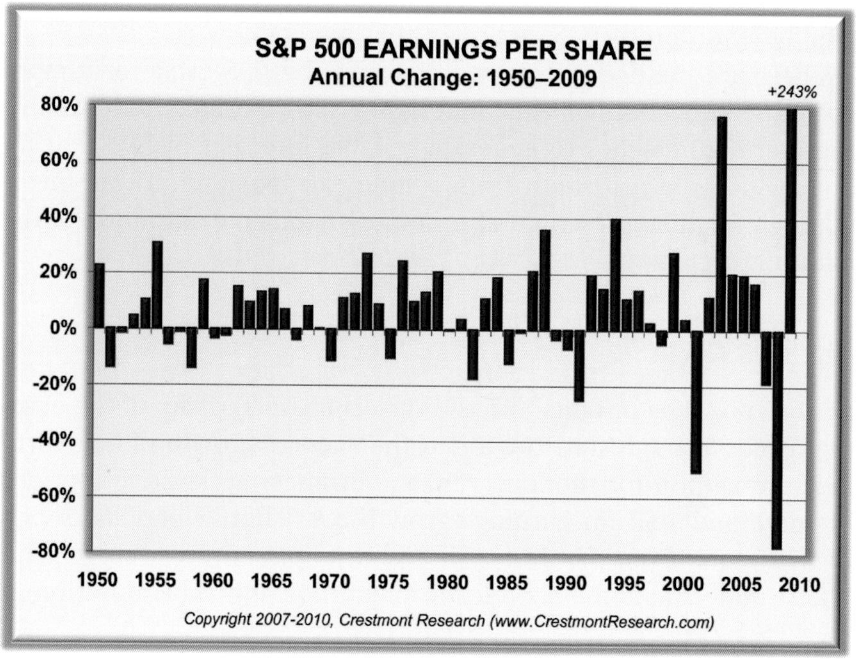

Copyright 2007-2010, Crestmont Research (www.CrestmontResearch.com)

in the mid-1990s. The declines are swift, and generally occur over a year or two; only twice did EPS fall three years in a row.

This choppy, somewhat irregular pattern has endured across periods of war, technological innovation, political issues, and change. To more accurately see the trends, the period of measurement can be extended by a few years to present the cycle as a multiyear average. This will help smooth the ups and downs to reveal a better indication of the underlying consistency of the cycle.

Figure 5.9 displays the three-year compounded average growth rate for earnings. While still somewhat erratic, the line begins to show the cyclical nature of EPS—and the tendency for it to return to a baseline growth rate. The average line across the swings is horizontal, reflecting the tendency for above-average growth to be offset by subsequent below-average growth. Therefore EPS is relatively anchored to a constant long-term trend line of growth, consistent with the previous assessment of GDP growth.

Figure 5.9. S&P 500 EPS Growth 3-Year Average: 1950–2009

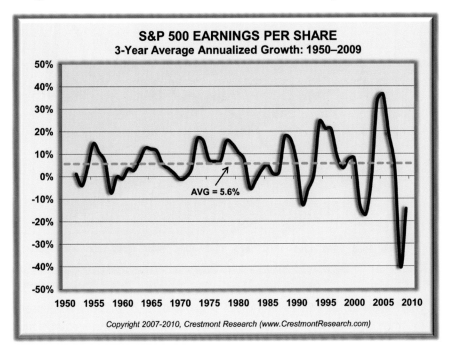

The next step is to transition from growth in percentages to growth in nominal dollars, the reported measure of EPS. Since the time horizon is relatively long term, the compounding effect reflects the exponential curve that was seen in prior series. The logarithmic scale can again be used to provide a more representative view for long-term compounding series. For shorter periods, say the past thirty years, the standard scale can be used without much apparent distortion.

Figure 5.10 presents the longer-term series of earnings per share for the S&P 500 on a log scale. The slope of the sixty-year line in figure 5.10 reflects the relative consistency of earnings growth over the period. Surges and stalls that appear with percentage moves from year to year calm considerably when viewing the series over such a long period.

Figure 5.10. S&P 500 EPS: 1950–2009 (Log Scale)

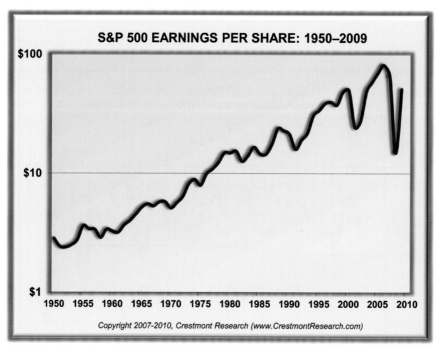

GDP growth, as the driver of EPS growth, is relatively consistent over time due to the underlying factors of population growth and productivity growth. The EPS cycle revolves around this more muted economic cycle and around its own core baseline trend.

Figure 5.11 focuses on the past thirty years, and highlights the significant variability in the cycle over relatively short periods, yet it reflects a consistent trend over the long term. The contrast of the two views in the figures emphasizes the need to employ techniques that can reliably filter the static of the cycle to reveal a credible and relatively accurate core baseline. Much like the fighter pilot executing a roll, investors need the focal point of an EPS baseline to provide a stable horizon to avoid the distracting gyrating effects of EPS cycles. The next step is to explore several methodologies that normalize earnings across business cycles.

Figure 5.11. S&P 500 EPS: 1980–2009

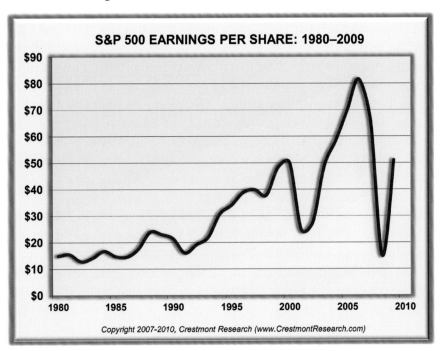

economic cycle and around its own core baseline trend.

Nearly Normal

The objective of normalizing or adjusting earnings for the business cycle is to provide a better indication for the underlying long-term trend. Without normalizing, the distortions to EPS from the business cycle cause most unadjusted values to be unreliable for analysis or future trends.

To illustrate, the reported EPS values for the S&P 500 index over the ten years from 2000 through 2009 were: $50, $25, $28, $49, $59, $70, $82, $66, $15, and $51. Though the long-term trends for GDP and EPS show a relatively high degree of consistency, the shorter-term annual changes are too volatile to be meaningful without a method to smooth the volatility.

If, for example, the long-term trend for growth is 5%, then a graph that uses the log scale will reflect a line with the upward slope of 5%. If the business cycle did not exist, then EPS growth would track the line. In reality, EPS growth is volatile cycle that fluctuates around the underlying baseline of growth. The previous figures graphically illustrate this dynamic.

There are various ways to normalize cyclical series. Two methods that are applicable to EPS are the use of a moving average and the use of a reference series. The moving average approach is represented by the methodology popularized by Robert Shiller at Yale University in his book *Irrational Exuberance*. The reference series approach is the methodology developed by Crestmont Research and presented in *Unexpected Returns*. The two series are similar, which reinforces the applicability of both methodologies. Analyses by Crestmont Research use one or both of the approaches depending upon what is most appropriate.

Each approach has nuances and limitations worth detailing. An understanding of both approaches can help investors use them appropriately and know when to apply further adjustments.

The approach popularized by Shiller uses reported net earnings for the previous ten years, as actually published in audited financial statements. Note that reported net earnings is also known as "As Reported EPS"; it is not the more recently developed and subjective version of EPS known as "Operating EPS." Under the methodology used by Shiller, EPS for each of the past ten years is adjusted forward, to the present, for the effects of the inflation rate. A composite value for EPS is then calculated by averaging the adjusted values for EPS across all ten years. The purpose of averaging the values across ten years is to offset the variances above and below the underlying trend.

The result is a trailing ten-year average for EPS in current dollars.

The advantages of this methodology include: (1) it is relatively simple to calculate; (2) it is a recognized and well-vetted approach; (3) it is effective at reducing the distortions to EPS caused by the business cycle; and (4) it is an objective quantitative methodology. The shortcomings include: (1) it generates only a historical series and does not provide future estimates or forecasts; (2) it produces a value that lags by real growth; and (3) it inherently assumes that the distortions on both sides of the baseline are equal.

When analysts compare values from this methodology to other values in this series (e.g., current P/E to a past year or to the historical average), the comparisons are consistent, and most of the shortcomings are moot since they appear throughout the series. This methodology, however, needs an additional adjustment to increase the comparability of earnings or the price/earnings ratio under this approach to values or averages from other methodologies.

Specifically, this approach produces a value that lags by nearly five years in real terms. Though the methodology adjusts for the inflation rate, it does not account for the underlying long-term real growth in the economy and earnings. The purpose of a normalizing methodology is to determine reasonable values within the long-term trend that reflect the underlying baseline to the business cycle. In most instances, the baseline value that is used for the recent month, quarter, or year needs to be representative of current values rather than a value lagged in time by nearly five years.

For example, assume that EPS in year 1 is $10, real growth is 3% annually, and inflation is 2% annually. The underlying trend would start at $10.00 and end at $15.51 in the tenth year. Keep in mind that the series would hypothetically end at $15.51; in the real world, the business cycle will inevitably produce a result somewhat higher or lower.

Figure 5.12 contains the details for this example. The values on the first line, Baseline EPS, relate to the underlying growth trend of EPS including the inflation rate. Baseline EPS, which relates to profitability at an equilibrium level, will generally correspond to the long-term economic growth rate.

In reality, reported earnings fluctuate significantly around the baseline level. A hypothetical cycle above and below the baseline

Figure 5.12. EPS Illustration: Concept of Normalizing

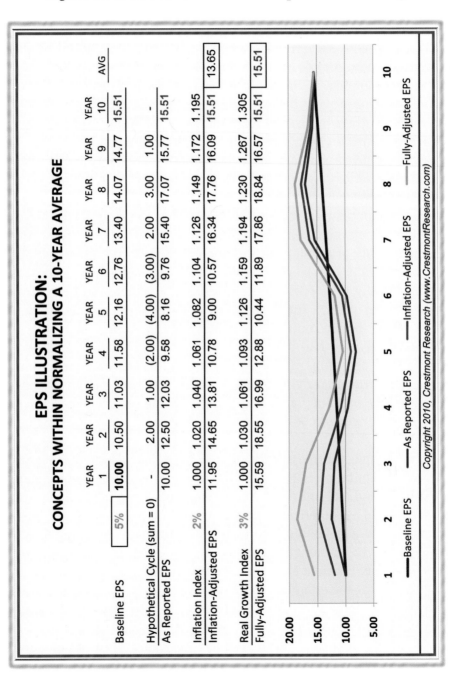

EPS ILLUSTRATION:
CONCEPTS WITHIN NORMALIZING A 10-YEAR AVERAGE

		YEAR 1	YEAR 2	YEAR 3	YEAR 4	YEAR 5	YEAR 6	YEAR 7	YEAR 8	YEAR 9	YEAR 10	AVG
Baseline EPS	5%	10.00	10.50	11.03	11.58	12.16	12.76	13.40	14.07	14.77	15.51	
Hypothetical Cycle (sum = 0)		-	2.00	1.00	(2.00)	(4.00)	(3.00)	2.00	3.00	1.00	-	
As Reported EPS		10.00	12.50	12.03	9.58	8.16	9.76	15.40	17.07	15.77	15.51	
Inflation Index	2%	1.000	1.020	1.040	1.061	1.082	1.104	1.126	1.149	1.172	1.195	
Inflation-Adjusted EPS		11.95	14.65	13.81	10.78	9.00	10.57	16.34	17.76	16.09	15.51	13.65
Real Growth Index	3%	1.000	1.030	1.061	1.093	1.126	1.159	1.194	1.230	1.267	1.305	
Fully-Adjusted EPS		15.59	18.55	16.99	12.88	10.44	11.89	17.86	18.84	16.57	15.51	15.51

Baseline EPS   As Reported EPS   Inflation-Adjusted EPS   Fully-Adjusted EPS is included in figure 5.12 to further this illustration. Note that it is equally above and below the baseline and sums to zero. The result is a series that is representative of As Reported EPS for the ten-year period. "As Reported" is the term used to indicate that EPS is the actual net income that companies report on their financial statements.

Shiller's approach adjusts EPS in each year of the ten-year series by increasing past values to the present by the rate of inflation. The result is that all past values are then stated in today's inflation-adjusted dollars. For example, in year 2, the inflation index was 1.020; in year 10, it is 1.195 (reflecting 2% inflation compounding over the nine periods of growth). Inflation, after compounding, accumulated to reflect a 19.5% increase in the series. Therefore, the As Reported EPS in year 1 of $10.00 is the equivalent of $11.95 in year 10 inflation-adjusted terms.

After all the years are adjusted for inflation, the results are averaged to generate a normalized EPS of $13.65. That value can be used to calculate the P/E ratio and other stock market metrics. Note, however, that $13.65 is lower than the Baseline EPS of $15.51 in year 10. This occurs because there was not an adjustment for the component of real growth over the ten years.

If all of the 5% increase had been driven by inflation, then the inflation adjustment would increase all the values for EPS to $15.51 and the resulting average would be $15.51. If none of the 5% annual increase related to inflation, then there would be no adjustments, and the average value would reflect the midpoint of growth over ten years, essentially a point around year 5.5.

In reality, EPS growth consists of both real growth and inflation. Further, real growth tends to average near 3%. As a result, the value for EPS driven by this methodology produces a value that is about 4.5 years of real growth behind the current value. In figure 5.12, the Baseline EPS for year 10 of $15.51 is almost 14% higher than the average Inflation-Adjusted EPS. This represents approximately 4.5 years at near 3% including compounding.

As a rule of thumb, therefore, the value produced by the methodology popularized by Shiller should have 15% added to it to bring Inflation-Adjusted EPS to the present in real terms.[1] This is appropriate when comparing EPS under this methodology with other measures of EPS that relate to the most recent year in the series. For example, it is appropriate to make the adjustment when comparing this moving average EPS to a current estimate of EPS.

Likewise, when calculating P/E using this version of EPS, the 15% adjustment enhances the comparability of this P/E to other P/Es that reflect the current period. This will be illustrated shortly following a discussion about the Crestmont Research approach.

There are other credible methods for normalizing EPS using moving averages across various periods of historical EPS and/or using various methods of period weighting or time adjustment. The methodology popularized by Shiller is the most recognized and accepted. Beyond the use of a moving average, another method is to use a reference series to determine the normalized EPS. Crestmont Research employs a methodology for EPS that is based upon a fundamentally related reference series.

The advantages of the Crestmont Research methodology include: (1) it is effective at reducing the distortions to EPS caused by the business cycle; (2) it can provide future estimates and forecasts as well as provide historical series; (3) it provides a value that is current in time; and (4) it is an objective and quantitative methodology. The shortcomings include: (1) the methodology is not simple to generate; (2) it requires an accurate measure or forecast of past or future GDP, which occasionally undergoes slight revisions; and (3) the vetting of the methodology is not as extensive as the method popularized by Shiller.

Though the methodology was presented in detail and explored in *Unexpected Returns,* a summary may be helpful for the context of this discussion. The Crestmont Research approach uses the fundamental relationship between GDP-N and EPS. A statistical regression of the two series produces values for EPS based upon the level of GDP-N. The high correlation between the two series produces a credible and relatively reliable value for EPS that can be used for historical analysis and assessments of valuation across secular stock market cycles.

Both of these approaches will be used in future chapters, and a comparison of the two should reinforce the applicability of both. In addition, a comparison of the two normalized EPS series to the actual reported EPS from the past ten years will highlight the value of normalized EPS.

Figure 5.13 shows the historical EPS series for both methodologies described previously. The moving average approach has been adjusted upward by 15%. Though there were periods over the past century when real economic growth varied from the long-term average of 3%, the rule of thumb is used to reflect the long-term average real growth rate. As indicated by the graphs, the two series are fairly comparable (and have correlation coefficient 99.5%). Note that when the moving average methodology is compared to other methodologies in later references and analysis, it will generally be adjusted by the 15% factor. When it is used on its own or compared to its average, the unadjusted value will be presented. The adjustment is only needed to make it comparable to methods that do not have the inherent real growth lag.

Figure 5.13. Normalized EPS: Shiller and Crestmont (1900–2009)

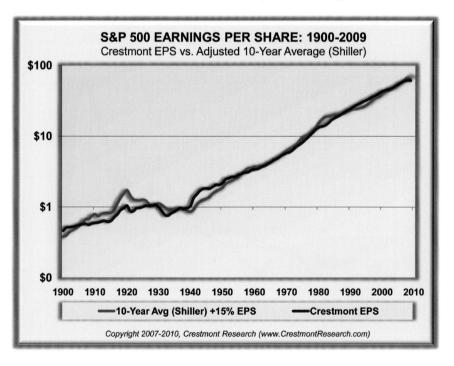

Both methods reduce the distortion of the business cycle. To illustrate, figure 5.14 includes the actual reported EPS for the past thirty years as well as the values from both methodologies, after adjusting the moving average value upward by 15%. Though the actual reported EPS is highly volatile and provides little confidence about the core baseline trend for EPS, the normalized EPS values reflect a much more stable indication of underlying earnings trends.

Normalized EPS serves a number of roles. It enables investors to more reliably assess historical earnings cycles and related measures of market valuation. On a more current basis, it can reflect the relative position in the earnings cycle. For example, after the big swings of the past few years, normalized EPS reflects that reported EPS in 2009 was still below the core baseline upon which it will grow in the future. Similarly, normalized EPS helps investors understand that the reported EPS of $81.51 in 2006 was a cycle distortion and well above

Figure 5.14. EPS:
As Reported, Shiller, and Crestmont (1980–2009)

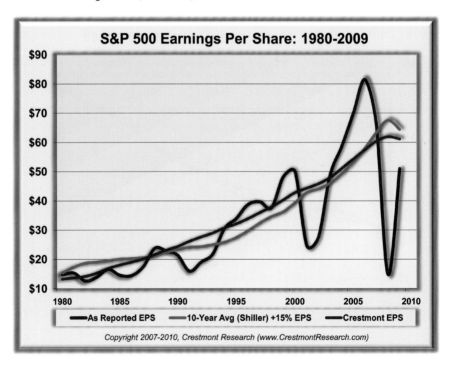

the baseline value. With a normalized EPS baseline, investors have a horizon against which to assess the wide range of recent values. Finally, with a reasonable forecast of GDP, investors have the means to extend into the future a credible estimate of future EPS. The baseline does not tell us the value that will actually be reported, but it does help frame a general range within which future EPS is more likely, and it provides baseline values from which future growth is driven.

Chapter 7 discusses the implications that distortions in EPS have on stock market valuations, and thus the need for a more consistent measure of the underlying EPS trend line. At this point, note that the As Reported quarterly or annual measurement of EPS is about as accurate as a random glance at the thermometer to determine the current season. Weathermen and climatologists use average daily temperatures and a variety of adjustment (normalizing) techniques to assess weather patterns and trends. Likewise with the stock market and EPS, appropriate techniques can enhance the validity and value of series that are by their nature prone to distortion.

POINTS OF EMPHASIS

- **Earnings (EPS) growth is driven by economic growth, as measured by nominal gross domestic product (GDP-N) over the long-term.**

- **The earnings cycle is distinct from the economic cycle; there have been numerous years when earnings declined despite increases in nominal economic growth.**

- **EPS can be normalized for increased relevance using a variety of methods, including moving averages and reference series. Both methods produce relatively similar results.**

SECTION III

FINANCE FOR FINANCIAL PHYSICS

Enigma [u-nig-ma]: something puzzling, perplexing, inexplicable, ambiguous, or contradictory by its nature.

CHAPTER 6

THE VALUE OF BEING PRESENT

A limited number of financial principles are needed to understand what drives secular stock market cycles and stock market returns. Ironically, the simplicity has probably contributed to misunderstandings about the stock market. As investors watch pundits try to explain the daily market swings, they understandably grow frustrated. On some days the pundits explain that the market rose because of a factor, while on other days they say that it fell despite that same factor. Further, there is a tendency for financial reporters and traders to attribute good news to the market on days when it rises and attribute bad news when it falls. As a result, logic leads us to believe that if the market is unpredictable in the short run, then it must be completely unpredictable in the long run.

As an analogy, consider the leaf that falls from the top of a tall tree on a breezy fall day. Next, introduce a pundit who tracks the leaf's path. The leaf will fall and rise as the breeze whisks it around in the air. If you were unaware of the force of gravity, it's very reasonable that you might cheer for the leaf to rise and fear for its fall as the pundit falsely attributes its every movement to unrelated factors when in fact its descent simply reflects a pattern of normal chaos. Yet when the situation is viewed in the context of physical principles, you know the leaf is ultimately coming down. Actually, you know that the leaf is destined to have a downward trend with intermittent lifts and plunges. The discussion can now shift from physics to finance to explain the principle that causes destiny for secular stock market cycles.

The first concept to explore is present value and its application to long-term secular stock market cycles. This includes a discussion about the effects of the inflation rate, interest rates, and risk premiums as primary drivers of present value.

Present Value

Rather than start with a dry, technical description for the concept of present value, imagine that you are dressed in a sufficiently embarrassing costume to get Monty Hall's attention on *Let's Make A Deal*, the popular TV game show that started in the early 1960s. Picture yourself with a wildly colorful and noticeable outfit.

You likely remember that the process on *Let's Make A Deal* is for you to trade with Monty. There are three doors with which he might tempt you, and he is also known to roll out the cash. Assume that you already own the contents behind door number 1: $110 paid to you one year from now. Monty asks, "Do you want to keep it"?

As you think about it, he waves a large roll of cash at you and says, "Or, I'll give you $100 right now!"

Would you rather have $110 in a year or $100 today? Assume that your local banker is offering 5% interest on a one-year certificate of deposit (CD); does potential interest income of $5 influence your decision?

Obviously, you see where this is going. You generally will be indifferent about $110 in a year only when the interest rate for one year is 10%. In this instance, the present value today for a $110 payment in a year is $100 when the interest rate is 10%. For those who are interested, the present value of $110 at a banker's rate of 5% is $104.76, since you would earn interest of $5.24 to total $110 in a year.

Therefore the concept of present value relates to the value today for money in the future based upon market rates of interest. The more descriptive terminology for "market rates of interest" in this case is known as the discount rate.

This is an important concept because it will ultimately explain why the inflation rate is the primary driver of secular stock market cycles. For now, it may be helpful to dig a little deeper into the details of present value for a more complete understanding to build upon.

The concept of present value relates not only to single payments in the future but also to any series of payments over time. This could include payments every month for a year, or periodic payments with a lump sum at the end.

For example, there are various types of payment streams common to most people's experience. Bonds pay interest quarterly or semi-annually, and then bonds repay the principal at maturity. Certificates of deposit often pay interest monthly, and then return the principal at maturity. Therefore bonds and CDs are payment streams in which the interest is paid periodically and the principal is paid at maturity.

There are other instruments that pay a fixed amount each month all the way through maturity, which is known as amortization. A home mortgage loan is a common example. The loan balance amortizes, or spreads out, such that the payment remains the same. Although the payment remains the same, the allocation to interest and principal changes over time. In the early months, most of the monthly payment is allocated to interest, and the small amount that exceeds the interest reduces the principal. Over time, as the loan balance declines due to allocations of the payment to principal, less of each payment relates to interest and more of it relates to principal. This cycle further accelerates the pay-down of the loan balance. In this instance, the monthly payment remains constant, yet the portions divided between interest and principal change.

All financial instruments are driven by the concept of present value. In many instances, like the ones above, the principal value is set at the start of the investment or transaction, and the interest rate is applied based upon current market conditions. In other instances, the investment or loan may already be outstanding, and the price of the investment is determined by current market conditions. Keep in mind that one person's loan is another's investment—they represent two sides of the same transaction.

In the previous example, you probably decided to keep the contents behind door number one—$110 in a year. The market value with interest rates at 5% was $104.76, and Monty Hall offered only $100. Assume that by the time you get home from the show, the interest rate rises to 15%. Certainly that's a bit extreme, but this is just an illustration.

At this point, your prize ($110 in a year) is worth $95.65—the amount that can earn interest of 15% ($14.35) and accumulate to $110 after a year. This is the same dynamic that impacts bond prices as market conditions and interest rates change. If you own or ever have owned bonds, you likely have seen their value change from one account statement to the next. As the then current market interest rate changes, which is the bond's discount rate, the value of the bond changes. For bonds, the relevant interest rate is related to the bond's maturity date and interest payments. Rising interest rates drive prices lower and falling interest rates drive prices higher.

The formulas and technical aspects of calculating present value are not needed to assess secular stock market cycles; just remember that the key to this principle is the concept of the point of indifference. Present value is the price at which you are indifferent, based upon market interest rates, about receiving one payment today instead of a series of payments in the future.

Further, the present value (the current price) changes as market interest rates change. Since market rates are almost always changing a little one way or the other, prices constantly change as the forces of buyers and sellers try to anticipate rising or falling interest rates.

Discount Rate and Inflation

From the previous discussion and examples, the primary driver to present value is the current market interest rate, known as the discount rate. The term "discount rate" is used because it represents the rate at which the future cash amounts are "discounted" to the present. The value today of future cash flows is less than the sum of the future amounts. In other words, from the previous examples, present value reflects the discount required to make the present value plus interest income (based upon market conditions) equal to the cumulative future payments. Alternatively, the difference between present value and the sum of future payments is interest income.

So how is the discount rate or market interest rate determined?

The purpose of interest rates is to protect the owner of cash from the adverse effects of inflation, which is the loss in value of cash due to a loss in its purchasing power. For example, assume that you accepted Monty Hall's offer of $100. When you arrived home, you began to think about all that you could buy with $100. By the end of the night, you had developed a widely diverse list of items, which government analysts refer to as a "basket of goods and services." Then, for some reason that surely would not sound like American consumerism, you decided to wait until next year to buy the basket of goods and services.

A year later, the composite price of the basket of goods and services is likely to be higher than it was when you first selected your items. Some items will cost more and others will cost less, yet overall the composite price is generally higher from year to year. That overall level of increase in the aggregate price of goods and services in an economy is inflation. This is the concept that was introduced during the discussion about economics. Since the inflation rate is the antagonist, further examples in the context of finance will help add emphasis to the culprit.

Remember that inflation is not the increase in individual prices. If the price of bread or gasoline rises, that is not inflation; rather, it reflects a simple price increase. Likewise, a decline in the price of computers or cell phones does not represent deflation.

Deflation, which is negative inflation, is the general decline in overall prices across the economy. Inflation and deflation are monetary financial concepts that relate to the value, or purchasing power, of money across an economy over time.

So let's go back to shopping with your winnings. If your basket of goods and services costs $102 a year later, then there will have been 2% inflation. In effect, your original $100 will have lost its purchasing power across the economy to buy as much as it did a year earlier.

If holders of cash in the economy expect that inflation will be 2% over the upcoming year, then they will require of potential borrowers or investors enough interest to cover the expected loss in purchasing power plus a premium for the use of the capital. The premium tends to vary depending upon the length of time related to the interest rate. This is why longer-term interest rates tend to be higher than shorter-term interest rates.

In addition, holders of cash demand a further premium for the risk associated with the borrower or investor. When the borrower is the United States government, investors generally accept the risk premium to be near zero. As a result, government debt represents the risk-free rate of interest. As the risk profile of an investment increases due to a decline in quality or a decrease in certainty, the risk premium related to the investment increases.

Ultimately, the market discount rate consists of the expected inflation rate plus a premium for the term of the investment plus a premium for the risk and uncertainty of the investment. As will be explored later, the discount rate for debt is more consistent and identifiable than the discount rate for non-debt investments such as stocks.

Debt generally has characteristics of specified interest payments and a fixed maturity date. Therefore the cash flows are more certain for these so-called fixed income securities. Fixed income securities consist of short-term instruments like Treasury bills, commercial paper, and bankers acceptances. Short-term instruments are known as money market investments; thus the term "money market fund" refers to investment funds that consist of money market instruments. Fixed income investments with original maturities between one and ten years are called notes. For maturities beyond ten years, the instrument is called a bond.

As the inflation rate falls, the value of the investment generally rises—reflecting a decrease in the discount rate. The less the instrument is discounted the greater its value. Since interest rates and discount rates conceptually don't fall below zero, the maximum value of a debt security occurs as the inflation rate reaches zero—even if the inflation rate falls further to deflation. In deflation, you have the ability to hold cash outside of financial instruments. As a result, the discount rate conceptually stops near zero and does not go negative. This is an important concept to appreciate at this point. Even when inflation declines into deflation, notes and bonds generally rise in value unless the credit quality deteriorates. The future stream of interest payments is valuable, and a bond has a fixed maturity value. In contrast, stocks don't do well as the inflation rate declines from low inflation to deflation. Their future stream of payments (earnings and dividends) declines due to deflation, and there is no fixed maturity value for stocks.

The Force

Chapter 5 included an example that highlighted the power of compounding. Relatively small changes in compounding growth rates had a significant impact on future values. Future values and present values are related by a common force, which in one circumstance is known as discounting and in the other as compounding. In one instance, the objective is to assess the value today of tomorrow's payments (present value). In the other, the objective is to assess tomorrow's payments based upon today's value plus market interest rates (future value).

Before leaving the subject of present value, because it is the principle that drives secular stock market cycles, consider the dramatic impact that changes in the inflation rate have on prices in the stock market. Unlike bonds, which have a fixed maturity, equity holdings in the stock market (owning common stock) are considered to be perpetual investments. Even though it often feels like your winners have short lives and your losers go on forever, stocks do not have a maturity.

When the value of a stock is calculated, it is therefore assumed that its cash flows continue indefinitely. In reality, an investor will receive dividends, or the company will reinvest earnings, as long as that investor owns the stock, and then the next investor will pay a value that is intended to reflect cash flows in perpetuity. With stocks, the assumption is that there will never be a final maturity. For the purpose of this discussion, rather than think about a single stock, assume that the example relates to an index of the stock market, which can add new companies as others cease to exist.

Next, stocks also are assumed to grow in size and profitability over time. When using a broad stock market index, the growth rate of earnings is expected to track relatively closely to economic growth. The historical growth rate generally has been slightly lower due to new business formations and the tendency for large public companies to have more consistent, albeit slightly slower, earnings growth.

The inflation rate affects both the overall growth rate of earnings and the discount rate for present value. The effect on both variables is not equal and thus does not offset in calculating the present value of earnings. The inflation rate does not always transfer completely into earnings growth. Further, the increase in inflation and related economic uncertainty can increase the discount rate by more than the inflation rate through an increase in the risk premium that is embedded in the discount rate.

For example, assuming that real growth remains the same, an increase in inflation can reduce P/E valuations in the market by half or two-thirds—this is what is experienced during secular bear markets. Commensurately, as high inflation subsides, P/E valuations can double or triple over time irrespective of earnings growth—this is what is experienced during secular bull markets.

These principles explain the financial relationship between the inflation rate and valuation. Valuation in the stock market is expressed by the P/E ratio. But sometimes P/E is not as simple as the two-variable ratio appears. The next chapter dives into details about P/E and how to make it relevant and reliable.

POINTS OF EMPHASIS

- Present value is the concept of cash today having the same value as payments in the future based upon market interest rates. Market interest rates are driven by inflation. Present value (the current price) reflects changes in the discount rate as driven by changes in inflation.

- As inflation declines, the values of financial investments generally rise — reflecting a decrease in the discount rate. Since interest rates and discount rates conceptually don't fall below zero, the maximum value of a debt security occurs as inflation reaches zero — even if inflation falls further to deflation. In deflation, you have the ability to hold cash. As a result, the discount rate conceptually stops near zero and does not go negative.

- As higher inflation subsides, market valuation can double or triple over time irrespective of earnings growth — this is what is experienced during secular bull markets.

- Future values and present values are related by a common force, which in one instance is known as discounting and in the other instance as compounding.

CHAPTER 7

GETTING TO P/E

The price/earnings ratio (P/E) is the investment industry's attempt to provide a single, simple measure of valuation for stocks and the stock market. P/E does provide an understandable way to translate the previous discussion about present value into a single number. The result is a tool that can provide valuable insights about fair value as well as future returns. As with any tool, it should be used appropriately and with awareness.

If P/E rarely changed over time, or if it changed randomly, then P/E would be nothing more than a phenomenon. Instead, the fundamentally driven cycle of P/E causes secular stock market cycles and determines whether the stock market has the potential for above-average or below-average returns. A more in-depth discussion of its nuances will clarify the outlook for the probable outcomes for stock market returns over this decade.

Figure 7.1, known as the Y Curve Effect, is a plot of the inflation rate and P/E for each year from 1900 to 2009. Historically, years with higher inflation and deflation tended to have a low P/E. During periods of relatively low inflation, P/E tended to peak in the low to mid-20s. The highest points to the right side of the graph reflect the late 1990s bubble, which is not a likely or reasonable assumption for the future. Why does the Y Curve Effect occur?

This discussion starts by applying the concepts and principles to bonds as financial assets. The inflation rate drives bond yields higher because investors demand compensation for inflation. As inflation rises, thereby increasing the yields of bond, the value of existing bonds with fixed interest rates declines. This is the function of present value. The decline in the price of the bond represents a loss in value to its investor until the bond matures. The buyers of bonds, however, can now purchase bonds in the market at lower prices, reflecting higher yields, to compensate for the increase in inflation. The key point to remember: higher inflation drives higher bond yields, which decreases existing bond prices.

Figure 7.1. The Y Curve Effect: P/E and Inflation (1900–2009)

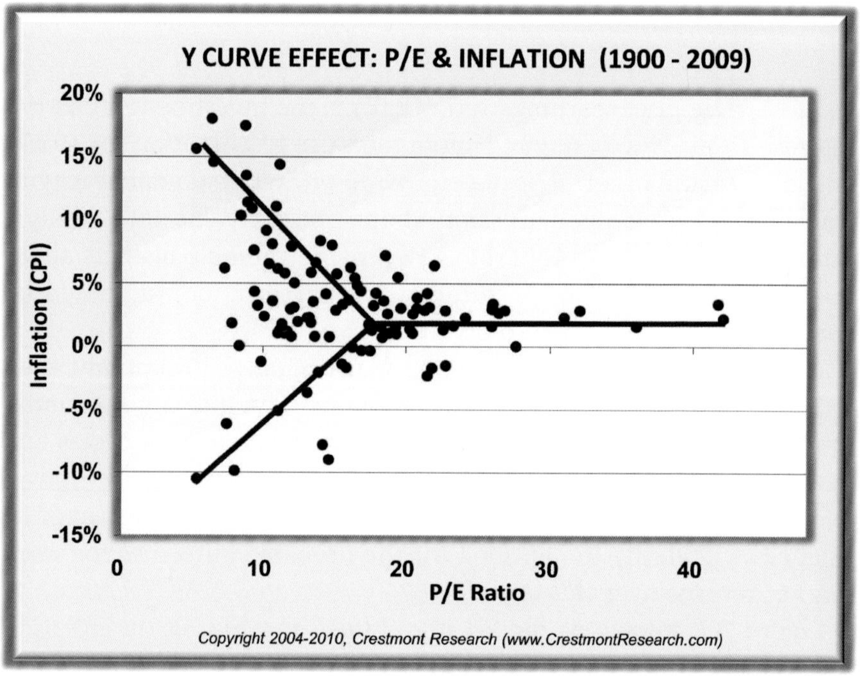
Y CURVE EFFECT: P/E & INFLATION (1900 - 2009)
20%
15%
10%
5%
0%
-5%
-10%
-15%
Inflation (CPI)
0
10
20
30
40
P/E Ratio
Copyright 2004-2010, Crestmont Research (www.CrestmontResearch.com)

Likewise, since stocks are financial assets, higher inflation drives stock prices lower. The effect of the inflation rate on the discount rate is greater than the effect of the inflation rate on earnings. The inflation rate does not always transfer completely into earnings growth. Further, the increase in inflation and the related economic uncertainty can increase the discount rate by more than the inflation rate through an increase in the risk premium that is embedded in the discount rate.

Similar to bonds, the higher discount rate from inflation therefore causes the current prices of stocks to decline as the present value of future earnings declines. Since stocks have no maturity, there is a loss in value to the owners of the stocks. The buyers of stocks, however, can now purchase stocks in the market at lower prices, reflecting a higher expected future return, to compensate for the increase in inflation.

In deflation, the value of a bond increases because its interest payments and fixed maturity price (known as par) are valuable under the effects of present value. For stocks, however, their present value declines. Though the discount rate (the desired rate of return to cover inflation) is low, deflation causes a decline in the nominal amount of future EPS. The result is that stock prices fall and thus P/E declines.

Though P/E declines during deflation and inflation, the reasons are quite different. The P in P/E is the market's determination of the present value of future earnings (or more accurately, the distributions from future earnings). The E in P/E relates to current earnings. Inflation and deflation do not affect the E in P/E; E is the current earnings amount rather than future earnings.

Inflation increases the future growth of E, but not by enough to overcome higher discounting; thus, the result is a lower P. Deflation drives the future trend for E negative, which despite the low discounting from deflation still results in lower P. In both instances, the lower values for P decrease P/E. Inflation's impact on P/E results primarily from discounting and deflation's impact on P/E results primarily from lower earnings.

The contrast of bonds and stocks during periods of inflation and deflation serves to dispel the myth that interest rates drive P/E. Though the association of P/E and long-term market interest rates is generally true, this mistaken association can lead to false conclusions under one of the scenarios. If the focus is only on the relationship between P/E and bond yields, then there will be a false outlook for deflation scenarios because high bond prices would diverge from falling stock prices.

The force of present value works on stocks just as it does on bonds. Since the inflation rate has been positive almost all of the time, analysts and pundits take the liberty of tying the common thread. As a result, the simplified relationship of bond yields and P/E is based upon the common relationship that bonds and stocks have to the inflation rate—but only when the inflation rate is positive. During periods when deflation poses a reasonable risk, the causes of divergence between stocks and bonds is especially important for understanding the impact of deflation on stock market returns.

In addition, there are implications for investment portfolios. Because bonds and stocks decline in value as inflation increases, bonds are poor diversifiers for stocks during inflation. During deflation, however, bond appreciation and yield can provide an offset to stock market losses.

There are several major points to recognize: First, rising inflation has an increasingly negative effect on bonds and stocks. Second, the negative inflation condition of deflation has a positive effect on bond prices and a negative effect on stock prices. Third, as deflation worsens, the increasing nominal decline in EPS drives P/E downward. Higher inflation and worsening deflation are increasingly negative to P/E. On the contrary, P/E peaks near the crossover point between deflation and inflation—when the inflation rate is low and stable (price stability). These points highlight the reason that inflation is Major Uncertainty #2 toward the probable outcomes for the stock market over this decade.

Morphing P/E

In addition to exploring P/E through a contrast to bond yields, consider P/E as the mechanism by which the price level of the market is determined. What are the principles that determine whether the Dow Jones Industrial Average, for example, should be 5,000 or 15,000, or 50,000? Though this discussion is conceptually similar to the bond yield comparison, it provides a perspective from an alternate direction.

P/E is a measure of relative market valuation. P is the market's value, and its multiple of E reflects whether the stock market has a relatively high value or a relatively low value. P/E of 20 is twice the valuation multiple compared to P/E of 10. Nonetheless, more than simply a measure, the concepts behind the ratio reflect the way investors determine the value of the stock market. Market value is not a mystery or an inexplicable phenomenon; it is determined ultimately by the investment decisions of buyers and sellers as they battle for position.

The P in P/E is driven by the concept of present value. There are several widely used approaches that use the principles of present value to determine the value for the P. Almost all of the models use two variables as the core driver for value. The first component is the long-term growth rate of earnings. As earnings grow at higher rates, the present value of P increases; more earnings in the future means more value today.

The second factor is the discount rate, the driver of present value. The discount rate increases or decreases primarily due to changes in the inflation rate. For example, higher inflation drives higher discount rates, which increase the amount of discount to the present value. As a result, higher inflation makes the present value for P lower.

Therefore P/E increases and decreases based upon changes to the present value of P. The present value of P is driven by earnings growth and the inflation rate. To illustrate the conceptual effects of various conditions on P/E, assume that P/E has a genetic DNA that enable it be part human and part machine.

When valuing the stock market, the P in P/E is the value of the index (e.g., S&P 500). There are three factors (genes to the DNA in this illustration) that determine the size of P: (1) the inflation rate; (2) the real growth rate without inflation; and (3) the discount rate, primarily driven by the inflation rate. The inflation rate is the gene that determines the level of bulk. Higher inflation adds more bulk. Deflation strips bulk and emaciates P.

The second gene is the real growth rate of earnings, excluding inflation. The real growth rate of earnings, over the long-term, is driven by the real growth rate of the economy (real GDP). This gene determines the level of muscle, the core body mass of P.

The third gene is the discount rate; it determines height. Discount is the key word; it represents reductions to height. With this gene, tall is normal unless something stunts it. There are two ways that height is compromised. First, as inflation increases, it creates excess bulk. As the level of bulk increases, the height gene stunts (the higher the inflation rate, the higher the discount rate). Second, as deflation gets worse, it devours the bulk and even offsets some of the muscle growth (deflation causes earnings growth to turn negative as it offsets real growth). The best condition includes solid muscle growth, a healthy layer of bulk, and maximum height. This occurs when the inflation rate is low and stable.

For humans, measurements of height and weight create a body mass index known as BMI. In this conceptual illustration for P/E, the height and weight of P create a price mass index (PMI). Therefore, a higher PMI increases P, which in turn drives P/E higher.

Though the inflation rate impacts the bulk gene and the height gene, the effects are not equally offsetting. The inflation rate does not always transfer completely into earnings growth. Further, the increase in inflation and related economic uncertainty can increase the discount rate by more than the inflation rate. As a result, in terms of the illustration, an increase in the inflation rate reduces the PMI because the reduction to height is relatively greater than the addition of bulk.

In summary, under the illustration, there are three genes: the inflation rate (bulk level), growth (muscle), and the discount rate (height). Height is suppressed by either excess bulk or excess lean. Muscle is increased by the real growth rate of earnings. The combination of height and weight influences the size of P, which drives the level of P/E. The suppression of height by too much bulk or too little mass causes the overall PMI to decline, thus P is driven lower. This effect drives the P in P/E upward and downward. Though the factors impact E (earnings) in the future, the ratio of P/E includes a current value for E that is not affected currently by future growth or future inflation. In effect, the PMI concept is the way that investors incorporate the inflation rate into the price that they are willing to pay in order to achieve an appropriate return.

Method Matters

The value for P/E in the Y Curve graph, figure 7.1, is normalized to adjust for the variability of the earnings cycle. As discussed in chapter 5, the business cycle creates distortions to earnings and thereby P/E, which can send false signals and produce skewed values if they are not normalized for the high variability of the earnings cycle.

Any ratio with two variables, including P/E, should be fairly simple — except when there are so many versions of the variables and
wrong choices can generate distorted results. There are several choices
for P and more than one credible alternative for E. The selection of
each variable is as important and relevant as the choice of fly and
rod when fishing the backwaters.

The most obvious P is the price of the index on any given day. If
P/E is intended to reflect today's valuation of the market, then there
is no better time than the present. Therefore, when a statement is
made about current valuations, whether the market is cheap or expensive, the most appropriate measure to use is the current price.
If the price from last month or last year-end is used instead, it will
not reflect the changes that have occurred since that point and will
only address the valuation of some point in the past that is no longer applicable today.

There are other instances, however, when the current price is not
the most appropriate P for P/E. When assessing historical periods,
for example, which version of P is appropriate? If the analysis uses
the index for December 31, then P/E will reflect the valuation level
for a single date rather than the general price level for the year. For
investors who contributed to or adjusted their portfolios during the
year, which is a significant number of investors, P/E on this basis
would not be representative.

To address this issue, there is a version of P that averages the closing price for each day of the year. The stock market is open for trading approximately 250 days each year. For the annual daily average,
the 250 closing prices are added together and the sum is divided by
250. This average reflects prices across the year. When it is used as
the P in P/E, the result is a valuation measure representative of the
full year. This is the approach used in Crestmont Research analyses
when the series or graph relates to annual data.

Some series, including the one generated by Robert Shiller at
Yale University, provide monthly data for the index as well as other
variables. EPS, for instance, which is reported quarterly, is extrapolated for the months between calendar quarters. P reflects the daily
average across the month. Keep in mind that annual analyses and
graphs that extract the December values rather than use all months

or average all months will represent a hybrid that will not be comparable to other annual analyses.

Further, the hybrid is an awkward cross between two intentions. The year-end value is most appropriate when references are being made to that date or when referring to yearly changes (e.g., to make statements about the gains or losses in the market for the year from start to end). In other instances, an average across each year will be more representative of the entire year for the reasons mentioned above and, therefore, the method of averaging daily data is appropriate. The hybrid approach of using an average for the month of December, however, seems to miss the objectives of each approach.

Nonetheless, there are many uses for the monthly average data set. For analyses and graphs that seek to provide more granularity than is available with annual data, the monthly average is a representative approach to reflect the activity for each month across the year, not just month-ends. Similarly, monthly data can be used to derive quarterly analyses when a quarterly series is not readily available. This latter comment merits a note: When using monthly data to construct annual or quarterly series, do not be surprised or frustrated by small variances to series or analyses produced using daily data. An annual average from days across the year will be slightly different from an average that uses the daily average from months—some months have more days than others and will be underweighted in the annual average, while others have fewer days and will be overweighted.

There are several versions of price (P) for P/E, as well as various methodologies for normalizing earnings (E). Many of the combinations can be appropriate depending upon the circumstances and measure that is needed. In summary, if the objective is to assess the current level of valuation, P/E should include the current market index and a version of normalized EPS. If the objective is to assess historical relationships or to develop a measure of the historical average P/E, the long-term series for P/E should be based upon the average index across each year and a version of normalized EPS. Further, when comparing values for P/E, it is important to use measures that have been developed similarly or that have been adjusted appropriately.

Figure 7.2 presents the historical series for annual P/E based upon the Crestmont methodology and the Adjusted 10-Year Average (Shiller) methodology. Though the two measures provide highly similar results, the Adjusted 10-Year Average series generally rides higher because of the periodic understatement of EPS, as described in chapter 5. The historical average P/E for the two series, adjusting for distortions from the extreme values, is approximately 14 for the Crestmont series and near 15.5 for the Adjusted 10-Year Average series.

Figure 7.2. S&P 500 P/E Ratio (1900–2009):
Crestmont & Adjusted 10-Year Average (Shiller)

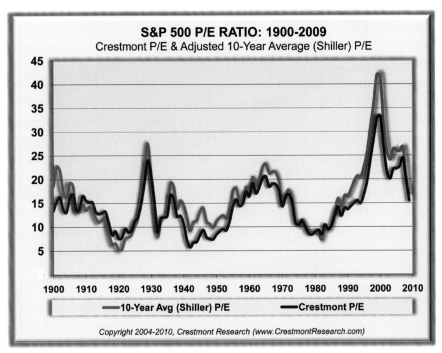

Chapter 5 highlighted the variability of earnings across its cycle, and the desire to have normalized measures of E to avoid distortions. The previous discussion addressed issues relating to EPS as an independent variable and the different approaches to P/E. The EPS cycle also has a significant impact on P/E, including effects on valuation and decisions.

Every Few Years or So

Prepare to expect it and understand how to recognize it; about every few years or so, P/E will not be as it appears. Cheap will be dear and dear will appear cheap. It is time to take another of life's journeys through Alice's looking glass to a world that occasionally operates upside down.

In a hypothetical perfect world, the economy would grow smoothly, earnings would grow consistently, the inflation rate would stay low and stable, and the financial markets would act rationally. Yields on bonds would stay the same, and stock prices would rise by the same amount each year based on the growth in earnings—since P/E would stay the same due to stable inflation and rational markets.

In reality, however, the economic cycle, the business cycle, and the inflation cycle operate independently, albeit with related influences. The economy has active cycles of expansion and recession. Additionally, the business cycle causes earnings to surge and stall. Finally, the inflation rate seems to have its own cycle, which the Federal Reserve is constantly fighting.

Most of all, the financial markets are far from rational. Today there is a field of research called "Behavioral Finance" that studies investor and market psychology. It is probably not a surprise to hear that investors and markets are sometimes irrational. As a result of the business cycle and market fluctuations, both components of the P/E ratio—price and earnings—therefore have a significant degree of short-term variability. This poses quite a challenge for those who seek a precise, or at least relevant, measure of valuation for the stock market.

When the goal is to assess the current level of valuation, investors should use the most recently available price to reflect current valuations in the market. It will not matter where prices were at the beginning of the month or year, or where they have traveled since then. If the quest is to assess the value today for a perspective on current investments or future returns, then the current price is more appropriate than a historical price or average.

Since the purpose of P/E is to measure the current level of valuation, the result should reflect a comparison of the market's price to a measure of the long-term earnings power of the companies in the market index. The reported values for EPS are not sufficiently consistent. Normalizing EPS provides a more valid measure of earnings along the continuum of its baseline trend.

For example, when reported EPS is at a trough in its cycle, P/E based upon the temporarily understated E will then indicate an expensive market. Ironically, an artificially low E makes P/E appear high just when the market might be a great value. Likewise, an artificially high E, at cycle tops, makes P/E appear low just when the market might be overpriced.

The challenge is that the P/E can at times send these mixed or false signals—not because the price (P) is distorted, but rather because the earnings (E) component does not accurately reflect the baseline trend in earnings. The words "baseline trend" should be emphasized because it is not today's earnings that matter; rather, it's the future stream of earnings that is relevant. When earnings is included in a ratio pertaining to stock market valuation, there is a critical assumption: the earnings (E) amount that is included should be representative of the baseline trend for future earnings.

An example can be used to further explore the concept of "baseline trend for future earnings" in the context of a discussion about P/E. Assume that the stock market index has earnings of $100 per share for the past year, and expect the growth rate of earnings to be 5% per year. In the theoretical world, as reflected by the blue line in figure 7.3, the future earnings stream would be $105, $110, $116, $122, $128, $134, $141, etc. The trend reflects a constant compounding growth rate of 5% per year. If the blue line occurred in reality, then for any year the reported earnings value could be used to accurately measure the P/E ratio.

In the real world, however, the earnings stream is never smooth—because of the economic cycle and the business cycle. As a result, the future earnings stream tends to surge for a number of years, then retreat for a year or two. Most important, the surge and retreat in annual earnings tends to fluctuate around the baseline trend for future earnings. As illustrated by the more realistic red line in figure 7.3, the future earnings stream for the example is $107, $115, $126, $138, $119, $130, $137, etc.

Figure 7.3. Earnings Cycle Illustration

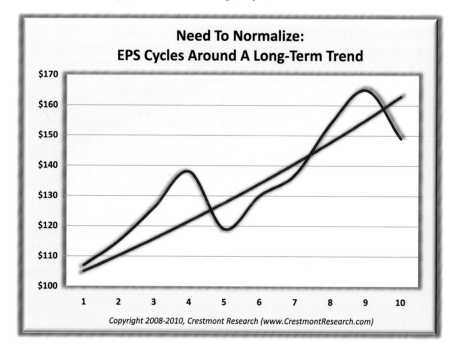

Rarely is the reported earnings value exactly on the baseline trend, yet much of the time it is relatively close. Then near the cycle peaks and troughs, about every several years or so, the value is far enough from the baseline that a significant distortion occurs. When the P/E ratio is calculated using a value near the peak or trough, it will reflect a distorted perspective of valuation and will not be an indication of current value. For the P/E to be valid and representative, it is important for the denominator of the ratio, earnings (E), to reflect the baseline trend for earnings.

As a historical example, in 2002 the market fell dramatically as the economy and the business cycle suffered weakness. The S&P 500 fell below 800. At the same time, earnings declined to $25. The result was a reported P/E of more than 30—irrationally high. Yet, using baseline earnings, P/E had fallen below 20—a somewhat low level for a relatively low inflation environment. Though the pundits were calling for significant further declines due to the overvaluation of the market, a more rational assessment using normalized EPS and P/E indicated that the market had become relatively undervalued.

Figure 7.4. S&P 500 P/E Ratio:
Crestmont, 10-Year + 15%, & As Reported (1990–2009)

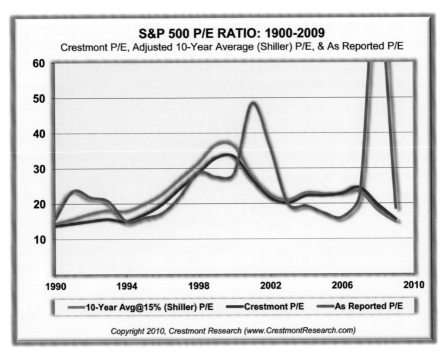

The distortion is evident in figure 7.4, which includes P/E based upon As Reported EPS as well as the two versions of normalized P/E. For this graph, to enhance comparability, the 10-Year Average P/E (Shiller) includes a 15% adjustment to E to compensate for the understatement of EPS under that methodology. Figure 7.2 did not include the adjustment in order to highlight the effect of not adjusting for the ten-year lag in real earnings growth.

Figure 7.4 therefore offers two messages: First, the two methodologies for normalizing P/E provide relatively similar results, each having the advantages and disadvantages that were previously discussed. Second, a normalized P/E is necessary to avoid the distortions and false signals from the As Reported P/E.

For example, troughs in the EPS cycle during the early 1990s, the early 2000s, and the late 2000s misrepresented P/E as overvalued while the normalized versions of P/E presented a more rational view of valuation. Likewise, peaks in the EPS cycle during the late 1990s and mid-2000s mistakenly lured investors to believe that the market was attractive.

Beyond the comparisons across the various methods for P/E, the level of P/E should be viewed relative to the level of the inflation rate, so even though P/E has been well-above average over most of the last decade, it was generally in the range associated with low inflation. Short-term distortions in P/E, not fully apparent in the annual data presented in figure 7.4, can provide indications of longer-term secular conditions or shorter-term cyclical anomalies.

If, for example, P/E is relatively high, and inflation is expected to trend higher over a number of years, then the stock market is likely to experience a secular bear period. If, on the contrary, P/E is extremely low when inflation is low, as it was in the spring of 2009, then the stock market is very likely poised for a surge once the short-term factors that are affecting the price of the market are resolved. The temporarily low P/E during the recent financial crisis did not position the stock market to move from secular bear to secular bull; it only provided a cyclical bull market once the crisis faded.

When the level of P/E is inconsistent with the expected trend in the inflation rate, it is more likely positioned for a short-term cyclical move. Secular cycles are driven by long-term trends in the inflation rate, not by temporary market surges or falls. The conditions that enable significant distortions between P/E and the inflation rate rarely persist. Once resolved, the market realigns with the fundamental drivers. Cyclical bull and bear markets are short-term surges or falls in valuation due to euphoria or crisis. Secular bull and bear markets are long-term periods of revaluation due to shifts in the overall inflation rate. Warren Buffett exalts Benjamin Graham's wisdom by emphasizing that the stock market in the short run is a voting machine subject to investor sentiment and crisis, but in the long run it is a weighing machine that is compelled by fundamental principles of valuation.

As an interim summary, foremost, the driver of secular stock market cycles is P/E as driven by the inflation rate. Second, an accurate measure of P/E is crucial; otherwise, there are relatively frequent false signals when the earnings cycle has passed through its baseline midpoint. When the false signals are most extreme, they send a strong and opposite message about valuation. For the assessment of current valuation and future returns, P/E based upon current prices and normalized earnings provides a relatively accurate measure of true valuation.

Natural High

The stock market bubble of the late 1990s forged new ground for P/E. Historically, P/E generally peaked at the end of secular bull markets at levels in the mid-20s. At the end of the 1990s, P/E didn't just find a slightly higher cloud—P/E left the atmosphere. Though it is now generally recognized that the stock market was in a bubble phase, it was not clear at the time to many analysts and investors.

By the late 1990s, many well-respected economists and policymakers believed the technology boom would deliver higher real economic growth for the future. Many "New Economy" pundits expected a lasting increase to productivity from inventions and information technology (IT) investments. Alan Greenspan, former chairman of the Federal Reserve Board, spoke on a number of occasions about the expected increase in productivity and economic growth. In remarks to the National Governors' Association in 1996, he said: "The rapid acceleration of computer and telecommunications technologies can reasonably be expected to appreciably raise our productivity and standards of living in the twenty-first century certainly, and quite possibly in some of the remaining years of this century." Later that same year, at the Federal Reserve Bank of Boston's 40th Economic Conference, Greenspan commented: "...as the infrastructure of the economy finally adjusts itself to the new semiconductor-based revolution, the rapid changes are likely to finally become more evident in increased measured productivity and growth." Then in 1998 testifying before a Joint Economic Committee of the United States Congress, he said: "The hopes for accelerated productivity growth have been bolstering expectations of future corporate earnings and thereby fueling still further increases in equity values." His comments not only represented his thinking at the time but also spanned multiple years and reflected a studied position, not just a momentary musing.

This and previous chapters have emphasized the impact of the inflation rate on P/E. Inflation increases the required rate of return, which in turn drives down P/E enabling investors to earn higher returns to offset inflation. The discussions further highlighted that P/E is vulnerable to deflation because deflation causes the growth rate of E to be negative. Declining cash flows are less valuable than rising cash flows. Therefore the fundamental principles that establish the level of P/E provide that lower inflation is better and higher growth is better—as long as higher growth does not occur because of higher inflation.

In the latter half of the 1990s, as reflected in Greenspan's comments, a general outlook emerged for higher productivity that was expected to bring an extended era of higher growth. As investors incorporated this outlook into the stock market, P/E rose to highs that were above previous peaks—the previous peaks had been based upon economic growth rates that were lower than the "New Economy" outlook. Though the historical growth rate for GDP of near 3% had endured over the prior century and particularly over the prior few decades, a more optimistic view challenged that assumption.

Even though the skeptical analysts ultimately were proven right, the stock market may have been rationally reacting to the expectation—or hope—that the New Economy was a new era. By mid-1999, even Greenspan became skeptical. In his comments to the Joint Economic Committee of Congress in June, he said: "The rate of growth of productivity cannot increase indefinitely. While there appears to be considerable expectation in the business community, and possibly Wall Street, that the productivity acceleration has not yet peaked, experience advises caution." It took the stock market several years to readjust the growth expectations that were being reflected in P/E back to the historical norm. P/E ultimately returned to levels appropriate for low inflation and average growth, back to the mid-20s in the early 2000s. Even without the bubble and readjustment, once valuations reached the mid-20s, without an up-shift in real growth, the stock market was destined for a secular bear cycle.

That period in history helps to highlight the effect that economic growth has on the ceiling for P/E. The historically average and relatively consistent growth rate of approximately 3% drove the ceiling for more than a century. P/E peaked at levels near the mid-20s. The hope of growth shifting above 3% "in the twenty-first century certainly," according to Greenspan, may have been assimilated by the market, thus rationally lifting P/E to new heights. If real economic growth and earnings growth had shifted to a higher level, then a higher level of P/E would have been justified.

The growth rate of the economy, and thereby the growth rate of earnings, sets the ceiling. Inflation and deflation set the range of decline from that ceiling. The impact of the economic growth rate on the range for P/E highlights the importance of the growth rate as Major Uncertainty #2 over this decade.

Since inflation increases the discount rate, and deflation turns earnings growth negative, both of which drive P/E lower, P/E has a peak at a point near the transition between inflation and deflation. That is the point at which secular bull markets end and secular bear markets begin. Once P/E peaks, ultimately the only way to go is down.

P/E reacts to the inflation rate. As a result, P/E must be viewed in that context. When the inflation rate is relatively high, investors should expect that P/E would naturally be low. At low inflation, a fairly valued P/E will be high. The earlier discussion about the "reversion-to-the-meanists" presented the contrasting view that the historical average P/E is the natural level. They consider the stock market to be overvalued whenever P/E is above the historical average, and undervalued when P/E is below average.

The reversion-to-the-meanists believe that the fair value level for the stock market is its historical mean, another term for average. Reversion is the concept of realignment back to a point, in this case the mean, so reversion-to-the-meanists are constantly reacting to P/E's position in relation to its long-term average. The result is that they will be right about half the time—pretty good odds for stock market analysts and weather forecasters. A more complete understanding of the drivers of P/E and stock market returns, however, can help investors to be right much more often. There's no reason to settle for even odds when your savings and retirement are at stake.

Validation

P/E is a thermometer of stock market valuation. It is subject to distortion, just like a thermometer mounted in full sun or near a leaky window in your home. Because P/E is susceptible to the distortions of the earnings cycle, various methodologies were previously discussed to adjust the variables in the ratio to mitigate those effects and provide a more reliable reading of valuation. Additionally in recent years, due to the use of operating earnings as E in P/E, the frequency of reports with a distorted P/E for the stock market has increased.

Operating earnings is derived by starting with actual reported earnings or forecast net earnings and adding back supposedly one-time expenses or gains. In theory, this is a good concept. During some years, companies will have expenses or income items that do not recur annually. If there is an expense that reduces earnings temporarily, then such a shortfall may not require a reduction in dividends. If earnings include one-time gains from the sale of a facility, for example, then a corresponding increase in the ongoing dividend may not be appropriate. Some analysts seek to reduce the distortion to reported earnings by adjusting earnings for the one-time charges and income that create single-year distortions. This is the concept behind operating earnings.

If the adjustments are applied consistently and accurately, then there should be equal positive and negative adjustments to reported earnings over time. If the adjustments are not equal, then the accountants and auditors have a lot of explaining to do about how to reconcile reported earnings with the equity account on the balance sheet — proper accounting does not have an account somewhere that allows perpetual adjustments for negative charges.

Over the past two decades, measures of operating earnings have shown significant positive variances to reported earnings. It is not unusual for operating earnings to exceed reported earnings by 20% or more, and during those two decades, the cumulative effect of operating earnings exceeding reported earnings has been significant. The effect on P/E is a significant reduction to the ratio. If, for example, the stock market index is 1,200 and normalized EPS is $60, then

P/E is 20. If operating EPS is used and is estimated to be $72 (20% more than $60), then the reported value for P/E is 16.7.

Further, analysts often include a forward-looking estimate for operating earnings, presumably to help investors understand where values will be in the future. Forward earnings can be an additional 10% or 20% higher than the prior year. In this example, the forward operating P/E would be based upon EPS of $85. The result is a P/E of 14.1, making the stock market appear cheap when that P/E is inappropriately compared to historical averages that are based upon trailing net earnings.

Operating earnings could be a valid measure of core earnings if the variances ultimately were zero, thereby reconciling with earnings, dividends, and cash flow over the long term. The consistent bias toward positive variances challenges the credibility of the measure. Additionally, forward estimates of earnings can offer additional perspectives about the trend and status of the earnings cycle, but only if they are consistently accurate. Currently, most measures of operating earnings and forward earnings are not sufficiently accurate as representations of the future baseline tend for net earnings. Measures of operating earnings and forward earnings are therefore not appropriate values for calculating a normalized P/E, especially not one that is compared to the historical average for P/E based upon net earnings.

The mixing of P/Es derived from alternate methods is in effect comparing apples to oranges. P/E based upon forward operating earnings should only be compared to the historical average for forward operating earnings, which does not exist since formal and consistent estimates of forward operating earnings is a relatively recent concept. If a fifty- or one-hundred-year average did exist for P/E based upon forward operating earnings, the value would likely be close to 10.

During periods when the simple P/E, the current market index divided by reported earnings, is different from the normalized versions of P/E, there is another way to validate which of them is more likely representative of the true valuation of the stock market. Unusual P/Es can result from the use of operating earnings, the use of non-normalized reported earnings, or from erroneous data. When you see a reading of P/E that appears suspect, a quick technique to assess the market P/E is to use the dividend yield as a proxy.

Dividends are paid from earnings, and over time remain much more stable and consistent than earnings. In recent decades, the normalized payout ratio of dividends is about 45% of earnings. To perform the validation, the reported dividend yield (D/P) can be converted into a price/dividend ratio (P/D) by inverting the ratio. If the dividend yield D/P is 2%, then P/D will be 50. When P/D is multiplied by the average payout ratio of 45%, the result of 22.5 can be used as an estimated P/E to compare to the reported and normalized P/E. Do not expect the values to be exactly equal; the objective is to compare the values for relative perspective. The P/E derived from the dividend yield should be relatively similar to the P/E using normalized EPS. Both the dividend-derived P/E and the normalized P/E can provide a better indication of market valuation than the As Reported P/E.

Early in the last century, the dividend payout ratio was closer to 65%. Over time, the dividend ratio has declined to near 45%. This reflects a variety of possible contributing factors, including a shift in the mix of less value-oriented companies to more dividend-retaining, growth-oriented companies, an increase in periodic stock buybacks rather than higher annual dividends, and perhaps that companies require higher internal reinvestments that have compromised dividend payouts. The research about the reasons is inconclusive, yet the data clearly reflect a historical trend toward a lower dividend payout ratio from earnings.

Regardless of the reasons that payout ratios are lower today than they were historically, the annual dividend payout rate is actually not as volatile as it appears when the payout rate is simply based upon reported earnings. When earnings are normalized to adjust for the business cycle, the dividend payout ratio is relatively stable as a percentage of normalized earnings. This provides an alternate benchmark against which to assess stock market valuation. Though the 45% payout ratio may change in the future, for now that factor appears to be representative of the current dividend payout rate.

Game Changer

The historical range within which P/E has cycled has been relatively consistent: generally with lows that were near 8 and highs in the

CHAPTER 7 · GETTING TO P/E   119

low to mid-20s. The historical average has been near 15, depending upon the method and time period used. The range of the P/E cycle, as established by the highs and lows, is largely determined by the real growth rate of earnings. The relative position of P/E within the range is what has been determined by the level of inflation and its trend.

The previous discussion about economics raised the possibility that future real growth, excluding inflation, may have downshifted from its historical trend of 3%. This major issue has not often been considered. In the past century, real economic growth has increased at slightly more than 3% annually. As a result of the relationship between earnings and the economy, EPS has increased at near 3% in real terms.

Therefore the range of the past P/E cycles has been driven by real growth near 3%. That level of growth has been considered a standard assumption. The recent decade and other factors are now challenging that assumption for the future.

One effect of slower economic and earnings growth is a lower level of earnings in the future. For example, over ten years, $1.00 compounds to $1.34 at 3%, but only to $1.22 at 2%. The difference is about 9.3% less EPS for the stock market under the slower growth scenario. Many analysts would consider that level of variance a minor forecasting error for EPS over a decade. Whether the stock market is 9% higher or lower in a decade is generally small change in the context of overall returns. But the implication of slower growth is far more significant than simply the ending level of earnings. Slower growth is a game changer.

There are three ways to assess its effect, all of which provide similar results. First, an extremely long-term model of earnings growth, dividend payouts, and present value can be constructed to assess the impact of changes in growth on P/E. Second, the academic formulas can be used to derive the effects on P/E based upon perpetual dividend growth. Third, the impact on P/E can be evaluated through the components of stock market return. Since all three approaches reflect comparable results, the more pragmatic third approach will be used to explore the implications.

Before examining the details, consider the significance of the issue. If the future growth rate of earnings decreases by 1% (i.e., near the reduction that would be expected if economic growth decreases by 1%), the historical average for P/E would decline from 15.5 to 11.5—representing a 26% decline in the stock market beyond the 9% shortfall from lower earnings growth. More dramatic, the typical peak in P/E falls from the low to mid-20s to the mid-teens; the adverse impact of slower growth increases at higher levels of P/E.

As previously discussed, inflation causes P/E to decrease because investors demand more return to compensate for higher inflation. Unlike the inflation rate, the growth rate of earnings does not necessarily change the return level that investors expect. They will still expect returns that are commensurate with the stock market and the expected inflation rate, but they will look to replace the contribution of slower earnings growth with another source of return.

To illustrate, assuming that a change in the growth rate does not change the inflation rate, the yields on government bonds can be expected to remain the same. Absent a change in credit quality from slower growth, the risk premium within corporate bond yields would not change. Likewise, the expected return from stock market investments can be expected to remain unchanged due to the growth rate.

When slower growth reduces the contribution of earnings growth to total return, another source of return is therefore needed to fill the shortfall. Stock market investors will not be willing to take equity risk without appropriate equity returns. If bond yields do not change, they will not compromise stock market returns. In this situation, stock market investors will step away until the price of the market declines to again provide appropriate returns. This is the function of markets—finding the price that provides a fair return.

This discussion relates to the effect from changes in the growth rate of earnings. To isolate that factor, several assumptions are needed, basically providing that the relevant relationships remain the same. First, based upon the previous economics discussion, a downshift in economic growth drives slower earnings growth. Second, long-term profit margins remain similar under both growth scenarios, thus the slowing of earnings growth is consistent with the downshift in economic growth. Third, the inflation rate remains constant across both scenarios for growth. Fourth, the expected return for stocks and bonds as well as the related equity risk premium for stocks does not change across both scenarios for growth. In other words, the relevant relationships remain the same.

Of the three components of stock market returns, two are available as sources of return, and the third one represents the way in which returns occur. The first source of return, EPS growth, is defined in this example as either providing 3% or 2% toward to the total return. As a result, the second source of return, dividend yield, will need to increase to compensate for lower earnings growth in the second scenario. Herein is the role of the third source of stock market returns: changes in P/E.

The dividend yield rises as P/E declines and vice versa. For the stock market to be positioned to provide equity-level returns, investors will look for the lower price that enables the dividend yield to rise sufficiently to offset the loss of earnings growth. The required decline in P/E varies based upon the starting level of P/E.[1]

If P/E starts relatively high, then a higher decline is required to provide the required dividend yield increase. For example, if EPS growth drops by 1%, then the change in P/E required to increase the dividend yield by 1% is 7 points from 22 to 15, 4 points from 15.5 to 11.5, and 2 points from 10 to 8.

This shift in P/E relates only to the change in earnings growth. P/E would then be further affected by changes in the inflation rate.

There will likely be, and needs to be, much debate about the accuracy of the estimates presented above, and about nuances that could add decimal points to the factors, or adjust the effects based upon further scenario assumptions. However, whether using long-term models, academic formulas, or the component-based method, all three approaches provide similar results. It is therefore important to recognize that slower growth will have a significant impact on P/E at all levels of the inflation rate. As the discussion evolves into implications and probable outcomes over this decade, slower economic and earnings growth will have a direct effect on the P/E range.

In closing, P/E is a measurement tool for market valuation. The level of P/E, driven by the principles of present value, reflects the price at which the stock market can deliver sufficient returns to compensate for inflation and risk. P/E is driven lower when conditions of inflation change the outlook for required returns. In addition, P/E declines when deflation changes the outlook for the level of future earnings. Of particular note, slower long-term economic and earnings growth reduces future cash flows and drive P/E lower. Conditions of solid long-term earnings growth and low inflation therefore provide the best conditions for a high P/E. In an environment where economic growth and the inflation rate are major uncertainties, an accurate and valid measure of P/E is more relevant and needed than ever before.

POINTS OF EMPHASIS

- P/E declines from inflation and deflation, but for completely different reasons. P/E is driven by: (a) the discounting of cash flows; and (b) the future stream of cash flows.

- Inflation attacks the first factor (discounting), yet it somewhat increases the second factor (future cash flows). The devastating force on discounting is greater than the increase to future cash flow. As a result, P/E declines as inflation increases.

- Deflation attacks the second factor (future cash flows), yet it delivers a very positive effect to the first factor (discounting). The positive effect on discounting is overcome by the negative effect on future cash flows. As a result, P/E declines as deflation worsens.

- P/E is highest during periods of low, stable inflation when there is the powerful combination of favorable discounting compounding positive growth in cash flows.

- Reductions in long-term EPS growth downshift the range for P/E.

CHAPTER 8

GREAT THEORIES AND
BUSTED MYTHS

In theory, theory and reality are the same;
in reality, they're not.
— *Attributed to Yogi Berra*

Several of the great theories of investment finance were
developed over fifty years ago. Some of them later received Nobel
Prizes and other high acclaim. Few, however, have been updated
following decades of use and a plethora of new information. These
theories relate to the functioning of the market, portfolio construction, and return assumptions. The purpose of discussing them is to
better appreciate how they have influenced the understanding of the
stock market and approaches to investing. This is especially important because these principles, widely used in practice, are too often
misused or misunderstood. With that perspective, it may be time to
rejuvenate these theories a bit to enhance their relevance and applicability by incorporating the past fifty-plus years of new information
and better understanding.

Efficient-Market Hypothesis

The review of investment theories will start at the roots with one theory
that influences many others. It serves as a fundamental assumption

for theories that will follow. The first theory of financial investments is the Efficient-Market Hypothesis (EMH), introduced by Eugene Fama at the University of Chicago in the 1960s.

EMH asserts that the markets are efficient—all publicly available information is immediately incorporated into the prices of securities; therefore, investors are unable to benefit from the skill of identifying and investing in mispriced securities. Fama's work proposed several levels of efficient markets and included considerations that allow for a market process, but EMH is often viewed as a market condition.

Imagine Professor Fama walking across campus one day, talking with a curious student on the way to class. There, in the middle of the sidewalk, lies a $20 bill. The student first notices it as they approach; Fama seems unaffected. The student, a bit reserved, does not want to distract his mentor and so ignores the temptation. After they pass by the $20 bill, the student, unable to resist, interrupts the professor to ask why he did not stop to pick up the money. Fama replies: "If the $20 bill actually existed, then someone else would have already picked it up."

Note in the description of EMH as well as the hypothetical story about Fama that this principle of market efficiency relates to a condition of the market rather than a process of the market. Though the theory evolved over time, it generally maintains that investment skill cannot beat the market because the market exists as an efficient condition in which all relevant information is recognized in stock prices.

After many years of market-beating performance by skilled investors, hedge funds, market traders, etc., there is mounting evidence that the market is a process of assimilating information rather than a state of information efficiency. As a result, the efficient-market hypothesis should describe a process rather than a condition, a process that includes the skills of speed, insight, and analytical prowess capable of delivering investment performance that exceeds market returns.

When this concept influences the other theories, bear in mind that markets assimilate information into prices. People who trade and invest in the market pursue a process of price discovery through bidding. Investors with different information or perceptions buy and sell securities such that the market price moves to reflect the balance between buyers and sellers. The ultimate condition of price efficiency in the market is the result of a process through which some market participants benefit from the early use of new information as it permeates into market prices.

Like onion and salt to many recipes, EMH is a part of most of the theories that follow. Some people still believe the original proposition of EMH. Others who now reject the rigidity of EMH have not yet incorporated that understanding into their thinking about the other EMH-driven theories. EMH appears to have been adopted rigidly by its name: Efficient-Market Hypothesis. Consider how different the understanding might be, and how the debate might have evolved, had it been called the Market Efficiency Hypothesis.

Modern Portfolio Theory

Modern Portfolio Theory (MPT), developed by Harry Markowitz in the 1950s, is a theory of tradeoffs between investment risk and return. The theory was groundbreaking and ultimately earned a Nobel Prize. MPT provides that a diversified portfolio eliminates risks related to individual companies, and synthesizes the pure risk of the market into portfolios. Because investors earn returns only for risks that cannot be diversified away, MPT provides the basis for a framework to develop investment portfolios.

The academic details are not needed for this discussion; however, the key concept to appreciate about MPT is that when markets are efficient, the market pays only for risks that you must take, and will not pay you for risks that you can diversify away. As a result, you are supposed to take only the risk for which you will be paid—which is overall market risk. In the end, this becomes the great justification for buying and holding stocks for the long term.

The reality of exposing your portfolio to this theory, however, is that MPT as presented by Markowitz has aspects that have been overlooked, and MPT has been widely misused. MPT should come with a warning label: Use with caution. It's only as good as your assumptions. What did Harry Markowitz intend to impart with his groundbreaking research, and what are the implications given a reasonable view of future long-term returns from today?

Markowitz published his research entitled "Portfolio Selection" in *The Journal of Finance* in 1952. He led with:

The process of selecting a portfolio may be divided into two stages. The first stage starts with observation and experience and ends with beliefs about the future performances of available securities. The second stage starts with the relevant beliefs about future performances and ends with the choice of the portfolio. This paper is concerned with the second stage.

Therefore, with emphasis from Markowitz, MPT leaves the first stage of developing the assumptions to the user. MPT is a highly powerful framework, but only if the assumptions are valid.

Many decades have passed since the article was first published. Many, many buy-and-hold advocates have reiterated their mantra in concert with Dr. Markowitz. But that may not have been what he intended. Yes, investors should be rewarded only for taking risks that cannot be neutralized. Yes, stocks have more risk than bonds, and over time have realized higher returns, but what if your timeframe is not seventy-five to one hundred years, and what if you are starting from a period of relatively high valuations and the expectation of below-average future returns?

To determine a reasonable assumption for stock market returns over this decade, it may be insightful to assess all ten-year periods over the past century. That is the first stage Markowitz referred to—before MPT can be applied to investment portfolios. Since 1900 there have been 101 rolling ten-year periods. The first was from 1900–1909, then 1901–1910, and ninety-nine decade-long periods thereafter. For simplicity in this discussion, the results can be sorted into two groups: those with above-average returns and those with below-average returns.

One characteristic that is prevalent for the two halves is the starting level of valuation in the market as determined by the price/earnings ratio (P/E), the leading indicator of prices in the stock market. Throughout the past century, when P/E started above average, subsequent returns generally were below average. Further, a below-average P/E generally delivered above-average returns. So when P/E is well above average, as it was at the end of 2009, should not the assumption for Markowitz's model be below-average returns?

Markowitz developed a valuable tool for portfolio management; conventional wisdom has forgotten or ignored the need to use appropriate assumptions—the essential "first stage" of portfolio management. Too often, MPT is used with the assumption of the long-term average return without regard to the impact of P/E on returns. As Markowitz emphasizes, it is the responsibility of investors to use "observation and experience" to develop "beliefs about the future performances." Though future performance of the stock market cannot be predicted with certainty, insights from observation and experience may be able to at least refine the assumptions into above-average or below-average territory. Since current market valuations are above average, it would be appropriate to include a below-average return assumption for the next ten years and possibly even longer.

Cousins CAPM and MPT

The Capital Asset Pricing Model (CAPM) builds upon the concepts of Modern Portfolio Theory (MPT). Whereas MPT provides the principles relating to the tradeoff of risk and return in constructing portfolios as well as the benefits of diversification, CAPM provides the model, or methodology, for optimizing the risk/return relationship of a portfolio. The formula for CAPM, including its Greek letters and function signs, is far too detailed for this discussion. The relevant point to take away is that the traditional application of MPT and CAPM may be well intended, but for investors its use in practice has been misguided.

If the first rule of portfolio management is diversification, why do most investors unwittingly concentrate their risks?

Many investors believe that a portfolio constructed with numerous stocks and bonds is diversified. That approach has its roots in the principles of MPT and CAPM. When, however, MPT and CAPM are misapplied, they do not provide the roadmap to secure investing, and leave investors vulnerable to substantial risk. Harry Markowitz developed MPT in the early 1950s. William F. Sharpe, Jack Treynor, and others, building on Dr. Markowitz's work, further developed these principles into CAPM during the 1960s.

CAPM explains that every investment carries two distinct risks. The first is general market risk, which Sharpe called systematic risk. Market risk, commonly known by the term for the second letter in the Greek alphabet ("beta"), is a pure risk unaffected by diversification. The second risk relates to individual companies, known as specific risk or non-systematic risk. As MPT provides, investors are compensated only through returns for market risk, since company-related risks can be diversified away. As a result, CAPM views beta as the source of expected return from a stock market portfolio. CAPM further provides the framework to measure the risk and expected return.

In combination, MPT and CAPM have been the basis for structuring investment portfolios for the past several decades. Based upon an investor's risk profile, allocations are made across the investment alternatives. Decades ago, there were stocks and bonds, and occasionally alternative investments like real estate or gold. As a result, portfolios were developed from a very limited palette. Investors and advisors have typically used the groundbreaking MPT and CAPM principles to structure diversified portfolios of stocks and bonds.

The Nobel Prize-winning team determined that market risk is the only risk that investors are paid to include in their portfolios. Since the risks associated with individual companies can be diversified away, the systematic market risk is the source of returns. Most investors have heard this principle stated another way: 80% to 90% of the returns come from being in the market, and a fraction comes from stock selection.

Actually, if an investor is sufficiently diversified to achieve academic theory, then CAPM indicates that the percentage should be the entire 100%. Proper diversification should provide investors with investment returns that are consistent with the market returns.

According to the CAPM model, these principles can be applied to both stocks and bonds. A diversified portfolio of stocks tends to provide the returns of the general stock market. Once individual company risk is diversified, the pure stock market risk remains. Thus the portfolio moves with the stock market. Stock market returns are driven by earnings growth and valuation changes, as measured by the price/earnings ratio (P/E). If P/E increases, stock market returns are generally high, since the P/E ratio multiplies the effect of rising earnings. If P/E decreases, stock market returns will be low or negative, since a declining P/E generally offsets the benefit of rising earnings.

Similarly, the principles of the model apply to bonds. Once the individual company risks are diversified, the portfolio moves in concert with the bond market. The bond market is largely driven by trends in longer-term interest rates. As many investors have experienced, when interest rates decline, bond values increase. Likewise, rising interest rates cause bond values to decline. Thus if interest rates are falling, the yield from the bond portfolio is supplemented with increases in the value of the bonds; or, if rates are rising, the decline in bond prices offsets some of the portfolio yield, resulting in lower total returns.

CAPM is a theory about structuring portfolios to optimize return in relation to risk. For decades, portfolios have been structured based upon the tradeoff between the lower risk and return profile of bonds, and the higher risk and return profile of stocks. Further, statistics show that bond returns are not correlated with stock returns over shorter-term periods. Because of the low correlation, the combination of bonds and stocks lowers the statistical measures of volatility, which is often used as a measure of risk. This combination of portfolio tradeoff and low correlation has led investors to incorrectly view portfolios of bonds and stocks as being diversified over their relevant investment horizons.

The model relies, in theory, upon assumptions and statistics that have unintended consequences in reality. An investment portfolio that is structured with traditional allocations of 60% in a diversified stock portfolio, 30% in a diversified bond portfolio, and 10% in other investments is concentrated 90% across two risks: stock market risk and bond market risk. And over longer periods of time, particularly during inflation, those two markets tend to move in the same direction. For example, in the 1970s, when inflation rose, both stocks and bonds performed poorly. In the 1980s, as inflation declined, both stocks and bonds soared. Stocks and bonds are financial assets that are driven by the force of present value — so it is not surprising that they move together over longer periods of time. Statistically, bonds and stocks have a low correlation across shorter-term periods, but the returns can be highly related over periods that are relevant to long-term investors. Consequently, while CAPM may optimize a portfolio on paper, the results at times may not be satisfactory on investors' account statements.

This does not indicate that the principles of MPT and CAPM are not valid. Issues arise at times when the principles are misapplied or when the application of the principles has not evolved as the financial markets have become more complex and sophisticated. Dr. Markowitz's publication of MPT in 1952 discussed the concept of "performances of available securities." In 1952, the available investment choices for investors were relatively limited beyond stocks and bonds, especially as related to liquid or publicly traded securities. A portfolio allocated across the two primary asset classes was about as diversified as it could be at the time.

Many investors today may not realize that mutual funds were uncommon before the 1980s (there were fewer than 300 in the 1960s; there are nearly 10,000 today). In addition, other investment choices and available securities have exploded over the past two decades. The menu now includes asset-backed securities, foreign investments, real estate, options, commodities, investment trusts, private partnerships, inflation-protected bonds, exchange-traded funds, etc.

Currently, the P/E ratio of the stock market is above average and relatively high. Interest rates and bond yields are near historic lows. Given the relatively high valuation level for both of the traditional asset classes, the risks related to stocks and bonds appear to be biased toward risk rather than return.

Returning to Dr. Markowitz, diversification in a portfolio applies to risks, not securities. Numerous investment alternatives and approaches are available today that can diversify exposure to various risks. Investment portfolios of all sizes and profiles can be diversified in ways that were not available historically, and as a result, investors can avoid being concentrated into the two major asset classes and their similar risks.

This discussion introduced three popular theories of investment, and explored the ways that they are sometimes misunderstood and misapplied. It should be recognized that a slightly modified, or maybe modern, perspective could yield greater value from these valuable theories and models.

In summary, markets are an efficiency process rather than an efficient condition; thus there are opportunities to benefit from skill in an investment portfolio. Diversification in portfolios should include the wide variety of investment alternatives (when they are a good value). Investment models are valuable for constructing portfolios — but most of all they require relevant and realistic assumptions.

One final concept needs to be considered before ending the discussion about investment finance. This tool is commonly used to evaluate portfolios. It relies upon some of the previous investment-theory misconceptions, and often leads to poor decisions by investors.

Monte Carlo Is a Bad Bet

Monte Carlo simulation, when applied to investment portfolios, is a methodology that enables analysts to assess the expected performance of the portfolio. The methodology evaluates the portfolio's results over an extensive number of scenarios relating to the investor's time horizon, to create a profile of likely outcomes. Essentially, Monte Carlo simulation takes a limited number of time periods and mixes and matches them into sets to create a lot of scenarios. With a hundred years of data, for example, Monte Carlo simulation can create millions of thirty-year scenarios. Then, by looking at the results of all of them, the portfolio can be analyzed for likelihood of success, portfolio gains, risk, etc. A key assumption underlying the methodology is that events are random, and therefore combinations of events are relevant representations of actual potential occurrences.

To illustrate Monte Carlo simulation, assume that you are going to Chicago for a week of vacation, and you want to know the likely weather forecast. Monte Carlo simulation would take a full year of daily weather data and generate millions of scenarios by mixing and matching random days during the year to create hypothetical weeklong periods. You can then supposedly analyze those weeklong scenarios to assess the probability of temperature, rainfall, snow, etc. for your trip to Chicago.

The weeklong scenarios from Monte Carlo simulation for your July 4 vacation could include, for example, a hypothetical week with the historical weather from the following random days: September 5,

February 21, June 15, April 1, October 8, May 29, and December 11.

Ridiculous? Yes. Weather is not strictly a random pattern of events—the seasons influence the general conditions of weather. It is implausible that your July week in Chicago could have the weather that follows the sequence listed above or could in any way relate to a hodgepodge of dates across seasons of the year.

When Monte Carlo simulation is applied to a stock or bond portfolio, the computer generates millions of scenarios by randomly combining various periods from history. The methodology incorrectly assumes that markets are efficient and market returns are random. Supposedly, arbitrary periods from history can be combined to simulate valid scenarios about the future.

It's not that Monte Carlo simulation is an invalid technique; rather, Monte Carlo is inappropriate to use for situations like weather forecasting or analyzing expected success from the stock market. Since randomness is a major underlying assumption for Monte Carlo simulation, similar periods would need to be combined to generate valid and reliable results.

For example, regarding your trip to Chicago, a Monte Carlo simulation that included only dates from July across many years should produce a result that has some validity. It would still have a few odd events, like matching a rainy day from one year with a dry spell from others. If the weather in Chicago tends to run in patterns, some of the results might not be totally applicable, yet at least you'll have eliminated the winter days from your scenarios.

Stock market returns are not a random pattern either. There are secular stock market seasons; the valuation level at the time of investment drives the ultimate level of returns. If, therefore, Monte Carlo simulation is applied to stock market returns (or any financial market), then it should include only data from relevant periods. Similar to the weather, not all scenarios would be entirely valid, yet this one step can greatly enhance the reliability of the results.

Since the valuation level of the stock market is a significant driver of future returns, the relevant periods for Monte Carlo simulation should be periods with a similar level of valuation. This can be accomplished by limiting the periods that are included in the analysis, based upon market P/E. The data history could be segmented into above-average and below-average halves or further refined into quartiles, quintiles, or deciles. These comments are not intended to provide a specific protocol for Monte Carlo simulation; rather, the objective is to raise a major shortcoming of a commonly used technique, and to encourage refinements that are appropriate for individual situations and market conditions.

Likewise, this chapter highlights the shortcomings of various investment theories to encourage a more modern application of the theories and to develop a better understanding of them within the context of secular stock market cycles. This is especially relevant today given the likelihood that the current secular bear will be prowling for another decade or longer.

POINTS OF EMPHASIS

- Markets are an efficiency process rather than an efficient condition; they seek to assimilate information into prices through the discovery process of buyers and sellers transacting.

- Modern Portfolio Theory (MPT) advocates diversifying portfolios to concentrate returns based upon market risk and returns.

- MPT specifically demands that investors take responsibility for the driver of the model — the assumption for future returns.

- The Capital Asset Pricing Model (CAPM) builds on MPT to assist investors in building efficient portfolios. When portfolios are concentrated into stocks and bonds, the short-term diversification effects can lead to long-term correlations.

- Monte Carlo simulation requires that its underlying events be random in nature, which in reality is not the circumstance for stock market returns. Relevant periods can help to make Monte Carlo simulation appropriate for analyzing stock market portfolios.

SECTION IV

SECULAR STOCK
MARKET CYCLES

Predicament [pre-dik-a-mint]:
a perplexing or troublesome situation
from which extrication is difficult.

CHAPTER 9

FROM SEVERAL PERSPECTIVES

As the current secular bear market continues into another decade, people are certainly beginning to wonder: "Is this secular bear market almost over?" and "How long before the next secular bull market starts?" The reality is that the current secular bear market likely has a long way to go, both in terms of magnitude and time.

The current high level of valuation indicates that the stock market remains in a secular bear period and far from a secular bull cycle. As a result, it's important to explore both types of secular cycles in a discussion of probable outcomes for this decade. Economic and financial conditions could deteriorate more quickly than expected and hasten the course for this secular bear. Likewise, economic and financial conditions could sustain low inflation and historically average GDP growth, thereby extending this secular bear cycle throughout this decade, delivering positive, albeit very modest, returns for the 2010s.

In addition, though secular bull and bear cycles have distinct periods with designated starting and ending dates, investors have time horizons that often overlap more than one cycle. Ten-year periods, which to most people are relatively long segments of time, have frequently included parts of both secular bull and bear cycles. In the graphs and analyses that follow, secular stock market cycles will be assessed from several perspectives.

The Long-Term View

Secular stock market cycles are long-term periods, often lasting a decade or more. When viewed over a century, the pattern of alternating cycles highlights the relative consistency, yet uncertainty, that drives surges and stalls in the stock market. In figure 9.1, secular bear markets are designated with red bars, and secular bulls are presented in green. The blue line in the lower section of the graph reflects the P/E ratio for the market. When P/E is rising, the increase in the valuation level of stocks multiplies earnings growth and creates the green-bar periods. When P/E declines, falling valuations offset earnings growth and create red-bar periods. This figure highlights the effect of P/E on secular stock market cycles.

It is a bit ironic that the first two decades of both the 20th and 21st centuries are burdened with secular bear markets. The revelry of 1899 continued one more year through 1900. For those stock market pioneers, the outlook must have been grand. By 1901, however, the crest in P/E marked the start of what would ultimately be a twenty-year secular bear market. After such a long period of market malaise and P/E compression, the market's coil was wound tightly to spring a roaring secular bull.

That roaring bull market era of the '20s, in retrospect and in the context of secular stock market cycles, was destined to deliver a decade of decadent returns because it started at such a low P/E. In the course of that decade, the stock market soared and ultimately ended with the Crash of 1929. The following year, 1930, marked the start of the next secular bear.

From this distance, the years almost appear to be moments, but for those living through those periods, it was just as frustrating and exhilarating as it is for us today. When viewed over the distance of decades, as reflected in figure 9.1, the years appear to be jagged points on a continuum. For investors in the market, however, each year represents over 250 days of slogging market moves.

Some analysts combine the shuffle-step of secular bulls and bears during the 1930s. They include the four-year secular bull from 1933 to 1936 as part of a supposedly longer secular bear from 1929 to 1941. Sometimes the date range is extended further to more conveniently

Figure 9.1. Secular Stock Markets Explained

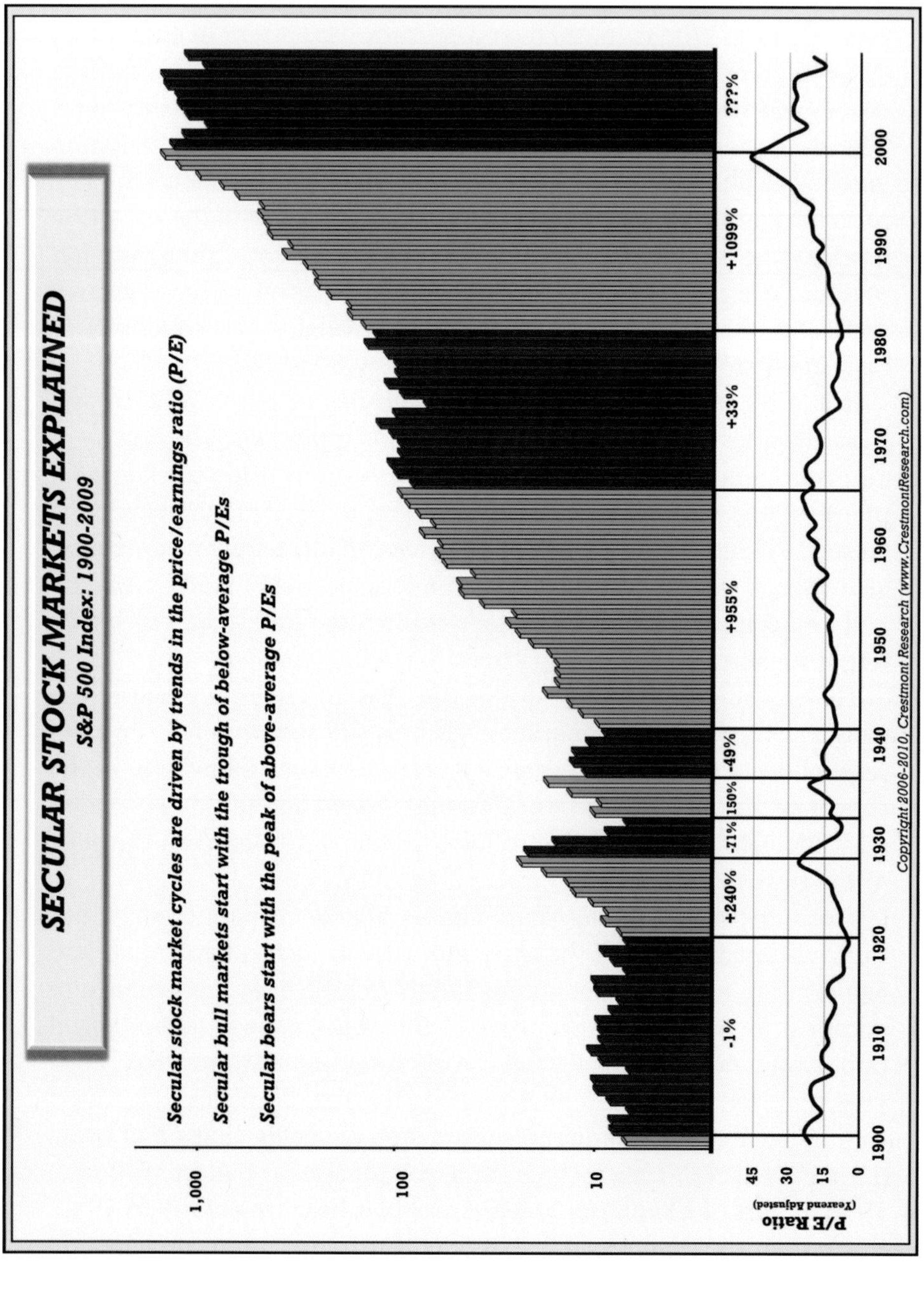

present a duration for secular cycles that is more commonly near or between fifteen and twenty years. That's an acceptable approach if the analyst believes that secular stock market cycles are driven by time. Many investors and advisors, however, seek a more fundamental explanation than the phenomenon of symmetrical waves of time.

Figure 9.1 shows the separation of the secular periods around the 1930s based upon the trend in P/E as driven by the trend in the inflation rate. By the late 1920s, inflation was near price stability, and P/E had increased into the upper 20s. Over the next four years, the inflation rate fell into deflation, and P/E declined to 8—clearly a secular bear market. From 1933 to 1936, deflation dissipated, and by 1936 inflation approached price stability at 1%. Responding consistently, P/E increased to an above-average 19. Then, from 1937 to 1941, inflation surged, ultimately peaking near 10% by 1942. As would be expected, P/E again fell and ultimately reached 9. Though that thirteen-year period was volatile and overall can appear to be a single secular bear period, it is more appropriately divided into three unique cycles. This is consistent with the tenets of inflation-driven, and thereby P/E-driven, secular stock market cycles.

The secular stock market cycles in figure 9.1 are delineated by full years. Practically, it could be difficult to distinguish the exact week, month, or quarter that reflects the point at which the stock market recognized the turning points for the inflation rate. To an extent, the stock market anticipates economic and financial events. Further, given that secular periods often last more than a decade, the convenience of annual breakpoints does not compromise the integrity of the analysis. Above all considerations, annual periods are more than sufficient to identify and relate the concept of secular stock market cycles.

For those interested in the nuances of cycle identification, the attribution of a year that is on the ends of the cycles to one secular cycle or the next requires rules of distinction. For example, the inflation rate was higher for 1933 than 1932, yet P/E reached its trough in 1932. Which year, then, should be the end of the secular bear, and which year should start the secular bull? As a rule of thumb, when a breakpoint is unclear, secular bear markets begin and end with a year of losses in the stock market. Secular bull markets begin and end with a year of gains in the stock market. This additional set of

Figure 9.2. Secular Bull and Bear Market Profile

SECULAR BULL & BEAR MARKETS PROFILE

Market Cycle From	Market Cycle To	(#) Total Years	Market	P/E Ratio Beg.	P/E Ratio End	Inflation Beg.	Inflation End	(#) Positive Years	(#) Negative Years	(%) Positive Years	(%) Negative Years	Max Pos. Yrs In Row	Max Neg. Yrs In Row	Avg Gain In Pos. Years	Avg Loss In Neg. Years	Change Begin To End
1901	1920	20	BEAR	23	5	-2%	16%	9	11	45%	55%	2	3	30%	-17%	2%
1921	1928	8	BULL	5	22	-11%	-2%	7	1	88%	13%	5	1	24%	-3%	317%
1929	1932	4	BEAR	28	8	0%	-10%	0	4	0%	100%	0	4	n/a	-32%	-80%
1933	1936	4	BULL	11	19	-5%	1%	4	0	100%	0%	4	0	34%	n/a	200%
1937	1941	5	BEAR	18	12	4%	5%	1	4	20%	80%	1	3	28%	-16%	-38%
1942	1965	24	BULL	9	23	11%	2%	18	6	75%	25%	4	1	16%	-8%	774%
1966	1981	16	BEAR	21	8	3%	10%	9	7	56%	44%	3	2	13%	-15%	-10%
1982	1999	18	BULL	7	42	6%	2%	16	2	89%	11%	9	1	18%	-4%	1214%
2000	????		BEAR	42		3%		5	5	50%	50%	2	3	14%	-13%	-9%
WEIGHTED AVERAGE BEAR (excluding 2000)										42%	58%	2.1	2.7	21%	-18%	-14%
WEIGHTED AVERAGE BULL										83%	17%	5.8	0.9	19%	-5%	810%

Notes: The index and returns reflect the Dow Jones Industrial Average at year-end from Dow Jones & Company. The P/E ratio is based upon the S&P 500 as developed and presented by Robert Shiller (Yale; Irrational Exuberance). Bull & Bear Market classifications are based upon Crestmont's assessment of cycles using peak and trough P/E ratios, inflation trends, and other analysis. The presentation does not include dividends, taxes, inflation adjustments, or transaction costs.

RETURN PATTERN (Red = down year; Green = up year; #% = annual change in the index; starting and ending DJIA index is presented on the ends of the rows)

1901–1920: BEAR	*71*	-9%	0%	-24%	42%	38%	-2%	-38%	47%	15%	-18%	0%	8%	-10%	-31%	82%	-4%	-22%	11%	30%	-33%					*72*
P/E Ratio		23	22	18	16	19	19	13	13	15	14	14	14	12	11	11	12	9	6	7	5					
CPI: Inflation		-2%	6%	1%	0%	1%	3%	6%	-4%	8%	4%	-8%	7%	3%	1%	1%	8%	17%	18%	15%	16%					
1921–1928: BULL	*72*	13%	22%	-3%	26%	30%	0%	29%	48%																	*300*
P/E Ratio		5	8	8	8	10	12	16	22																	
CPI: Inflation		-11%	-6%	2%	0%	2%	1%	-2%	-2%																	
1929–1932: BEAR	*300*	-17%	-34%	-53%	-23%																					*60*
P/E Ratio		28	21	15	8																					
CPI: Inflation		0%	-2%	-9%	-10%																					
1933–1936: BULL	*60*	67%	4%	39%	25%																					*180*
P/E Ratio		11	12	13	19																					
CPI: Inflation		-5%	3%	2%	1%																					
1937–1941: BEAR	*180*	-33%	28%	-3%	-13%	-15%																				*111*
P/E Ratio		18	14	16	15	12																				
CPI: Inflation		4%	-2%	-1%	1%	5%																				
1942–1965: BULL	*111*	8%	14%	12%	27%	-8%	2%	-2%	13%	18%	14%	8%	-4%	44%	21%	2%	-13%	34%	16%	-9%	19%	-11%	17%	15%	11%	*969*
P/E Ratio		9	11	11	13	14	11	11	10	11	12	12	12	14	18	18	16	15	18	17	20	19	20	23	23	
CPI: Inflation		11%	6%	2%	2%	8%	14%	8%	-1%	1%	8%	2%	1%	1%	0%	1%	3%	3%	1%	2%	1%	1%	1%	1%	2%	
1966–1981: BEAR	*969*	-19%	15%	4%	-15%	5%	6%	15%	-17%	-28%	38%	18%	-17%	-3%	4%	15%	-9%									*875*
P/E Ratio		21	22	21	19	15	17	18	16	11	10	12	10	9	9	9	8									
CPI: Inflation		3%	3%	4%	5%	6%	4%	3%	6%	11%	9%	6%	7%	8%	11%	13%	10%									
1982–1999: BULL	*875*	20%	20%	-4%	28%	23%	2%	12%	27%	-4%	20%	4%	14%	2%	33%	26%	23%	16%	25%							*11497*
P/E Ratio		7	10	9	11	13	16	14	17	16	18	20	21	20	23	26	31	36	42							
CPI: Inflation		6%	3%	4%	4%	2%	4%	4%	5%	5%	4%	3%	3%	3%	3%	3%	2%	2%	2%							
2000–????: BEAR	*11497*	-6%	-7%	-17%	25%	3%	-1%	16%	6%	-34%	19%															
P/E Ratio		42	32	26	24	26	26	26	27	21	17															
CPI: Inflation		3%	3%	2%	2%	3%	3%	3%	3%	4%	0%															

objective rules seeks to further remove subjectivity or visualization from the determination of secular stock market cycles.

For more details related to secular stock market cycles since 1900, figure 9.2 offers a tabular presentation of data related to the individual cycles as well as the individual years within each cycle. In addition, the coloration of years with positive and negative returns (green and red respectively) helps to show the consistency of generally positive returns in secular bull markets and generally alternating years or sets of years of positive and negative returns in secular bear markets.

In the top section of figure 9.2, the starting and ending years for each secular bull and bear period are shown along with the total years in the cycle. The chart further presents the starting and ending P/E ratio, the number and percentage of positive and negative years, and other statistics for each period. Secular stock market cycles have ranged in duration from four to twenty-four years.

Secular bull markets start with P/E well below the historical average, generally under 10. Over the course of the secular bull, P/E typically doubles or triples, and at times has more than quadrupled. In contrast, secular bear markets start with P/E well above the average, generally more than 20. Over the course of the secular bear, P/E typically declines by two-thirds or so.

The generally rising P/E trend in secular bulls results in a high percentage (83%) of positive years, while in secular bears, generally less than half of the years are positive. Secular bulls reflect long runs of positive years occasionally punctuated by a negative year, whereas secular bears tend to have relatively short runs or alternating ups and downs. Though both secular bulls and bears tend to average 20% returns during positive years, the loss years are relatively small for secular bulls in contrast to secular bears. By the ends of the cycles, secular bears on average finish about where they started, while secular bulls have averaged an eightfold increase.

The bottom section of figure 9.2 shows annual details for each year organized by secular cycle. The figure highlights that the trends in the inflation rate and P/E are not smooth, but rather tend to move in a general direction. This is analogous to temperature across the seasons. Each day does not reflect a consistent step upward or downward on the thermometer. Instead, the temperature wavers back and forth along a general trend that is apparent when measured over weeks and months. Likewise, the economy and markets are too volatile and sporadic to reflect a melodic wave for the inflation rate, P/E, and many of the other elements. Because the economy and markets are subject to natural trends and forces, the cycles are neither symmetrical nor random in their course.

The long view of secular stock market cycles presents the alternating periods of above-average and below-average returns. These periods are driven by the trend and direction of the inflation rate and P/E. When inflation or deflation is calming, the tailwind of rising valuations multiplies the growth in earnings to create dramatic returns. On the contrary, when inflation or deflation ignites from the calm state of price stability, P/E declines and creates a headwind for the market. The effect of declining valuation in the stock market offsets much or all of the contribution from earnings growth, thereby creating a choppy market with disappointing returns.

Decades, Not Centuries

Some people will identify with the long-term view; others will be curious to see the effect that the secular cycles have on their own investment horizons. Ten years is generally considered long enough to smooth the yearly ups and downs in the market. Many people expect that the cumulative return over ten-year periods will begin to concentrate near the long-term average return of 10%.

There have been 101 rolling ten-year periods since 1900, covering more than a century of stock market history and numerous secular stock market cycles. Many of the ten-year periods include years from both secular bulls and secular bears, while others are exclusively within an individual secular cycle. The result is not a muted or random profile of returns — the secular cycles have a profound impact across periods of ten years and longer.

Of course, very few if any ten-year periods will have total returns (including dividends) of exactly 10%. Instead, consider your expectation that annualized returns fall within a range around 10%. What percent of the time across the 101 ten-year periods did annualized returns, including dividends, fall within the fairly wide range of 8%–12%?

This is clearly relevant to the probable outcomes for stock market returns over this decade. Many investors and advisors either implicitly or explicitly assume that stock market returns for this decade will be inside the 8%–12% range. This is especially true considering that the assumption by many investors for overall investment portfolio returns is 8% or more.

Consider that the expectation for returns from a portfolio includes a blending of assumptions, combining relatively higher stock market returns with much lower bond investment returns and, for some investors, returns from alternative investments. For the blended portfolio to generate overall returns of 8% after expenses, stocks may need to return 12% or more to offset bond returns that are likely to be less than half that. Alternatively, some investors are concentrating more heavily in stocks because of the low bond yields.

Nonetheless, many investors assume that stock market returns over this decade will be inside the range of 8%–12%. As figure 9.3 reflects, the annualized total return from the stock market over ten-year periods has been inside the 8% to 12% range less than one-quarter of the time!

Just over one-third of the time (36%), annualized ten-year returns exceeded 12%. The remainder of the ten-year periods, 43%, delivered annualized returns over the decades that were less than 8%.

As reflected in the graph, the columns list the respective ten-year periods. The periods are not random; rather, they run in series that reflect the fluctuating trend in P/E as driven by the inflation rate. Returns in the rightmost column, reflecting periods with returns in excess of 12%, are all periods when P/E started at less than 15. For the leftmost column, with returns below 8%, the starting P/E was generally above 15. With P/E starting this decade near 20, it is almost certain that the next ten years ultimately will find its place in the left column.

Figure 9.3. Frequency of 10-Year Returns by Ranges

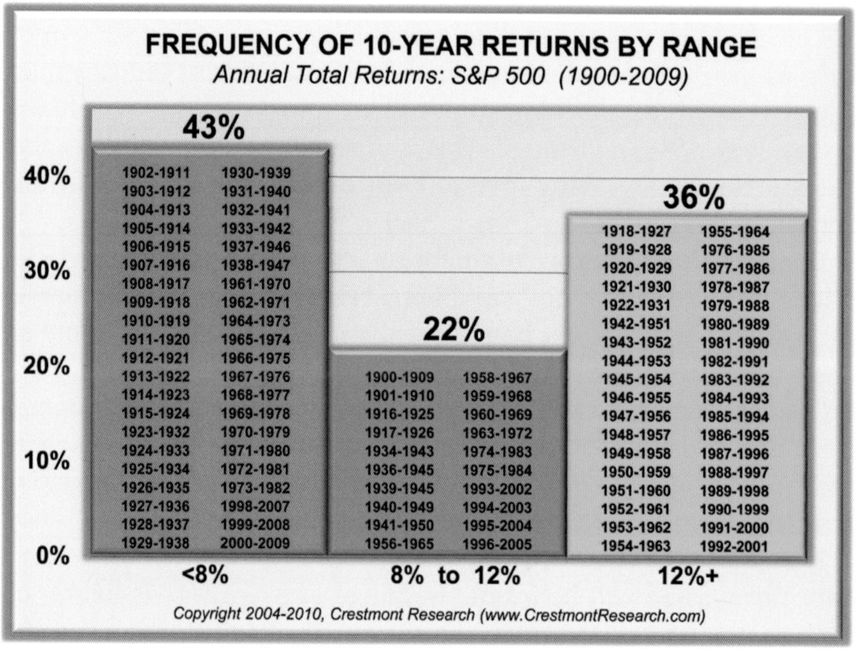

FREQUENCY OF 10-YEAR RETURNS BY RANGE
Annual Total Returns: S&P 500 (1900-2009)

40%	43%					36%	
	1902-1911	1930-1939					
	1903-1912	1931-1940					
	1904-1913	1932-1941					
	1905-1914	1933-1942				1918-1927	1955-1964
	1906-1915	1937-1946				1919-1928	1976-1985
30%	1907-1916	1938-1947				1920-1929	1977-1986
	1908-1917	1961-1970				1921-1930	1978-1987
	1909-1918	1962-1971				1922-1931	1979-1988
	1910-1919	1964-1973		22%		1942-1951	1980-1989
	1911-1920	1965-1974				1943-1952	1981-1990
20%	1912-1921	1966-1975				1944-1953	1982-1991
	1913-1922	1967-1976	1900-1909	1958-1967		1945-1954	1983-1992
	1914-1923	1968-1977	1901-1910	1959-1968		1946-1955	1984-1993
	1915-1924	1969-1978	1916-1925	1960-1969		1947-1956	1985-1994
	1923-1932	1970-1979	1917-1926	1963-1972		1948-1957	1986-1995
10%	1924-1933	1971-1980	1934-1943	1974-1983		1949-1958	1987-1996
	1925-1934	1972-1981	1936-1945	1975-1984		1950-1959	1988-1997
	1926-1935	1973-1982	1939-1945	1993-2002		1951-1960	1989-1998
	1927-1936	1998-2007	1940-1949	1994-2003		1952-1961	1990-1999
	1928-1937	1999-2008	1941-1950	1995-2004		1953-1962	1991-2000
0%	1929-1938	2000-2009	1956-1965	1996-2005		1954-1963	1992-2001
	<8%		**8% to 12%**			**12%+**	

Copyright 2004-2010, Crestmont Research (www.CrestmontResearch.com)

Alternatively, stock market performance can be evaluated over time. Figure 9.4 presents stock market returns across the 101 rolling ten-year periods. The year on the horizontal axis reflects the ending year for all ten-year periods starting with 1900–1909 and ending with 2000–2009. When the performance from all 101 periods is averaged, the result is the long-term average return of 10%. Yet, as highlighted in this figure and the previous one, average rarely happens. History reflects a barbell-shaped profile of returns, more often either well above average or well below average. It certainly is not the bell-shaped curve with most years concentrated near the average that many investors expect or hope to see.

Note that the most recent decade has slipped below the line for 0%, which has not happened since the two occurrences in the late 1930s. Keep in mind that this reflects a loss including dividends, not simply a decline in the index. Further, the most recent decade may be getting a sibling at the end of 2010—a second negative decade bar beside the most recent one in the chart. P/E had risen so high in

the late 1990s and early 2000s that another decade-long stock market loss is likely for the decade ending 2010. Even when decade-long
stock market returns again move back into positive territory, the relatively high level of P/E during the 2000s will very likely result in
an extended trough with relatively low returns for the bars ending
over this decade.

Figure 9.4. Rolling 10-Year Stock Market Returns

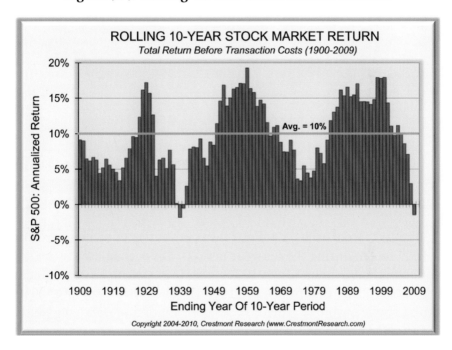

The rolling-period bar graph provides a framework to highlight the
dynamics of secular stock market cycles. Sometimes it is helpful to
break things into their component parts to assess the constants and
the drivers of the whole. For total return in the stock market, there
are three components: EPS growth, dividend yield, and the change
in P/E. Figure 9.5 highlights the contribution that each part makes
to the whole.

Figure 9.5. Rolling 10-Year Stock Market Returns: Components

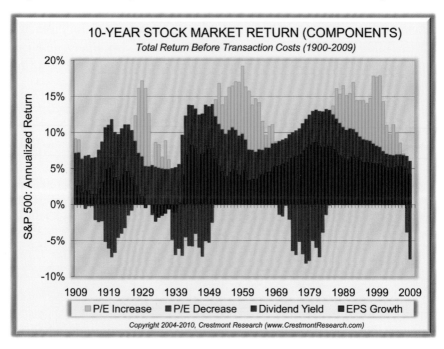

The blue part of each bar reflects the contribution of earnings growth to total return during the ten-year periods. Other than during the deflation and depression of the 1930s, earnings growth has provided a core base to the total return from stocks. The brown part of the bar sitting above earnings growth is the contribution of dividend yield.

The most significant determinant of whether returns were above or below average, however, was the change in P/E. If P/E increased over the period, the effect is reflected as a green-bar extension to returns. If P/E declined, there is a red bar plunging into negative territory offsetting much or all of the return from earnings and dividends. The effect of the offset creates the troughs in figure 9.4.

Ironically, when earnings growth was strongest, returns were weak. The periods of the 1910s, '40s, and '70s included a number of years with relatively high inflation. Inflation adds to the nominal growth of earnings, thus reflecting a strong nominal contribution from EPS to total return. Nonetheless, the effect of a declining P/E in response to rising inflation more than offset the extra growth in earnings from inflation.

While the analysis is focused on rolling bar graphs, there is one additional version that can be used to gaze into the future. Figure 9.6 overlays the P/E ratio at the start of the 10-year periods with the rolling 10-year bar graph. The graph aligns the starting P/E with returns over the subsequent ten years. The bars reflect annualized returns for the 10-year period. The line is the level of P/E at the start of the period represented by each bar. Since the starting P/E is a major driver of subsequent returns, the return bars move inversely to the P/E line. Further, this graph includes the starting P/E for the next ten years; obviously, the bars will fill in over this decade. As a result, this figure provides an opportunity to anticipate the future. The seeds of destiny for ten-year returns, within a general range, are somewhat already sown.

Figure 9.6. Using P/E to Gaze into the Future

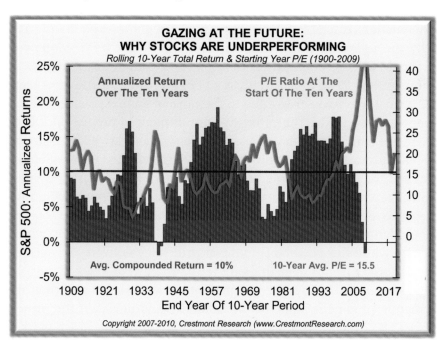

The good news is that the peak in P/E at the start of the rolling decades is passing; therefore the return bars should begin to show positive results after the next period is added. There is probably little consolation in knowing that portfolios planted in the early 2000s will show little yield after a decade in the stock market. Even more disappointing, however, is that this decade (ending 2019) will also reflect poor trailing-decade returns. P/E is still not low enough to assure even average returns for the future from the current level of valuation.

After looking at the components of return and assessing the effect of secular stock market cycles from various perspectives, this is a good time to emphasize just how significant P/E is to ultimate returns. The change in P/E certainly is a major part of the 10-year return bars; additionally, P/E has implications for the other two components: dividends and earnings growth.

Influence and Power

The previous discussions and charts have sought to explain how and why the inflation rate drives P/E over the longer term. Moreover, it should also be emphasized that P/E is not a reliable indicator of short-term returns. P/E actually is a poor indicator for the short term (less than five years or so) due to the normal annual volatility of the market. Though short-term returns are difficult to predict with P/E, there are market technicians using various quantitative and charting techniques to anticipate short-term market trends. The techniques can be, and for many investors are, very effective at generating trading gains, implementing risk management, or enhancing investment timing. The technicians are able to tune in to the underlying currents of sentiment that drive sloshing and volatility in the short term, which occurs while the power of financial principles delivers the secular stock market trends over the long term.

Further details about the components of total return and their interaction provide insights to the influence and power of the principles. P/E has a direct impact on multiplying or muting stock market returns. Further, P/E interacts with the other two components of total return — dividend yields and earnings growth.

The influence of P/E on the first component, dividend yields, is direct and fundamental. Figure 9.7 graphically highlights the relationship between dividend yield and P/E. The values for the P/E ratio are presented on the vertical axis and the values for dividend yield are presented on the horizontal axis. The dots represent the values for dividend yield and P/E for each year since 1900. For example, in 1957 the dividend yield was 4% and the P/E was 15.6, so you can find a dot at the intersection of 4% and 15.6 on the graph. The rest of the 110 years are plotted similarly. This approach helps us visually assess the trends or relationships between two variables.

As reflected in the graph, as P/E rises, the dividend yield falls. Likewise, P/E declines drive higher dividend yields. This relationship is no coincidence or phenomenon; rather, math determines it. Though changes in dividend payouts over the long term have an impact, the level of P/E is the more significant driver of dividend yield.

As with any math example, the explanation requires a few formulas. For this discussion, however, there are few variables and limited calculations. Figure 9.7 compares the P/E ratio to the dividend yield. A walk between the two measures explains their relationship.

P/E is price divided by earnings. Dividend yield is dividend divided by the stock price (D/P). P/E, when turned upside down, becomes the earnings yield (E/P)[1]. Thus the comparison is earnings yield (E/P) and dividend yield (D/P). The level of valuation in the market does not affect dividend policy; earnings drive dividends. The payout of dividends is typically about half of earnings. As a result, the dividend yield is about half of the earnings yield (if D is 50% of E, then D/P will be 50% of E/P, since P remains the same in both fractions). The key point is that dividend yield necessarily declines as the earnings yield declines.

The portion of earnings that companies pay as dividends is called the dividend payout ratio. Note that earlier in the century the dividend payout ratio was somewhat higher than 50%. In recent decades and years, the dividend payout ratio has been somewhat lower than 50%. For simplicity in this discussion, and to reflect more recent decades, the dividend payout ratio for this illustration is assumed to be 45%.

As P/E rises, thereby mathematically reducing the earnings yield, the dividend yield therefore necessarily falls. Consider the following

Figure 9.7. P/E Influences Dividend Yield

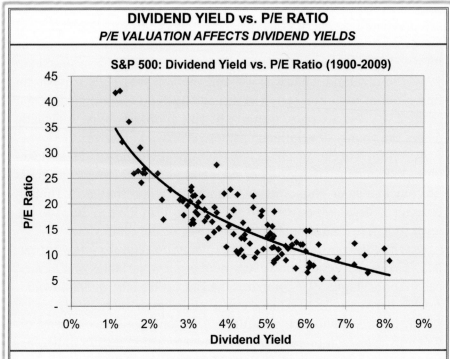

DIVIDEND YIELD vs. P/E RATIO
P/E VALUATION AFFECTS DIVIDEND YIELDS

S&P 500: Dividend Yield vs. P/E Ratio (1900-2009)

IMPACT OF VALUATION ON DIVIDEND YIELDS
P/E does not change EPS nor Dividends, only the price; and thus the dividend yield.

Assumptions:
Earnings Per Share (EPS)	$2.00	
Dividend Per Share (DIV)	$0.90	
Payout ratio	45%	

P/E RATIO	EPS	DIV	(EPS x P/E) PRICE	DIV YIELD
35	$2.00	$0.90	$ 70	1.3%
30	$2.00	$0.90	$ 60	1.5%
25	$2.00	$0.90	$ 50	1.8%
20	$2.00	$0.90	$ 40	2.3%
17	$2.00	$0.90	$ 34	2.6%
15	$2.00	$0.90	$ 30	3.0%
13	$2.00	$0.90	$ 26	3.5%
10	$2.00	$0.90	$ 20	4.5%
7	$2.00	$0.90	$ 14	6.4%

Note: This partially explains the reason for currently low dividend yields. Further, the payout ratio of dividends to earnings has historically been 35% to 60% and is currently near the bottom of the range.

two examples: When P/E is 20, the earnings yield is mathematically 5% $(20/1 \leftrightarrow 1/20 = 5\%)$. If the dividend payout ratio is 45%, then the dividend yield is near 2.25% $(1/20 @ 45\% = 2.25\%)$. On the contrary, when P/E is 10, the earnings yield is mathematically 10% and the dividend yield is near 4.5%. The major point to remember from this example is that the level of P/E directly drives the dividend yield.

Reported dividend payout ratios will appear to vary more than the underlying dividend trend. This occurs due to the variability in the earnings cycle that was previously discussed. Though the numerator (dividends) rises relatively consistently, the denominator (reported earnings) varies significantly across the earnings cycle. This concept emphasizes the earlier discussion about the need to normalize earnings when calculating stock market ratios that include EPS, including the dividend payout ratio.

The boards and management teams of corporations, however, inherently understand that earnings swing more dramatically than long-term cash flow from the business — the source of dividends. Investors in publicly traded corporations want consistency through a stable growth in dividends. As a result, dividend reductions often have a negative effect on stock prices.

Corporations therefore tend to constrain dividend increases during the up-cycle of earnings, thereby reducing the necessity to cut dividends during the down-cycle. In effect, dividends and dividend growth tend to track the underlying core baseline of earnings growth. Dividends tend to naturally normalize to a more stable long-term growth trend.

This discussion leads to the question: How does the relationship of dividends and P/E affect secular stock market cycles?

The level of valuation across secular stock market cycles, as reflected in P/E, makes dividend yield an intensifying factor rather than a counterbalancing offset. When P/E is low and positioned for a secular bull market with above-average gains, the relatively low valuation level raises the yield from dividends, thereby adding to returns. On the contrary, when P/E is high and positioned for below-average gains, the relatively high valuation level lowers the yield from dividends just when investors would be hoping for help. In summary, a low P/E drives above-average gains and higher dividend yields; a high P/E drives below-average gains and lower dividend yields.

One of the reasons that there is such a significant difference in the level of returns in secular bulls and bears is that dividend yield, recognized as a significant contributor to total return, exacerbates the outcome from the secular cycle.

Ironically, dividend yield has a greater relative impact when it is lowest, since the other parts of the return end up being so low. Even though the dividend yield reflects a higher return percentage for secular bull markets, the outsized positive addition of gains from the increase in P/E lowers the relative significance of dividends.

For the second component, earnings growth, the relationship is indirect. P/E does not cause a change in EPS, but the interaction between the two elements for stock market returns means that factors that influence both should not be isolated. One of the most significant examples is the impact of the inflation rate on EPS and P/E.

Some analysts will say that the stock market is a good hedge against inflation because companies pass inflation into their earnings. During periods of rising inflation, one of the effects of inflation is that overall prices in the economy rise—including the revenues and costs of companies. As a result, when overall revenues and costs increase by inflation, then earnings too increase somewhat in response to inflation. For many companies, however, future earnings do not increase equally as inflation accelerates, due to accelerating labor costs and other factors that seek to get ahead of inflation.

In particular, inflation affects more than the just the growth rate in EPS. If the only result of inflation were higher earnings, then the stock market would respond accordingly and move higher, but it does not. Inflation also drives down P/E and thus offsets all and more of the inflation-driven growth in EPS.

Figure 9.5, the bar graph that separates the components of return into four colors, highlights that the waves of earnings growth from the inflation of the 1910s, '40s, and '70s were more than offset by the undertow of inflation. The historical periods when earnings grew best were among the worst in terms of stock market performance.

To make matters worse, the total return from the stock market was not only below average but inflation also reduced the purchasing power value of the investment portfolio. Higher inflation brought a decade or more of low returns, and further lessened the value of what was left.

The analysts who present the inflation-hedge argument are limiting their perspective to the basic concept that (1) earnings growth drives stock prices higher, (2) inflation drives earnings growth higher, and (3) ergo, stocks are either immune to—or even benefit from—inflation. In their defense, there is not a substantial amount of published information about the effect of inflation on P/E.

A Look Inside

The view of a secular bear market across a decade or longer tends to mute the significant swings that occur during the period. Normal market volatility, directed by short-term economic factors and investor psychology, drives cyclical periods of surge and fall. As you reflect back upon the first secular stock market chart in this chapter, figure 9.1, remember how calm the red-bar periods appeared. The variations across the 1960s and '70s secular bear market period hardly put a wrinkle in the trend. Beware that it does not lure you into a sense that secular bear markets are periods of quiet hibernation.

Hardly anyone with exposure to, or an interest in, the stock market limits his or her interest to long-term periods. Very few investors are patient enough just to watch the market monthly, and many people experience it daily. Figure 9.8 provides a real sense of the course within secular bear markets by presenting a daily graph of the most recently completed secular bear market. The statistical volatility of the 1960s and '70s secular bear cycle is similar to other secular bear periods.

It is striking to see the magnitude of the swings. Statistically, the volatility of secular bulls and bears is similar. The difference, however, is that the upward skew of returns in secular bulls masks the feeling of volatility. The secular bulls provide bigger gains and smaller gains each year, with an occasional scare. Secular bears, however, gnaw back and forth between the gains and losses. There is a significant difference in the way that investors feel during periods of smaller and larger gains compared to periods of losses and gains.

Figure 9.8 also demonstrates that the effect of gains and losses on cumulative returns is disproportionate. Mathematically and financially,

Figure 9.8. Last Secular Bear: Magnitude of Cyclical Swings

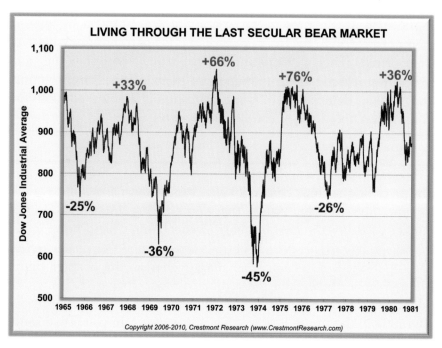

LIVING THROUGH THE LAST SECULAR BEAR MARKET

Copyright 2006-2010, Crestmont Research (www.CrestmontResearch.com)

a 33% gain is required to compensate for the effect of a 25% loss. For example, a portfolio that starts at $100 and declines by $33 to $67 requires a 50% gain ($33 divided by $67) to recover to breakeven. As the losses increase, it takes an ever-increasing and disproportionate gain to make up for the loss. To return to breakeven, a loss of 20% requires a gain of 25%, a loss of 40% requires a gain of 67%, and a loss of 50% requires a gain of 100%. Likewise, the same dynamic works in reverse. The chart shows that relatively larger gains can be completely wiped out with disproportionately smaller losses. The pairs that were just mentioned (−20%/+25%, −40%/+67%, −50%/+100%, etc.) are offsetting regardless of which side comes first.

The magnitude of the swings in figure 9.8 is striking. Equally dramatic, as presented in figure 9.9, there is a relatively short duration between the peaks and troughs. The short-term swings are known as cyclical periods. Both secular bulls and bears have many interim short-term cyclical periods. In secular bear markets, these periods typically last a few years to the upside, followed by a year or two

Figure 9.9. Last Secular Bear: Duration of Cyclical Swings

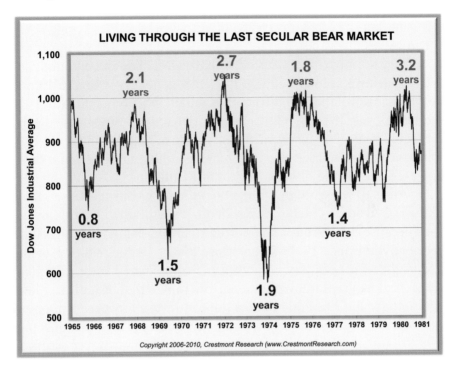

of decline. This is another indication that the stock market is much more volatile that most investors realize.

Volatility in Perspective

Volatility matters for several reasons, especially in secular bear markets. An understanding and appreciation for the normal levels and cycle of volatility can help shield investors from the emotional roller coaster that often leads to bad decisions. Further, some investors perceive that the volatility of the prior decade portends a new era. Others wonder whether volatility is a recent phenomenon caused by globalization, hedge funds, exchange-traded funds, or any factor from a long list of attributed issues.

Some people say that wisdom comes with age; in reality, age brings experience that often leads to wisdom. Secular stock market cycles and long-term volatility cycles occur over such long periods that investor wisdom often comes too late. A disciplined study of the lessons of history can therefore provide insights and wisdom about the stock market, its secular cycles, and volatility.

During secular stock market cycles, volatility is one of the characteristics that most investors experience viscerally and emotionally. When, during a secular bull, the market is generally rising, investors nearly ignore volatility and treat it as a daily phenomenon. Since almost every year in secular bulls has positive returns, investors quickly forget the years with losses since they cause minimal damage to portfolios. When the market does not have the tailwind of a secular bull, however, the profile of volatility is quite different.

Figure 9.10 presents the frequency of changes in the Dow Jones Industrial Average (excluding dividends) within ranges. The Dow is used because it is the most recognized stock market index with actual year-end data since 1900. The purpose of using a range is to provide an indication of volatility without using complicated statistical measures. If most years fall within a narrow range, then it indicates low volatility for the stock market. On the contrary, if most years are outside of a wide range, then stock market volatility is high. As reflected in the figure, stock market volatility is relatively high and consistent.

Note the range at the top of the figure, relating to years when the market ended within or outside of –10% and +10%. The historical frequency of years within the range, the single-digit years, is close to 30% for bulls, bears, and the total. It is surprising to many investors that only 30% of years end within the range. Obviously, almost 70% of years move up or down by more than 10%. That reflects many double-digit years.

Figure 9.10 further reflects an extended range of –16% to +16%. That is the equal range away from zero required to include half of the years. Yes, half of the years historically have either been up more than +16% or down more than –16%. Forecasters may not always be able to predict what the market will do this coming year, but they can say that based upon history there is a 50% chance that the stock market will be up or down more than 16%!

One of the most interesting insights occurs when the data separates into secular bull and secular bear market periods. The overall magnitude of volatility, based upon the frequencies inside the ranges,

Figure 9.10. DJIA: Magnitude of Volatility by Ranges

Dow Jones Industrial Average
DISPERSION OF ANNUAL STOCK MARKET CHANGES
Percent Of Years During Secular Cycles
(8+ Cycles: 1901-2009)

RANGE	109 Yrs AVG	54 Yrs BULL	55 Yrs BEAR
<-10%	21%	4%	38%
-10% to +10%	31%	30%	33%
>+10%	48%	67%	29%

RANGE	109 Yrs AVG	54 Yrs BULL	55 Yrs BEAR
<-16%	16%	0%	31%
-16% to +16%	50%	50%	49%
>+16%	35%	50%	20%

is similar across secular bulls, secular bears, and the total of all periods. The differences, however, occur outside of the ranges, especially between the secular periods.

While P/E is generally rising during secular bull markets, only two of the fifty-four secular bull years experienced a decline of more than 10%. Further, none of the years in secular bulls experienced a loss of more than –16%. Yet when P/E is generally declining during secular bear markets, there are numerous years with declines and quite a few beyond the –16% threshold. As the table reflects, however, even secular bear markets have their share of years with strong gains, like 2003 and 2009. Unfortunately for investors, many of the good years are more than offset by years like 2002 and 2008.

The next look at volatility uses the traditional measure known as standard deviation. It is not important for this discussion to go into detail about the statistic—it is only necessary to appreciate that it's the most common measure of volatility, and to recognize that a higher value means higher volatility. For this analysis, the monthly percentage changes in the S&P 500 index are used, and then the result is annualized to reflect the level of variability in the market. Financial market professionals often use this measure as a measure of risk in models that assess risk versus return.

Figure 9.11 presents the twelve-month rolling standard deviation for the S&P 500 index going back six decades to 1950. The concept of rolling periods for this analysis means that the value used for each month is the standard deviation for the most recent twelve months. As the market goes through periods of higher and lower volatility, the measure reflects those changes.

Figure 9.11. S&P 500 Index Volatility: Rolling Volatility (1950–2009)

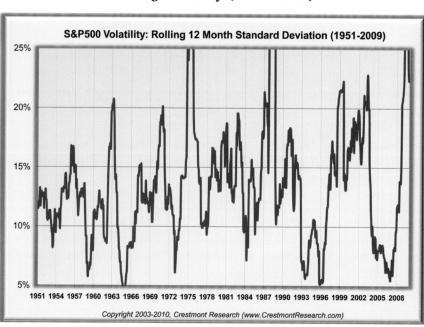

One of the most noteworthy aspects from the history of volatility is its tendency to move around dramatically. Though most periods generally fall within a band of 10%–20% volatility, the average is near 15% (the statistic that many models and academics use for stock market volatility). There have been periods, however, when volatility was unusually high and periods when it was unusually low.

Sometimes the extreme periods in one direction follow oppositely extreme periods. The light-gray vertical bars on the graph divide three-year periods, so it is apparent that some of the extreme periods can last for a while, yet few last a long time.

For most of the mid-2000s, volatility was unusually low. By late 2006 and early 2007, volatility fell into the lowest 3% of all periods since 1950. No wonder investors and market spectators had become complacent about market volatility—or maybe complacency about risk led to the low volatility. In either case, the waters of the market were unusually calm.

Shortly thereafter, volatility surged to startling and anxiety-inducing levels. Though volatility increased to more than 25%, fairly high by historical standards, that high level was not unprecedented. If history is again a guide, volatility will likely spend most of this decade in the mid-range, yet not without several more spikes in both directions.

The extremes of ultra-low and ultra-high levels of volatility over the prior decade have not been unique; such periods have occurred in previous decades. A historical perspective of volatility reflects that higher-volatility periods are normal and can extend for quarters or years. Some investors anchored on the previous extreme low-volatility years as a normal condition and were surprised by the subsequent period of high volatility. A true understanding of history provides a more rational perspective, and can help investors take action to protect their portfolios when high volatility prevails, and to be cautious during periods of low volatility.

Early Conclusions

Before considering the practical implications of the continuing secular bear market, there are a few early conclusions. First, when viewed across time, secular stock market cycles reflect periods of surge and stall; the pattern coincides with the cycle of inflation. Second, the effects of secular stock market cycles on periods of a decade and longer create a barbell profile of well above-average and well below-average returns. Third, the results are accentuated because the effects of inflation and changing P/E valuations compound through the components of return. Fourth, the shorter-term periods inside secular cycles are much shorter and more variable than most investors expect. Finally, general volatility in the stock market is higher than most investors realize.

POINTS OF EMPHASIS

- The current secular bear market is not near its end. P/E remains relatively high, and secular bear markets cannot end until P/E declines due to significant inflation or deflation.

- The profile of decade-long returns reflects periods that are either significantly above average or significantly below average.

- The primary cause of the variability of above-average and below-average returns over longer-term periods is the change in P/E over the period.

- When P/E is higher, dividends yields are lower and vice versa.

- Secular bear market cycles are filled with shorter-term periods of cyclical bull markets and cyclical bear markets, which are dramatic, with significant swings over relatively short-term periods.

- Volatility in the stock market varies from very iow periods to very high periods, but it tends to spend most of its time in the mid-range.

CHAPTER 10

BETTER THAN HOPE

Too often, investors have been led to believe that hope and faith in the long term are appropriate investment strategies. Instead, investing should be treated like a business, its constant objective to produce profits while remaining respectful of adverse periods.

Businesslike investing requires a philosophy of profits over participation. Investments should seek to make money, not simply to passively participate in the markets. Toward that end, the first rule of making money is to avoid losing money. A carefully selected and appropriately diversified mix of investments can improve the likelihood of success.

Some investors fail by making decisions that seem rational at the moment but do not take into account that conditions and patterns never continue without change. Success is as much about avoiding the pitfalls as it is about being right. The difference between investment success and failure requires truly rational decisions rather than irrational ones that only seem rational in the moment.

For example, consider the flip of a fair coin. If the payoff is $2.25 on a one-dollar bet for heads and $2.00 on a one-dollar bet for tails, what's your pick for the first flip? Unless you are an irrational contrarian or a cynic, you obviously pick heads. But what if heads comes up three times in a row? Are you tempted to go with tails? What if heads appears ten times in a row? It's tempting to think that the next one must be tails, even if the odds of a fair coin remain 50/50 regardless of past events.

Sometimes inconsistent or irrational events happen, and tempt investors to shift their thinking into inconsistent terms. A shift away from rational principles takes the fork in the road away from likely success.

Sophisticated investors and professionals know that it requires more discipline to avoid mistakes in the heat of stress than it does to make good decisions in the comfort of time. Good decisions during periods of stress are often the result of careful planning in advance. Success also requires a combination of wisdom from experience and instinct about the markets. Trends that do not have a history of continuing indefinitely generally don't; history is a wise source of insights.

During periods of high volatility and declining market trends, it is all too easy to get caught up in the mindset of extrapolating the bad times well into the future. Likewise, periods of low volatility and steady climbs often build a false sense of confidence about the market, and an attitude of heightened complacency toward risk. One element for long-term success is to avoid making emotional decisions during the rare periods. For example, periods of anxiety and complacency often lead investors to concentrate on the investments that appear to be working. At the same time, they may dump nonperforming investments that are generally winners.

Beware the elf of human nature perched on your left shoulder, whispering irrational recommendations when rationality is most needed. Even if the elf of best practices on your right shoulder espouses great wisdom, the comfort food of emotion may lure you to the wrong choice. The elf of human nature is a magician with sleight of hand skills that will seek to divert with backward logic and the luring trio of hope, fear, and greed. The elf of best practices, however, can help to control his counterpart and remind you that even after ten heads in a row, tails has not become more likely no matter how tempting.

The trio of hope, fear, and greed distracts investors from discipline. The mere decision to purchase an investment invokes a sense of commitment. Upon execution, feelings of cognitive dissonance drive the tendency for people to justify their actions. This either reinforces confidence about winners, or fosters hope for the recovery of losers.

An investment starts with a sense of hope—the hope that the first steps upward will continue or the hope that a slight slide will soon recover. A further slide can move the emotions from hope to fear, which creates an empty feeling of anxiety, the uncertainty associated with the possibility of losing money on an investment. Fear and the desire for the antidote of hope drive investors to hold on to losing investments. There is no better feeling than coming from behind to break even. The all too common result, however, is an increasing loss that ultimately leads to despair.

On the topside of break-even lurks greed. Too often, as well, an unexpectedly quick rise in an investment can tempt an investor to sell for the simple rush of success. When that investment slips by the quick trigger and mounts larger gains, greed teases the investor to wish for ever-higher prices. All along, hope, fear, and greed take turns encouraging missteps and discouraging discipline.

The result often leaves investors with a majority of winning positions, a set of losing positions, and one or a few big losses. Many investors find that the overall portfolio return, while often acceptable, would have been far superior without the few big losses. Each of the big losses yields a lesson—one the investor swears never to repeat. Yet every year seems to have its few big losers, every time with the hope that it will not recur. Most frustrating, the exercise of discipline may have helped to avoid many of those losses. The goal of businesslike investment discipline is to reduce the instances of big losers, enable more of the winners to extend, and apply rational decision-making through the investment process.

Market conditions change, especially in secular bear markets. The cylinders of the portfolio engine that lag today may be the leaders tomorrow. The challenge of applying discipline to investment selection is determining which cylinders have good potential and which to overhaul.

Portfolios will inevitably include apparent solid performers that are simply riding a market without actually functioning well. Those holdings may not do their duty when conditions change. In contrast, there also may be lagging cylinders that conditions hold back from fully performing. They could be tomorrow's workhorses. Invariably, the elf of human nature will encourage you to sell the latter to buy more of the former. Differentiating between the two is a key to long-term investment success.

If discipline were easy, then everyone would use it. The lack of consistent discipline by all market participants creates opportunity, but it also creates noise. The objective of a businesslike approach to investing is to squelch the background noise and apply discipline and best practices to investing. There is no specific set of rules to follow, nor is there one right way to invest. As a result, this chapter cannot conclude with a specific action plan or investment approach for investors. There are, however, several principles that can help investors to seek and develop their own disciplines or to identify experienced and understanding professionals.

Coming Back In Style

Investing, especially in the stock market, has not always been viewed as a profit-driven activity. Although it started that way, early modern theories of investing and markets temporarily led investors astray. The ravages of the current secular bear market and its associated challenges to the long-accepted buy-and-hold approach are leading to a resurgence of Old School investing, the approach that Benjamin Graham described in the seminal book *Intelligent Investor* (1949).

Intelligent Investor is a complement to Graham's first classic, *Security Analysis,* coauthored with David Dodd in 1934. For decades Graham highlighted the differences between investing and speculation. He espoused the tools and approaches that recognized the stock market as a venue for investing in companies rather than a theoretical place to invest in financial securities. Graham warned investors not to treat securities as the source of profits from investing, but rather to recognize that the ownership interest in the underlying companies produced the returns.

Just three years later, in 1952, Harry Markowitz published "Portfolio Selection" in *The Journal of Finance,* and planted the seeds for Modern Portfolio Theory (MPT). Suddenly the investment universe was out of balance. MPT represented a portfolio approach to stock market investing, one that treated stocks not just as financial assets, but as portfolios of risk and return.

Over the subsequent decades, value-based investors—including disciples of Graham and Dodd—continued their trade privately as the modern approach swept like a tsunami. Had there been wrestling matches between Markowitz and Graham during the 1960s or '70s, neither of them would have been a decisive winner, and across the secular bear market of that period, both may have been losers. The 1980s and '90s, however, changed the course of the debate. The currents in the market shifted to create significant upward momentum for the stock market. The simplicity of passively managed portfolios, especially stocks and bonds, became the mainsail in the tailwinds of the secular bull market.

As conditions have shifted from secular bull to secular bear, discerning investors and advisors in the 2000s are beginning to challenge the passive buy-and-hold approach. Investors are getting serious—out of knowledge or fear—about preserving savings as well as stewarding it as their resource for retirement and other needs beyond. Unlike conditions around 1950, retirement has become "long term" as life spans have extended considerably. Though investing historically may have been a long-term process toward a short-term retirement, today's retiree faces a much longer tail of needs. Investment success is again regaining the focus of profitability over patience.

Diversification

Graham and Markowitz had different ideas about the role of diversification. Graham used it to build a businesslike portfolio with the expectation that each component was unto itself a source of return. He chose each stock carefully based upon disciplined analysis of its prospects and evaluation of its valuation, recognizing that diversification in the portfolio provided multiple opportunities to profit from the skill of investment selection.

With Graham's approach, the goal is to have a portfolio that represents an eight-cylinder engine that can run effectively on six cylinders at any given time. Since all conditions of the market, economy, inflation, commodities, etc. cannot be reasonably anticipated, it would be speculative to attempt to structure a portfolio for perfect results across all environments. A diligently diversified and value-selected portfolio includes components that perform well under some conditions, yet underperform under other conditions. The application of

skill to investment selection as well as portfolio structuring can enhance overall success.

Markowitz uses diversification differently. His diversification seeks
to eliminate the effects from individual companies and concentrate
the power of the market as the driver of performance. His theory asserts that the market will not pay investors for risks that can be eliminated. Since the inclusion of numerous stocks eliminates the risk of
any individual company to the overall portfolio, then diversification
serves to distill the driver of returns to stock market risk. With returns then based upon the market, skill is limited to achieving sufficient diversification rather than to selecting individual companies.

When investors accept the stock market as the driver of returns,
they are left with the choice of either timing or patience. The traditional approach, based upon some of the academic theories, quickly
accepted patience as the virtue and timing as speculation. Regardless of whether investors find short-term timing to be speculation or
technique, an understanding of secular stock market cycles delivers
insights for reasonable expectations from this approach.

Both Markowitz and Graham have much to offer. Many investors are
likely to lean toward Markowitz for secular bull market periods, and
then decide whether to use Graham as an all-weather philosophy or
as the complement to Markowitz during secular bear markets. If you
have yet to decide, you will likely have many years to think about it
as the current secular bear progresses. In the meantime, if you employ a Markowitz approach, be sure to include—as he emphasized
in his first stage to MPT—appropriate assumptions. In this environment, that will generally mean below-average stock market returns.

Further, whether one follows the principles of Graham or Markowitz,
be sure not to use the Rip Van Winkle approach with your portfolio.
Even under the Markowitz mandate, traditional investment management includes many techniques of portfolio structuring and oversight.
For example, institutions and individuals often use the technique of
rebalancing across the various asset classes of the portfolio. Rebalancing is the reallocation of assets from one or more asset classes to
other asset classes as their relative value changes. For example, assume a portfolio that is allocated half to stocks and half to bonds.
When the value of the stocks increases to 55% of the total, thereby

resulting in 45% allocated to bonds, the technique of rebalancing would require selling stocks and buying bonds to adjust the components back to 50%. Alternatively, the portfolio could receive or distribute funds to realign the portfolio to its original equal weighting. There are many subtleties for implementing rebalancing, including frequency, triggers, and other considerations. For this discussion, the key is to recognize that even the more passive approaches to investment management still require care and attention.

Graham had different ideas about rebalancing: he enlisted the wisdom of a hypothetical character that he referred to as Mr. Market. Graham believed that companies should be owned while they represented good value, then sold or replaced with more attractive opportunities. To Graham, it is time to rebalance the capital allocated to that company when it is no longer an attractive, businesslike investment.

Graham recognized that investing in the stock market required not only an evaluation of businesses but also an evaluation of the market. Each day, the market assesses the value of each company. Investors, likewise, hold an opinion about value. According to Graham, when Mr. Market is more enthusiastic than you are about the prospects of your holding, Graham believed that it was best to sell. When Mr. Market shows less interest, however, Graham saw the opportunity to buy.

These timeless principles apply to bonds and other investments as well as stocks. The key takeaway is that investors can choose to approach investing either as allocations to the markets or as investments within the markets. The approach determines whether the investor seeks relative returns, in relation to what the markets passively provide, or absolute returns driven by the businesslike approach of profit-driven investing.

Absolute vs. Relative

The absolute return approach and the relative return approach have differences, strengths, and weaknesses. Each approach can be appropriate in certain market conditions. Relative return investing has been used over the past few decades as the traditional approach. As this secular bear market has continued, however, the absolute return approach has been gaining recognition among investors.

The terms "absolute" and "relative" refer to their respective benchmarks of success. Absolute refers to a standard of positive results. Performance under absolute return investing is assessed in relation to breakeven. Relative refers to a standard of results that is in relation to another series. Performance under relative return investing is assessed in relation to a stock market, bond market, or other index related to the investment. Both approaches include the risk of not achieving their objective, but only the absolute return approach starts with the constant goal of profitability.

Absolute return investing is a philosophy as well as an approach. It incorporates the objective of investment gains regardless of broad price changes in a market benchmark or an asset class. Absolute return investing uses active skill for returns, rather than a more passive participation in general market trends. As a result, investing becomes businesslike, seeking profits from the activities of the investment manager rather than gains from general market moves and passive sources of income from the asset categories. Further, absolute return investing defines risk as the potential for a loss; the threshold for success in absolute return investing is profitability. It does not concentrate on either the direction of the markets or the performance of investments in relation to a benchmark—a loss is a loss.

As with any businesslike activity, however, profits are not assured. There will be years and periods when even diversified and well-managed portfolios experience a loss. Such periods often reflect highly adverse market conditions. In many of these instances, absolute return investments will serve to reduce losses and better position the portfolio for recovery.

Relative return investing is a somewhat recent practice driven by much scholarly research and popularized over the past several decades. The objective is to seek investment gains from the performance of an asset class or benchmark. An asset class is a group of assets whose value tends to change similarly. Stocks are an example of an asset class. An increase in the overall value of the stock market has a comparable effect on most portfolios of stocks. As a result, a diversified portfolio of stocks will be highly correlated to the stock market. In other words, the price of the portfolio will move similarly to its market benchmark. Likewise, bonds are an asset class. Generally, passive portfolios of bonds are correlated to the overall bond market. Therefore the relative return approach to investing offers investors the returns of the market—when the market provides returns. This approach requires a long-term view and patience as the investor endures volatile market swings on the way to long-term success.

Relative return investing does require skill, but the skill is directed to effective participation in the asset class and realizing the benchmark return. Since investing for relative returns depends upon the performance of the asset class, a primary measure of risk relates to the deviation from a benchmark known statistically as "tracking error." If the portfolio is down 10% when the market is down 12%, there has been 2% of positive tracking error. If instead the portfolio declines 13%, then the negative tracking error is 1%. This explains why relative return practitioners cheer when they are "beating the market." Their goal is to have a cumulative series of positive tracking errors to ultimately outperform the market. In practice, very few relative return managers beat their benchmarks consistently over time.

As a result, some investors have shifted their strategy to "indexing." This approach uses passive funds that closely track the market index. The passive funds replace active money managers that seek to beat the market while maintaining a close relationship with the index. Whether the portfolio uses active managers or passive indexes for the relative return approach, the investor will be highly dependent on the direction of the market. A relative return strategy in a below-average environment generally produces below-average results.

At the start of each year, as you consider the expectations for your investment portfolio, assess whether it is invested with the objective of making a profit regardless of the direction of the stock market, interest rates, and other markets. Ask yourself or your investment manager whether the investments are expected to make money this year. If the response includes "that depends on the direction of the markets," then you are pursuing a relative return approach. When it reflects an objective of positive returns each year, you are more likely pursuing an absolute return approach.

Risky Business

The absolute return approach to investing includes not only an objective for returns but also a perspective about risk. Risk can be friend or foe, and investors succeed or fail depending on how they deal with it. An inherent condition of all investments, risk should be respected, assessed, managed, and prudently controlled. You may have heard "If you want greater returns, you have to take more risk." The implication is that risk creates returns—as though risk were an element that mixes with investment capital to morph into returns. In reality, risk represents a condition that drives investors to demand compensation and protection. Risk is not the knob that you turn to increase returns.

As a result, in the financial markets, higher returns tend to be as-sociated with higher risks, which is far different from the notion that risk drives returns. Risk is not a fertilizer for returns; rather, it repre-sents weeds in your investment garden. Investment strategies need to adapt to the market environment. This is especially true when market conditions reflect the above-average valuations of a secular bear market.

Risk is not an assumption based on historical averages; it is unique to each situation. Though risks can often be assessed in the context of history, the future does not necessarily mirror the past. A caution readily recognized (and often ignored!) appears in most investment documents: "Past performance is not an indication of future results." Likewise, past levels of risk do not necessarily indicate future risk.

Risk is the uncertainty of loss. Without uncertainty, the situation would already be a loss and not a risk. Further, without the possibility of loss—if the uncertainty is only about the size of your gain—there is hardly risk. Some investors assume that higher risk merely means near-term volatility rather than the possibility of permanent losses to their accounts. Despite all of the ways that risk can be assessed and measured, risk is the likelihood that your investment will lose money. It is often measured in terms of probability and magnitude. For ex-ample, an investment might have a 20% chance of a loss. Further, it could have a risk of losing 50% of the investment. As the probability of a loss increases, and as the magnitude of potential loss increases, investments become more risky. The result is that investors should require greater potential for returns as risk increases — if they wish to take that risk at all.

Assessed together, returns and risk are elements that investors consider to determine the price and terms of an investment. If the assessment of return and risk is accurate, a properly structured port-folio of investments should deliver its expected return. Bear in mind, however, that on the other side of your transactions may be someone as diligent as you. As a buyer, you will believe that you have found great opportunity; while the seller on the other side of the transac-tion believes that the opportunity was not worth the price. This cap-italistic tension will be similar when you are the seller. Be careful, therefore, to use the diligence of a business decision to accurately assess the risks and potential returns.

Rational investors generally expect riskier investments to offer higher returns than less risky investments. This bedrock financial concept governs much investment thinking, and is the reason that lower-quality bonds yield more than higher-quality bonds. But the risk/reward relationship is not always as direct as many might assume. Did Jack Welch at GE or Warren Buffett at Berkshire Hathaway take on higher levels of risk to achieve their higher-than-average levels of return? Most analysts would say that Welch and Buffett achieved higher returns by exercising higher levels of skill than their coun-terparts at competitors. Analysts might even argue that a portion of their success lies in their ability to reduce risk by identifying particu-larly high-quality companies to add to their investment and corporate portfolios. Some investment strategies employing an absolute return approach have generated higher returns over market cycles while as-suming much less risk than the overall market.

Another misconception is that higher risk automatically means a potential for higher rewards. Risk is what rational investors assess and price into the expected return of an investment. For example, the price or yield of the lower-quality bond is set by rational inves-tors who will only pay a price that compensates for risk. It is the function of the market to set the price and terms of assets or invest-ments with the expected financial payback based on the anticipated level of risk and losses.

The term "expected returns" is used in the financial community to refer to the rate of return that an investor should require from a certain investment given its risk profile. When Markowitz published his paper on MPT in 1952, he referred to the "expected returns—variance of returns" rule, where the expected returns "include an allowance for risk."

Expected returns, other than yields from risk-free Treasury bills, therefore include a risk premium—a gross yield before any losses. In comparing higher- and lower-quality bonds, the lower-quality bond is priced to yield higher interest payments due to its greater risks. Compare, for example, a higher-quality U.S. Treasury bond yielding 3% with a lower-quality bond issued by a risky company. Due to the greater risk of loss, investors should require that the corporate bond have a higher yield, say 7%. Since there is generally no risk of loss on the Treasury bond, the expected return of 3% will be realized as a 3% return. But the expected return of 7% on the corporate bond may be realized at 7%, or it may be less if there is a credit loss.

In a portfolio diversified across numerous corporate bonds yielding 7%, investors should expect that the realized portfolio return would be less than 7%. It is likely that at least a few losses will occur given the higher risk profile of the bonds. As a result, there will be a difference between "pre-risk expected yield" and "post-risk probable yield." Investors are often seduced into higher-yielding investments without considering the likely post-risk return. It is important to understand this when considering the risk premium of asset classes, especially stocks.

There are many ways to assess and measure risk, including methods for quantifying the probability or magnitude of a loss. Investors use these measures to determine the likelihood of losing money on an investment, and to estimate how much they could lose if the investment fails to perform as expected.

Risks can be categorized as general risks of an asset class or as risks associated with individual investment choices. For example, the risk of the stock market as a whole is different from the risks associated with individual securities. It is important to understand this difference in order to manage the risks and the source of your returns.

Probabilities are only true if they are statistically valid. Without a preponderance of evidence, a probability is little more than an edu-cated guess. For example, one investment with a 10% probability of a total loss will result in either a total success or a total loss. A 10% probability of total loss over 100 transactions, however, usually results in losses of close to 10% across the portfolio. Until your portfolio is sufficiently diversified, most measures of risk will not accurately as-sess the threat to your portfolio.

Assume that you have the opportunity to invest in an oil well with a 25% probability of success and a payoff of ten times your invest-ment (a 1000% return). Your expected return, the probability times the potential payoff, would be 250%. If you invest $12,000 across a portfolio of a dozen ventures at $1,000 each, you can expect to lose $9,000 across nine of them. From the three in which you invested $3,000, however, the payoff is $30,000. Your net return of $30,000 represents a 250% return on your $12,000 investment.

If, instead, you invest all $12,000 in just one project, the proba-bilities may be the same, but the outcome is binary — it will either succeed or fail. If you succeed, your return is 1000% (ten times the investment) and if you fail, your loss is 100% (all of the investment). The statistical probabilities may be the same, but the risk and return profiles are quite different. This is one of the benefits and strengths of diversification.

For the stock you buy today, risk can be regarded as the probabil-ity and magnitude of a loss tomorrow, or whenever you sell it. As a result, many investors assess risk against the absolute level of break-even. In the short run, over days or even a few years, break-even can be a close proxy against which to assess risk. In the longer run, however, risk takes on additional meanings.

Figure 10.1 displays again the chart of total return for the S&P 500 before transaction costs and taxes over the 101 rolling ten-year pe-riods starting with 1900–1909 and ending with 2000–2009. Market pundits will comfort you with the statistic that over ten-year periods investors have lost money only three times since 1900. Therefore, they contend, there is little risk to stock market investments over the long term.

Figure 10.1. Rolling 10-Year Stock Market Returns: Losses

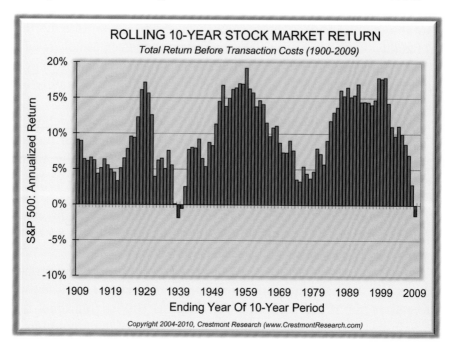

Their contention ignores two significant issues that become much more relevant over longer periods: inflation and liabilities. Since money represents purchasing power, an investment that breaks even over a decade returns only a fraction of the purchasing power, after inflation, than it had when it was initially deployed for an expected return. Over short periods, the effects are minimal, but over longer periods, the effect of inflation compounds. Given the historical average inflation rate of 3.3%, in the course of a decade, items that cost $1 will cost $1.38. If your investment breaks even over that period, you will be almost 30% short of meeting your obligations or needs. In some instances, obligations rise at a higher rate than inflation. This can apply to institutions as well as to individuals.

Institutions, including pension plans and endowments, have liabilities that they are required to fund with returns from their investment portfolios. Individuals have retirement goals or family responsibilities that demand an expected rate of return. If the investment return over a decade or two is break-even for an institution or an individual, risk of loss has not been avoided; rather, risk has been experienced in the loss of the required return. Though the investment may not have lost money, the institution or individual could be bankrupt as liabilities outstrip break-even or small-return assets.

If, for example, a pension plan has $1 billion in assets and is required to fund $2 billion in liabilities in ten years, it will need to earn 7.2% a year. Likewise, if an individual has a ten-year retirement plan or education goal and expects a certain return, simply breaking even can be not only disappointing but also disastrous.

For assessing portfolio risk, a measure and assessment other than break-even is necessary. Rather than simply recovering the principal, investors should assess the probability of achieving the required or expected rate of return. Risk, therefore, can represent the uncertainty of a shortfall in funding a projected liability.

Figure 10.2, Rolling 10-Year Stock Market Returns: Obligations, recognizes the demands of institutional and individual future obligations and assesses the performance of the stock market over the

Figure 10.2. Rolling 10-Year Stock Market Returns: Obligations

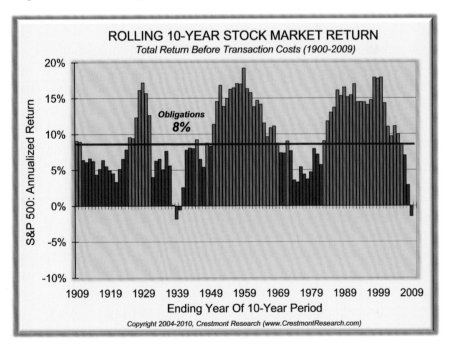

past century for its ability to meet these obligations. Figure 10.2 is identical to the chart in figure 10.1, with a line reflecting a required return of 8% and red highlights for the periods that fell short. The threshold of 8% provides some level of cushion to cover transaction costs, etc. and still enable the investor to achieve near 7% net returns. Keep in mind that many institutions currently assume an 8% net return across their entire portfolio, which would require even higher returns from stocks to offset much lower bond returns. Figure 10.2 reveals the historical probability of achieving success without risking funding shortfalls for obligations or planned uses.

Over the 101 decade-long periods since 1900, only 56 have achieved annual returns of 8% or more—merely a 56% probability of success! Further, of the 56 periods that do reflect sufficient returns, 47 (84%) are periods with price/earnings ratios (P/E) that increased from the start of the period to the end of the period. Not only were there a significant number of periods that did not reach the threshold of success, but also the vast majority of success periods required a rising P/E. The change in P/E over the investment period is the most significant driver of variability in stock market returns.

Under current conditions, the likelihood of success over this decade for an investor with an 8% threshold is very low despite the high probability of some level of return. Often, the appropriate assessment of investment success is not whether there is a loss, but rather whether there are sufficient gains to meet obligations. Insufficient returns represent failure as much as absolute losses.

Beyond probabilities and actual losses, many market experts measure risk by volatility of the returns. The most common measure is standard deviation, a statistic that reflects the width of the range for returns. A low value indicates that returns are expected to be in a narrow range, while a higher value indicates that the returns are more dispersed.

Volatility matters over time because it diminishes compounded returns compared to average returns. Volatility also affects the quality of the ride. Sharp downdrafts and roller-coaster volatility can drive many investors to divest their stock holdings at the wrong time. As a result, investors experience the decline but not the recovery.

Investors cannot spend the average returns that are often cited to promote stocks as consistently good investments. Investors can only spend compounded returns. The distinction between the two is important, and an example can clarify the differences.

A simple return is the mathematical average of a set of numbers. For instance, the simple average of 10% and 20% is 15%. A compounded return is the single percentage that provides the cumulative effect of a series of returns. If an investment grows by 10% and then again by 20%, its cumulative increase is 32%. This is greater than the sum of 10% and 20% as a result of compounding; however, the single percentage that would grow to 32% over two periods is 14.9%, slightly less than the simple average of 15%.

The difference between simple average gain and compounded average gain is significant for the stock market over the long term. During the period 1900–2009, the simple average of the annual gains for the stock market, excluding dividends, was 7.1%. The compounded annual gain excluding dividends reflects a more accurate view of realized annual returns. At the start of 1900, the Dow Jones Industrial Average was 66.08, and in 2009 it ended at 10,428.05, compounding at 4.7% over the 110 years. Though total returns were somewhat higher, since dividends generally were greater than transaction costs over that period, the difference between simple gains and compounded gains is dramatic.

Excluding dividends, transaction costs, and taxes, the simple average gain of 7.1% provides the illusion that, had you invested $1,000 in the market in 1900, you would have $1,891,654 by the end of 2009 ($1,000 compounded at 7.1% annually over 110 years yields $1,891,654).

An investor in the stock market over that same period, however, would net $156,363. An initial investment of $1,000 increased by 4.7% annually over 110 years compounds to only $156,363. The average gain is quite different from the compounded gain. Compounded gains are the relevant gains that generate cash in your account that can be spent.

Though the average gain was 7.1%, if your investments are compounding at only 4.7%, the financial results will be significantly lower. The difference between the average return and the compounded return is the result of two effects denoted by Crestmont Research as "volatility gremlins." These volatility gremlins can reduce the dollars you actually receive by more than 90%!

The volatility gremlins erode the average return into the compounded return, and the simple return into the actual return. Negative numbers and the dispersion of returns are mathematical mites. Each has a significant effect on realized returns. By understanding their impact, investors can appreciate the benefits of reducing volatility and increasing the consistency of investment returns. Investors can then realize higher compounded returns, and experience a more enjoyable and less stressful investment ride.

The first volatility gremlin is the impact of negative numbers on compounded returns. To illustrate the effect, consider an investment over two years. If an investment portfolio makes 20% the first year and loses 20% the second year, the simple average return is zero. When +20% is added to –20% the sum is 0%. The investor, however, has actually lost 4%. To break even, it takes a greater positive return than the offsetting negative loss. For a –20% loss, the offsetting gain is +25%. It works the same whether the positive or the negative occurs first. A +25% gain can be wiped out by a –20% loss.

The second volatility gremlin is the impact of the range of returns on the average. As the returns in a series become more dispersed from the average, the compounded return declines. The following example demonstrates this second dynamic. The compounded return from three periods of 5% returns is greater than any other sequence that averages 5%. Figure 10.3 illustrates this mathematical phenomenon. If you earn a return of 5% per year for three years in a row, your simple average return is 5% and your compounded return is 5%. If, however, you earn 6% the first year, 5% the second year, and 4% the third year, your simple average return remains 5%, but your compounded return drops to 4.997%. While this minor difference appears insignificant, consider the ramifications.

As the variability of a return series increases, there is a decline in the beneficial effects of compounding returns. Consider a case in which you earn 9% the first year, 5% the second year, and 1% the third year. Your simple average return remains 5%, but your compounded rate of return—the return that gives you dollars to spend—drops to 4.949%. The actual volatility of the stock market is greater still, and

Figure 10.3. Volatility Deteriorates Returns

Impact Of The Volatility Gremlins: Dispersion & Negative Numbers

	CASE A	CASE B	CASE C	CASE D	CASE E	CASE F
Year 1	5.0%	4.0%	9.0%	15.0%	25.0%	30.0%
Year 2	5.0%	5.0%	5.0%	-10.0%	-15.0%	-25.0%
Year 3	5.0%	6.0%	1.0%	10.0%	5.0%	10.0%
Simple Average Return	5.000%	5.000%	5.000%	5.000%	5.000%	5.000%
Compounded Return	5.000%	4.997%	4.949%	4.419%	3.714%	2.361%

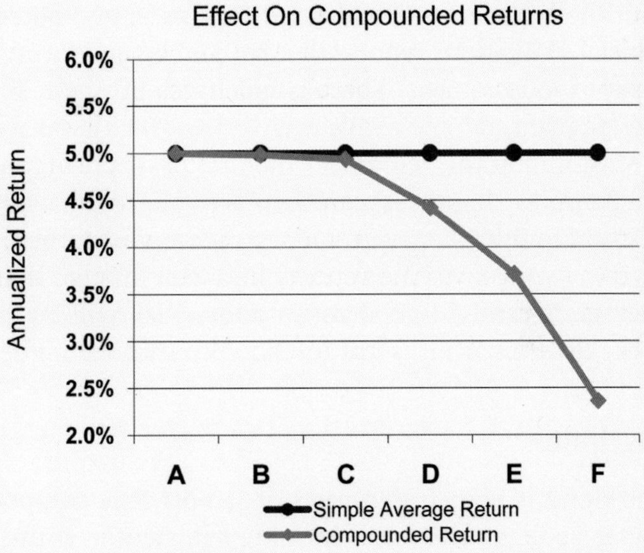

Effect On Compounded Returns

(chart: Annualized Return vs. Cases A–F; legend: Simple Average Return, Compounded Return)

the impact on compounded returns is much more significant. Keep in mind that half of all years in the stock market occur outside a 32% range, from –16% to +16%. As the level of dispersion increases, the impact from the second volatility gremlin increases.

Whether you take the traditional approach of relative return investing or the progressive approach of absolute return investing, risk is integral in your portfolio. Savvy investors understand the risks and their underlying assumptions and adopt a more businesslike approach to investing, reducing or hedging unwanted or undesirable risks. Investors are too often surprised by losses from unexpected or unintended risks. A well-constructed investment portfolio, like a well-run business, addresses its vulnerabilities and reacts to the ever-changing environment.

Risk, when it becomes a loss, undermines the value of previous or future gains. The power of losses exceeds the power of gains, requiring ever-greater gains to restore increasing losses. As risk and the variability of returns increase, the force of Albert Einstein's eighth wonder of the world—compound interest—is diminished.

Beware the pundit who cheers an investment for not losing money over the long term. The effects of inflation and potentially rising financial obligations require that success be measured by the achievement of solid returns. There is much risk in simply breaking even in the long run.

Most important, remember the first principle of Markowitz's Modern Portfolio Theory: assumptions are your responsibility. Be sure that your assumptions rationally assess risk as you develop, structure, and diversify your investment portfolio. Keep in mind that the long-term average is rarely a good assumption. Risk will be an ingredient in every investment; it is not the knob to turn for higher returns.

Discipline

The trend is your friend, until it is not. This paraphrase of the old trader's adage serves as a warning against one of the most powerful forces in human nature, especially as it relates to investors. It is Siren calling you into the market at the top and scaring you out near the bottom. It is one of the powerful reasons that undisciplined investors want to start each year by selling what has not worked in a portfolio so as to double down on what has.

Market and economic conditions are constantly in a state of change, which has cyclical impacts on parts or all of a portfolio. As a result, the more disciplined approach to investing is to invest based upon the underlying fundamentals rather than the current position in the cycle. Graham knew this when he encouraged the constant revaluation of the business's fundamentals and its constant assessment against market value. A rising price is not an indication of rising value, no more than a falling price reflects a bargain.

The key to successful investing in the environment of uncertainty presented by secular bear markets is the businesslike discipline of consistency based upon fundamentals. This was one of Jack Welch's top business tenets. Welch was the legendary chief executive at General Electric from 1981 to 2001. Though he had the benefit of a secular bull market for most of his tenure to multiply his operating success, Welch is recognized for business acumen that built GE into the largest and most valuable company in the world under his leadership.

Consistency, however, does not imply perfection. Consistency of principles and discipline sometimes meets the unexpected. Occasionally, due to human nature, even the best intention for discipline will confront unexpected events and thereby result in mistakes. As a result, not all good investment decisions have good results, but consistently good decisions generally yield good results over time. In the end, rational discipline leads to investment success.

Success is dependent not only upon the gains that are achieved but also upon the risks that are controlled and the investment process that is employed. To that end, it is important to recognize the environment and conditions of secular bear markets. This is the distinction between anticipation and prediction.

Generally, markets do not decline or rise at one time or on one line. Market movements are choppy, volatile, and often without regard for the immediate economic or financial conditions. Over time, however, markets see the completeness of the forest, not the interim distraction of individual trees. Nonetheless, the experience of investors is quite the opposite—constant distraction from individual trees that often distorts the forest.

Though the shorter-term cyclical periods at times may last only one or a few years, with dramatic surges and falls, these periods tend to feel like an eternity for long-term investors. There are over 500 market days across just two years, representing several thousand hourly data points for those people who watch it more closely. Though the overall trend may have direction, like a good story that takes time

Figure 10.4. The Impact of Losses

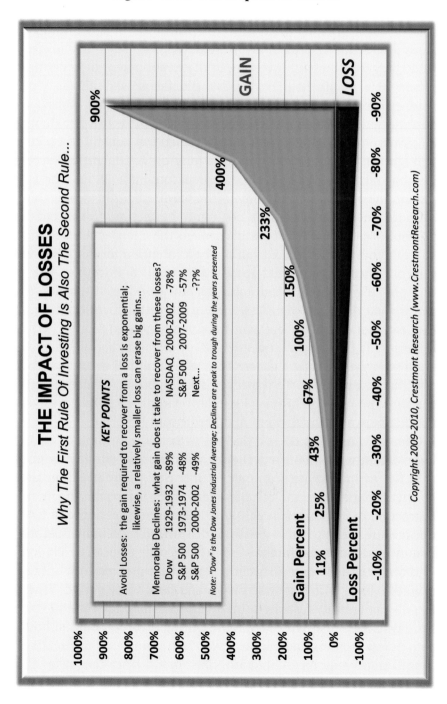

THE IMPACT OF LOSSES

Why The First Rule Of Investing Is Also The Second Rule...

KEY POINTS

Avoid Losses: the gain required to recover from a loss is exponential; likewise, a relatively smaller loss can erase big gains...

Memorable Declines: what gain does it take to recover from these losses?

Dow	1929-1932	-89%	NASDAQ 2000-2002 -78%
S&P 500	1973-1974	-48%	S&P 500 2007-2009 -57%
S&P 500	2000-2002	-49%	Next... -??%

Note: "Dow" is the Dow Jones Industrial Average; Declines are peak to trough during the years presented

GAIN

LOSS

Gain Percent: 11%, 25%, 43%, 67%, 100%, 150%, 233%, 400%, 900%

Loss Percent: -10%, -20%, -30%, -40%, -50%, -60%, -70%, -80%, -90%

Copyright 2009-2010, Crestmont Research (www.CrestmontResearch.com)

to develop, there will be many subplots that will create distraction if one does not remain focused on the overall script.

In the course of the market's script, there will be many instances when the fundamentals will be in charge, and there will be other times that may appear to be confusing exceptions. Another goal for investment success is to learn to avoid false lessons from exceptions. History uses repetition as a way to convert experience into wisdom. It helps to discern the false signals and misinformation as markets naturally take their course through the short-term cyclical periods and across the long-term secular cycles. A portfolio that is appropriately structured helps to protect investors against the uncertainties of market action and to position investors with patience for performance.

Capture and the Impact of Losses

Consider 1931, the worst year for the stock market in the past century—actually the worst year in the history of American financial markets. Stocks were down 51%. To recover, the market had to gain more than 100%. Many investors never held on to experience the recovery.

Herein are two of the primary reasons to control risk in a portfolio. First, significant volatility from an investment portfolio can cause investors to react irrationally and exit holdings just when the better decision is to hold on or buy more. Second, the amount of gain required to recover a loss is disproportionately large compared to the loss incurred. Likewise, gains are erased by disproportionately smaller losses.

For example, if an investor in 1931 had a portfolio that limited its decline to half of the 51%—say 25%—then the required recovery is only +33% rather than +100% (to recover from the 51% loss). The detriment of losses is disproportionate to the benefit of gains.

To illustrate further, as reflected in figure 10.4, a gain of +11% is required to recover from a loss of –10%, +33% to recover from –25%, +67% to recover from –40%, and +400% to recover from a NASDAQ-level decline of –80%. During challenging periods like secular bear markets, when gains are sporadic, risk management to limit losses can be invaluable toward the process of achieving investment success.

This concept has significant implications for stock market investments. Since the volatility of the stock market is so important, there are many instances when a reduction in losses can be very beneficial in reducing the amount of the recovery needed to match the market.

In the 1990s, many investors pursued a strategy known as "beat the market." The philosophy behind this strategy is to remain fully invested, try to lose a little less than the market when it declines, and try to make a little more than the market when it rises. In essence, accept all of the downside and all of the upside to try to beat the market over time. Of course, when the stock market is averaging 17% per year, as it did during the recent secular bull market, who cares if the strategy varies a bit from actual market results?

Since the 2000s, the strategy has been shifting to an approach that could be called "achieve returns." In the current secular bear market period, even beating the market may not be sufficient if, for example, this means accepting a loss of 2% when the market loses 6%. Moreover, investors have become much more sensitive to risk. The reward-to-risk relationship has shifted significantly since the 1990s.

Investors are beginning to realize that risk management, especially in secular bear markets, can drive returns in addition to the other return-drivers in a portfolio. For example, assume that you could structure a portfolio with investment approaches or managers that would generally experience 40% of the downside of the market. Using a stock market measure, this is known as having a market beta of 0.4 ("beta" measures the ratio of a security's or portfolio's movement in relation to the overall stock market). Assuming, therefore, that your portfolio can be structured with the intention that its decline will be approximately 40% as much as the market declines, how much of the upside of the stock market must you capture to match market returns over time?

If the portfolio is expected to decline by only 40% of the market's decline, then the portfolio will not need to match the market's gains as it recovers. Figure 10.5 reflects the relationship between losses and recoveries for investments in the stock market. To match market returns over time, the level of participation on the upside is dependent upon the exposure to downside losses. Avoiding losses significantly reduces the portion of upside needed to match or exceed stock market returns over time. From the example, if you could contain losses to 40% of the market decline, you historically needed only 54% of the recovery to achieve market returns. If you can achieve more than that, the portfolio should exceed the market's return over time.

Figure 10.5. Capture:
Returns Needed to Recover Losses in Stocks Over Time

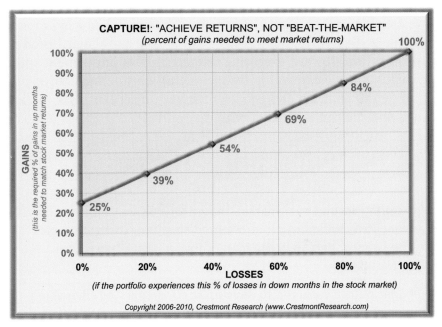

This is important for two reasons. First, good risk management not only reduces the volatility and uncertainty of your portfolio but also positions the portfolio to require less recovery than the market to exceed the market return. Second, this is instructive to reset expectations about the need to beat the market. An investor who is positioned to minimize some of the downside can be satisfied and successful during market surges with less than the market return. A solid 10% return during a year when the market surges 16% can be successful over time if the portfolio sufficiently limits losses during years of decline.

Hope Is Not A Strategy

In closing, the uncertainties integral to secular stock market cycles, especially secular bear markets, heighten the need for a businesslike approach to investing. This requires a delicate balance between a long-term perspective and a shorter-term sense of urgency for discipline and fundamentals. This does not require a new way of investing; rather, it involves the use of long-held and time-tested principles. Investing for most investors, therefore, is the art of deploying capital with the goal of gains, the management of risk, and the inclusion of diversification. Toward executing the tactics of an investment strategy, it is important to recognize the overall environment by understanding the financial and economic drivers of secular stock market cycles and the characteristics of those cycles.

POINTS OF EMPHASIS

- During secular bear markets, when returns are muted or negative, the more profit-oriented absolute return strategies are appropriate over the market-following relative return strategies.

- Discipline is required to develop and manage well-diversified portfolios and to avoid the common errors of human nature.

- The first rule of investing is to not lose money. The second rule is to never forget the first rule, and then all of the other rules follow.

- The volatility gremlins of losses and disperse returns reduce the benefits of compounding.

- Risk is not only the chance of a loss; it is also the possibility of shortfalls in meeting income needs or liability obligations.

- A portfolio in the stock market that limits losses does not have to beat the market to exceed market returns over time.

SECTION V

THE BIG DILEMMA

Consternation [kon-stur-ney-shun]:
A sudden overwhelming fear and alarm
resulting from the awareness of danger that
results in confusion and dismay.

CHAPTER 11

PRACTICAL IMPLICATIONS

Winston Churchill could have been talking about this decade in the stock market when he said, "Let our advance worrying become advance thinking and planning." The practical implications of another secular bear market decade should be a call to action rather than a call for retreat. Churchill offers wisdom that acknowledges challenging conditions and provides a solution toward success. His advice encourages investors to seek the benefits of preparation and risk management, the essential elements for investing through this secular bear toward the next secular bull market.

The current environment has significant implications for a broad group of people. Below-average returns from the stock market certainly impact those who are saving for retirement, whether personally or in retirement accounts. It also affects retirees who are already living on savings. For these investors, the keys to success in a secular bear market lie in: (1) early recognition of the financial market landscape; (2) a well-managed investment approach; and (3) a realistic expectation for lifestyle spending.

Beyond individuals, there is a wide range of institutional investors. These include endowments, foundations, corporate pension funds, government pension funds, and other investing entities. Some of these institutional investors do not have a readily available source of funding to supplement spending when investment returns are lean. In an environment of below-average returns, these entities in particular need realistic return assumptions for planning and a well-managed investment approach. Additionally, because this decade will not be as fruitful as some past ones, these institutions will operate with lower incomes and thus lower distributions to constituents.

Other institutional investors have alternate sources of funding to draw upon. Corporate pension plans are the obligation of the related corporation. Public pension plans are the obligations of the related government employer and, ultimately, taxpayers. Unlike many of the other institutions, the liabilities of pension funds are generally fixed obligations. Shortfalls from incorrect assumptions about returns therefore impact the alternate funding sources rather than spending levels. The risks are substantial. As a result, over the past few decades, corporate employers have replaced fixed-obligation pensions with retirement plans that hold individual balances for employees. In other words, for current employees, defined contribution plans replaced many of the previous defined benefit plans. Public employers, however, continue to use fixed-obligation pensions and operate them with assumptions for relatively high investment returns.

Although there are thousands of public pension plans, the nature of their operations and commonality of purpose lead the segment to operate with similar assumptions and investment approach. Therefore, the public pension plan segment represents a collective issue more so than a series of individual issues. The current magnitude of the shortfalls in public pension plans is substantial, and it impacts a broad base of constituents. The most significant problem is the unrealistic expectation for investment returns that is delaying action and further increasing the shortfall.

An unexpected irresistible force is about to meet a seemingly immovable object. For many of these pension plans, the assets currently held and additions that are expected will not be able to generate sufficient income to meet the currently committed liabilities. Already, local communities are implementing new fees and taxes on residents, even those without taxable income, to address annual operating budget shortfalls that are worsened by increases in required pension contributions. Shortfalls that might have remained a local or state issue with early recognition are becoming large enough to now be a national issue.

Tax revenues, even at higher rates, are unlikely to be a sufficient source for the magnitude of shortfalls under most outcomes for the secular bear market. Though some of the burden can be cast forward upon future generations, there are likely to be significant reductions in government programs, including support for lower-income families, schools, police, and other state and local services. The situation is already severe; a more urgent recognition of reasonable return assumptions and appropriate planning can keep it from worsening.

This discussion explores the practical implications of below-average returns for three sets of constituents: pre-retirees, retirees, and public pension plans. Each of them has a somewhat unique circumstance, yet all of them share similarities. Pre-retirees have time for planning, the benefits of future contributions, and the prospect of a future secular bull market. Retirees are confronting the realities of retirement in a secular bear market. Public pension plans have too few assets to cover extensive liabilities. Further, they continue to use unrealistic assumptions for investment returns, and aggressive accounting under special rules that mask the full extent of their shortfalls.

Nonetheless, the three sets of constituents operate within a similar framework. All of them are trying to confront the practical implications of funding: cash in and cash out. Cash in, past and future, is savings. Cash out, present and future, is either payments toward obligations or income for retirees. Both cash in and cash out have growth factors associated with them: for cash in, for example, the growth factor is the assumed rate of return on investments.

Figure 11.1 provides an illustration to use as the framework for discussing the practical implications of a secular bear market. Contributions represent current or future additions to savings. Savings is the amount of capital available for investment, and investment income is the assumed future return from accumulated capital in savings. Distributions represent the starting and ongoing base payments from savings upon retirement or upon benefit payouts from retirement or pension plans, while the inflation adjustment is the annual rate of increase that distributions must grow to cover inflation or promised increases in payments. Basically, contributions and savings are the available funds, distributions are the amounts expected

Figure 11.1. Model for the Practical Implications of a Secular Bear Market

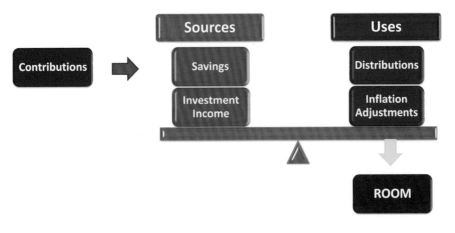

in the future, and the assumptions for investment income are what determine whether the sources will be sufficient to cover the uses.

If the inputs are insufficient to meet all of the outputs, you end up in the ROOM—you have Run Out Of Money. The ROOM is the shortfall between contributions and distributions based upon the assumptions for investment income and an inflation adjustment. Obviously, the ROOM means that you have exhausted savings before meeting all needs and obligation. For individuals, this means that you will be out of savings before you are out of time. For institutions, it means that you will have distributed all assets before satisfying all liabilities. The result will be compromises to beneficiaries, or, for public entities, additional demands from taxpayers.

If the variables are a bit unclear at this point, the illustrations that follow will color them with details. First, it is important to identify the overall impact that secular stock market cycles have on the constituent groups. Then, the discussion will proceed to specific issues and considerations for pre-retirees, post-retirees, and institutions—especially public pension plans.

Chunks, Not Streams

Al Pacino, Dionne Warwick, Fran Tarkenton, Jack Nicklaus, Mario Andretti, Peter Fonda, Raquel Welch, Ringo Starr, and Smokey Robinson—what do they have in common with secular stock market cycles?

They were all born in 1940 and were subsequently impacted by secular bull markets. The choice of that year, which is not precise but was chosen for illustration, is that people born around 1940 aged into their forties by 1980. Most people and families accumulate savings slowly, if at all, during their twenties and thirties. By their forties, and certainly fifties, they begin to build retirement nest eggs. Therefore those born around 1940 had the opportunity to build sizable retirement savings during the 1980s and '90s if they invested well as they reached their prime saving period.

David Brinkley, Shelley Winters, Walter Matthau, and others born in 1920 were saving during the secular bear market of the 1960s and '70s. With little stock market gain over that period, their savings would be filled with contributions that earned little additional investment income. That modest capital base, however, then encountered the secular bull market of the 1980s and '90s, and though the nest was small, the eggs from it were abundant.

This walk down memory lane illustrates several points. First, secular stock market cycles deliver returns in chunks, not streams. Second, most investors live long enough to have the relevant investment period extend across both secular bulls and secular bears. Third, investors do not get to pick which type of cycle comes first. Fourth, investors need to be aware that they will likely encounter both types of cycles. Those who experience secular bears during accumulation are generally better prepared than investors who are spoiled by a secular bull. A secular bull market is a pleasant surprise to retirees who endured a secular bear on the way to retirement. For retirees who grew to expect a secular bull during accumulation, the unexpected secular bear can be considerably disruptive.

Given where the stock market and valuations are today, the circumstances are quite different for people across different age groups. The following discussions about the three sets of constituents explore the concepts that affect each category. This chapter does not provide the tools needed for effective financial planning or for investment policy and portfolio construction. There are many qualified professionals and writings that can provide expertise for implementation; this chapter seeks to sow seeds of understanding about the relevant issues.

Accumulation

The outlook for the current secular bear market is uncertain. It could last a decade or longer with mediocre returns, or end in a blaze of fury within five years or so. Either way, current pre-retiree accumulators are in a period of below-average returns and above-average risk. This group of investors therefore has two major issues: The first is market risk, the risk that their investments will perform poorly; second, this group is at risk of underperforming their expectations for investment returns and accumulation.

The implication of the first risk is a shortfall of returns, whereas the second risk is a shortfall of contributions. As investors near retirement, their ability to recover from the second risk declines. Reasonable expectations about market returns for the foreseeable future can, therefore, enable accumulators to modestly increase their contributions to savings if necessary. Otherwise, they may be required to radically increase it later once the shortfall is apparent and inevitable.

Given the time horizon, the accumulators can be separated into two groups. Some people are many years or decades from retirement; the current decade represents only a part of their pre-retirement accumulation. This group can be designated as the Early Accumulators.

For people who have many years to go, the keyword is patience. This decade or so will be a slog of accumulation. It is a period for careful and consistent additions to savings, and it's a very good time to be contributing. If you are in this group, then you will want lots of savings in the future when returns on savings (investment income) are positioned to be above average. Do not accept the conventional wisdom that you can afford to take more risk because you have more time.

Conventional wisdom about the stock market provides that if you stay invested long enough, you can expect historical average returns.

This fallacy has led many investors astray. The stock market is not a game of chance that relies upon longer periods to tip the odds in your favor, and the odds are not the same for all periods. Secular stock market conditions are not random events; the market's valuation level significantly influences subsequent returns.

For example, a coin flip is a game of chance in which the odds of each flip are 50% that heads will result and 50% that tails will result. Allow heads to represent investment success and tails to represent investment failure. Though each flip of the coin comes with the same odds for heads, as the run of tails grows, there is a sense that heads is due. Therefore those who bet on games of chance often rely upon staying power to ride out long runs of tails for the ultimate payout from heads. Staying power is not as relevant for investing across secular stock market cycles. While it may be true that later contributions will benefit from the heads of a secular bull, existing investments will carry the burden of a secular bear for a long time.

In reality, the reasoning about long-term investors taking more risk relies upon the ability of those investors to sacrifice with extra contributions, or to delay retirement in later years if the early years do not work out as expected. There is no reason to play a game of chance with your life savings when the odds are weighted against success. When armed with a reasonable expectation of return based upon market conditions, investors do not need to take long-shot risks that are weighted against them.

Importantly, this does not mean that investors should avoid the stock market—rather it highlights the need to alter their approach away from passive buy-and-hold investing to more actively managed and diversified investment strategies. The stock market provides solid opportunities for returns during secular bear markets, but during those periods, portfolios require an enhanced level of risk management to complement return generation.

Early Accumulators should therefore recognize that the current environment presents the challenges of below-average returns and other secular bear market characteristics. As a result, they can look to the near term as a period of conservative accumulation. For now, this group should include no more than a modest assumption for investment income, and be willing to change that assumption later when conditions change. This represents an opportunity to add extra contributions with the patience and understanding to know that it will be available to perform later. Further, it is not too early to assess the expected distributions and include a factor for an inflation adjustment. This planning will help to realistically assess the amount of savings that will be needed at retirement. Given the long-term horizon and an ability to address the other variables, there should be ample ability and time to avoid the saving deficit of the ROOM.

Long-term accumulators have many moving parts that affect their retirement planning. The complexity of this group's planning deserves careful consideration to avoid hasty oversimplification, which can result in underdeveloped risk management. A long-term perspective is not a justification to accept higher risk.

Though the extra time before retirement enables accumulators to supplement retirement funds with increased contributions, shortfalls in savings from losses leave accumulators vulnerable. An investor who is mauled by a bear due to poor risk management may have insufficient assets to capitalize on the subsequent secular bull market. Further, while an accumulator may be able to rebuild losses though additional savings, the timing may be too late to participate in a more favorable market to build sufficient wealth for retirement.

The second group in this set, the near-retirees, will be called Late Accumulators. People in this category are within a decade or so of retiring. They are investing in the last lap of accumulation toward a marathon of retirement, and have likely started planning for the next stage of life. Many in this group made tremendous progress in the 1980s and '90s, only to have the proverbial gold ring pulled away over the past ten years. Many in this group are still hoping that this decade will not only make up the lost ground of the prior decade but will also reach their original projections.

The appropriate strategy for investors in this group needs to start with assumptions based upon reasonable expectations. The stock market is not positioned to start a secular bull ascent or achieve even historically average returns. Rather than view the past and current decades as fallen periods, think of them as pauses resulting from the stellar surge of the prior two decades. This group of people has a sobering near future, one that requires wealth preservation rather than

wealth accumulation. In a decade or two, this group will likely realize solid returns from the next secular bull market—the goal is to
have all, or more, of their current savings available to invest. Great
returns generated from half as much capital can still deliver a disappointing lifestyle in retirement.

Under the illustrative model, Late Accumulators should focus on
further growth in savings, with the focus on additional contributions
rather than the near-term returns on savings. They will want to have
a confident sense for the expected income represented by distributions, and a reasonable assumption for the growth of income in the
future from an inflation adjustment for what hopefully will be a
long retirement period. This does not mean that Late Accumulators
should avoid the stock market; instead, they should have reasonable
expectations and should focus on stock market strategies that deliver more consistent income. They may be particularly interested,
as well, in the next discussion about safe withdrawal rates from retirement portfolios. Though the remaining horizon for contributions
is more limited, with careful planning and diligence there should be
ample ability and time for near-retirees to avoid the saving deficit
of the ROOM.

Distribution

The distribution phase marks the transition point between additions
to savings and withdrawals from savings. Some retirees will begin to
withdraw before completely ceasing to make additions. If a person
or family has begun to take withdrawals, then they have entered the
distribution phase. For these investors, some of the variables from
the model in figure 11.1 are becoming fixed or significantly limited
in the range of alternatives.

For this part of the discussion, the assumption is that the investor
has made, or expects to make, a full transition to the mode of retiree.
As a result, the investor no longer has contributions to use for planning. Most likely, recent retirees may be deciding the initial level of
distributions, and existing retirees may be rethinking their distributions after a decade of poor returns. At this point, retirees know their
level of savings; the most significant assumption relates to expected

returns and investment income from the investment portfolio. Above all, retirees want to avoid the ROOM.

Since the number of active variables has been reduced, and since the driver for retirement portfolio distributions is highly dependent upon investment income, it is important to explore in detail the concept of withdrawal rates. Safe Withdrawal Rate (SWR) is the term that investment advisors, financial planners, and do-it-yourself investors use to represent the acceptable rate at which funds can be withdrawn from an investment portfolio while still providing a high confidence of income for the balance of a retiree's lifetime.

SWR is often stated as the percentage of an investor's initial portfolio that can be safely withdrawn annually after retirement to cover life's expenses. In the earlier diagram, this is essentially distributions divided by savings for the first year, including an assumption that the distributions will change annually by the inflation adjustment factor. The main variables are: (1) success rate, as reflected in the percentage likelihood of not running out of money; (2) portfolio mix and return assumptions for investment income; (3) how long the retiree assumes that he or she will live; and (4) a variety of other variables including tax rates, investment expenses, etc.

A retiree today has a relatively long-term horizon, with an average retirement age near sixty and an expected lifespan for the last surviving spouse of almost thirty years. Relatively healthy retirees today can expect one or both spouses to live well past ninety. Whether you are retired now or on the cusp of retirement, your savings has been built over many years of toil and saving to provide or supplement your income during retirement. For pre-retirees who are still building the nest egg, this analysis can provide insights about what to expect in the future. The objective is to determine a safe assumption for investment returns, and a safe level of income or withdrawals from savings each year to sustain a desired lifestyle—the rate at which it is safe to withdraw golden eggs from the goose.

Some advisors or planners will go so far as to advocate that today's long-term retirees invest heavily in the stock market. Those pundits say, "A market that has never lost money over thirty-year periods won't let you down in the future." It's true that there has never been a thirty-year period when stock market investors overall have lost money, yet there have been quite a few thirty-year periods that have bankrupted senior citizens who were relying upon their stock portfolios for retirement income.

Most analysts and models suggest that a retiree can withdraw 4% to 5% of the original balance each year, increased annually to cover inflation, and still have a very good chance of not running out of money. The models, however, often do not use reasonable assumptions and do not sufficiently consider risk. Generally, such high withdrawal rates relate to investment portfolios that are significantly weighted toward stocks, especially during the current and recent environment of low bond returns.

For illustration, assume that a retired couple invests exclusively in the stock market because they "need" the extra return and should feel "safe" that the stock market will not let them down over a thirty-year period. Further, assume no income taxes, investment fees, commissions, or other charges. Admittedly, these assumptions probably deliver the best-case scenario and conclusions.

For the analysis, the portfolio includes a diversified stock market portfolio using the S&P 500 index including dividends. The time horizon is thirty years, which assumes that the last surviving spouse will need money for at least thirty years after the retirement date. What, therefore, are the chances of success, of not running out of money, and avoiding a job search after age eighty?

Many models use historical average rates of return. As previously reflected across multi-decade periods in the stock market, average rarely happens. Most often, returns from the market are either well above average or well below average. Regardless, as far as retirement success is concerned, each retiree's results will be binary—the retiree either will be successful or will run out of money. It doesn't matter whether the retiree—on average—has a 75% chance of success. The reality for each retiree is that success will be either 100% or 0%. Though probabilities are interesting, retirees should thus be keenly focused on the implications of the assumptions and their likely impact on the outcome.

Using history since 1900 as the laboratory to assess the likelihood of success, a retiring couple who start with withdrawals of 4% have a 95% chance of success. In other words, they have a 95% chance of not running out of money before the last surviving spouse no lon-ger needs withdrawals. For example, this represents an initial an-nual withdrawal of $40,000 for a retiree with $1 million, increasing the $40,000 at the start of each year by the inflation rate. By the way, about half of retirees will live past the expected average lifes-pan; thus the success rates are actually lower for the half of retirees in the lucky group.

A 95% chance of success sounds pretty good—on average. The 95% success rate, however, means that you have a 1-in-20 chance of having to find a job at age eighty. If you have enough money to be thinking about SWR, you likely have a lifestyle that you don't want to compromise. When you think about last-to-survive issues, it has even greater significance.

To further emphasize the concept of success rate, assume that the doctor comes into your hospital room and says that your upcoming surgery has a good success rate: a 95% chance of success. The doc-tor performs this procedure five times a day. Since that's twenty per week, how many of you will immediately hope that you will not be the one that week who does not make it.

A 95% success rate sounds good to all those who are standing around the operating table, but it is quite different for the one who is actually on the table. The patient will be thinking about his or her particular circumstances—whether the odds are more likely to be above or below the 95%. A high success rate may still represent a significant risk.

Before digging into the details, what does the overall average look like? Over the 81 thirty-year periods since 1900, on average across all periods, the retiree who started with $1 million could have with-drawn 4% plus the inflation rate each year and still ended with $7.0 million. The average retiree accumulated seven times his initial sav-ings, even after withdrawing 4% plus inflation every year for thirty years. As for the failure rate, only 4 of the 81 periods resulted in the retiree running out of money.

What are the implications for investors, especially at this stage of a secular bear market? For retirees who are primarily invested in the stock market, the most significant factor determining future returns is the level of valuation at the time of initial investment, as measured by the P/E ratio. So the level of the P/E at retirement has a significant impact on the individual investor's chances of success in retirement.

To better understand the potential success rate for a couple entering retirement, stock market history can be dissected into five ranked sets called quintiles. These sets are organized from the highest to the lowest P/E ratio at the start of the respective thirty-year periods. The result is that the highest quintile (the top 20% of all periods) includes the thirty-year periods since 1900 that started with P/Es of 18.7 and higher. The second set (the next 20%) cuts off at a P/E of 15.1, the third at 12.2, the fourth at 10.4, and the last at 5.3.

Why does this matter? While the success rate for the entire group was 95%, for a retiree who enters retirement with a portfolio dedicated to stocks when P/E is 18.7 or higher, the expected success rate based upon history is 76%—analogous to more than one loss per day for the surgeon, rather than one per week using the overall average.

When P/E started at relatively high levels historically, thereby fundamentally positioning the stock market for below-average returns, there was a significant adverse impact on future success. When P/E started at relatively lower levels, returns were always sufficient for 4% withdrawals—100% success from periods that started with a low P/E.

As figure 11.2 reflects, the starting level of P/E has a direct impact on retirement success and on ending capital. The implication for today's investor is that the likelihood of financial success in retirement is considerably less than most pundits advocate. Twenty years from now, a response of "who knew?" won't be much comfort for retirees in the employment line at the local job fair. This is especially true since a rational understanding of history and the drivers of longer-term stock market returns can help today's retiree avoid that surprise.

As presented in figure 11.2, covering the 81 thirty-year periods since 1900, the top 20% of the periods based upon the beginning P/E started with P/E at 18.7 or higher. Within that 20% of the periods, about 1 in 4 (24%) of the thirty-year periods resulted in the retiree running out of money before the end of the period. When that occurred, the retiree was out of money on average during the 27th year and as early as the 23rd year. For those 76% who were fortunate enough to not run out of money, the average retiree that started with $1.0 million ended the thirty years with almost $2.8 million.

Figure 11.2. SWR Profile By P/E Quintile:
4% SWR, 30-Year Periods Since 1900

Safe Withdrawal Rate From Stock Market Portfolio
4% Withdrawal Plus Inflation: 30-Year Periods Since 1900

STARTING P/E QUINTILES	STARTING P/E RANGE	SUCCESS RATE	AVERAGE ENDING $s	AVG YRS IF OUT OF $s
Top 20%	18.7 +	76%	$ 2,555,842	27.3
Second 20%	15.1 to 18.6	100%	$ 5,517,179	n/a
Third 20%	12.2 to 14.9	100%	$ 7,009,735	n/a
Fourth 20%	10.4 to 12.0	100%	$ 10,779,456	n/a
Bottom 20%	below 10.4	100%	$ 9,317,929	n/a
ALL PERIODS	14.4 avg	95%	$ 6,980,717	27.3

Keep in mind that success provides a wide path, but failure is a thin line: those who succeed will end with a little or a lot; those who fail get to zero, or start counting pennies as their savings dwindle. Further, in reality, for retirees who invest during top quintile periods, the chance of suffering the painful effects of failure is even higher than 24%. Since a few of the periods ended relatively close to zero, fear forced some retirees to drastically reduce spending as their portfolios dwindled toward the end.

For most retiree investors over the past century, those fortunate enough to have retired when stock valuations and P/Es were lower, the results were much better. As reflected in figure 11.2, the benefits were directly and inversely related to the starting level of valuation. As the starting valuation declines, returns increase, and the resulting average balance in the portfolio at the end of the thirty years increases. This is another tangible example of the way that starting valuation significantly impacts future results.

A number of advocates and studies promote initial withdrawal rates of 5% or more of the starting portfolio: "You can have $50,000 a year from your million dollars, and have it increase annually by inflation and still last thirty years." The calculated success rate historically is 75% for retirees using a 5% initial withdrawal rate from stock market portfolio. For many retirees, that probability of success would be marginally acceptable. When the impact of starting P/E is included in the analysis, however, the odds change significantly for most of the quintiles.

As figure 11.3 shows, though the average may have been 75%, one of the sets reflects success as low as 41% while another had everyone making it safely through the thirty years. As you reflect upon the figure to assess the likely odds of either financial success or failure during your retirement, it is crucial to recognize the importance and impact of the starting level of P/E. Most important, it does not matter how many of the scenarios provide your heirs with multimillions; you will likely be most concerned about reducing the chances

Figure 11.3. SWR Profile By P/E Quintile:
5% SWR, 30-Year Periods Since 1900

Safe Withdrawal Rate From Stock Market Portfolio
5% Withdrawal Plus Inflation: 30-Year Periods Since 1900

STARTING P/E QUINTILES	STARTING P/E RANGE	SUCCESS RATE	AVERAGE ENDING $s	AVG YRS IF OUT OF $s
Top 20%	18.7 +	41%	$ (1,141,148)	21.8
Second 20%	15.1 to 18.6	75%	$ 1,624,058	22.0
Third 20%	12.2 to 14.9	69%	$ 4,421,662	24.0
Fourth 20%	10.4 to 12.0	94%	$ 8,175,391	26.0
Bottom 20%	below 10.4	100%	$ 6,889,885	n/a
ALL PERIODS	14.4 avg	75%	$ 3,930,573	22.6

of being forced to work again at eighty. Risk management is not just about enhancing success; it is about avoiding the unacceptable failures.

Though a statistical analysis of history provides averages across a wide variety of market conditions, the relevant periods for analysis are those with similar characteristics. Given the significant impact of P/E on returns, that factor will be a major driver for retirees over this decade and beyond. When individuals or couples retire with P/E in the upper quintiles, thereby driving below-average returns, their expected results will be below average. In some instances the risks will be so great that they may need to adjust their expectations, or they may need portfolio management to enhance potential success.

Retirees during secular bear markets may be limited to withdrawal rates that are less than 3%, or in some scenarios as much as 4%, to sustain their desired lifestyle successfully throughout retirement. Retirees who want to withdraw 5% or more will need a more consistent and higher return profile for their investments than passive investments in the stock market or bond market can provide when starting valuations are high. For those retirees, it will require a more actively managed and value-added approach to their portfolios, including investments in the stock market, even then with no guarantees of success.

There is no magic solution, no one way to achieve success. Given that retirees over this decade and longer are confronting the conditions of a secular bear market, it is important to start with a reasonable expectation about future returns and market conditions, then to apply appropriate investment strategies and approaches. Early personal planning and ongoing investment discipline can help toward avoiding the ROOM.

Institutionalizing Pensions

There are two general types of pension plans at private companies and across public government entities. One of them, called defined contribution plans [e.g., 401(k) and 403(b)] holds contributions on behalf of employees until retirement. Retirement benefits are based upon employee contributions and the employer's contributions on behalf of the employee, often called matching. The contributed amounts generally are invested based upon the employee's selection from the employer-determined investment alternatives. For this type of plan, the variables (contributions, savings, investment income, distributions, and inflation adjustment) are the same as for the first two groups previously described, the pre-retirees and retirees. Thus pre-retirees and retirees who are in defined contribution plans can refer to the earlier discussions in this chapter.

The other type of plan is a defined benefit plan. In general, these plans specify the benefits that retirees will receive upon retirement. The employer is responsible for ensuring that there are sufficient assets to pay the benefits. Private sector employers, which include publicly traded and privately owned companies, have significantly reduced their use of defined benefit plans, and have shifted to various forms of defined contribution plans. Public sector employers, however, continue to extensively use defined benefit plans or hybrid plans that include characteristics of defined benefit plans and defined contribution plans.

The remainder of this chapter discusses the practical implications for pension funds in the public sector. The objective is to highlight their vulnerability to the remainder of this secular bear cycle. Further, this discussion relates to the issues confronting every institutional investor who has limited additional sources and extended obligations.

It is a crisis that is developing slowly, like watching a train wreck occur in slow motion. It likely will not happen immediately, but will at some point become unavoidable. The collision path was set earlier in the last decade when the secular bear cycle began. Despite the warning signs, investment officers and boards neither adjusted their expected return assumptions nor increased annual funding requirements for these public pension funds.

Defined benefit plans are intended to have sufficient funds in savings to cover expected future obligations. In the terms of the model, the amount in savings plus the growth from investment income is supposed to cover the defined distributions, including annual changes at the inflation adjustment or other specified rate.

In August 2010, the Government Accountability Office (GAO) delivered a report titled "State and Local Government Pension Plans" to the Ranking Member of the U.S. Senate Committee on Finance.

According to the report, there are 2,547 public defined benefit plans in the U.S. covering nearly 20 million employees and over 7 million retirees—collectively representing almost 10% of the nation's population. Many of the pension plans are relatively small or are administered by local government employers. The 73 largest plans had $10 billion or more in assets as of 2008 and represent over eighty percent of all pension assets.

The GAO further reported—based upon survey data in 2007, before the 2008–2009 decline and partial recovery of the stock market—that the average public pension plan holds assets that are less than 85% of the current value of future liabilities. Pension liabilities are the benefits due to employees and retirees in the future.

Pension fund analysts determine the funded status by calculating the present value of the future obligations by discounting those liabilities at the rate of return that is assumed for the plan's investments. In other words, the key assumption for estimating the present value of the liabilities (the discount rate) is the assumption for future returns from investments. If the present value of the liabilities is equal to or less than the assets, the plan has fully funded its obligations. For the average plan, however, the assets are less than the liabilities; thus the plans have an unfunded liability. The fund's analysts are permitted to use whatever rate of return assumption they believe is appropriate. Reflecting the commonality of the entities, there is a relatively high concentration of return assumptions among public pension plans. Though the range in the GAO sample includes returns from 3%–10%, slightly more than one-half assume returns between 8% and 8.5%. Two-thirds of the plans assume returns of more than 8%, and less than one-tenth assume returns below 7.5%. The median in the GAO sample is 7.8%.

Each plan determines a return assumption based upon its profile of investments and individual considerations. The typical pension plan in the GAO report, based upon aggregated investment data, invests 50% of its assets in equities, 30% in bonds, and 20% in other investments. The other investments include real estate, private equity, hedge funds, commodities, and cash.

The discount rate for calculating the present value of the liabilities is a single percentage. It is based on the composite return from the investments across all asset classes in the portfolio or a general assumption for overall returns. The investments are assessed at market value; thus, for instance, the return assumption for bonds is the current market yield and not higher yields from purchases during previous higher interest rate periods. To illustrate the concept of a composite return, a plan with the typical mix of investments and an 8% return assumption might assume 10%–12% returns from the other investment category, 3%–5% returns from bonds,[1] and 8%–9% from the stock market.

The return assumption, however, is a net return after all investment fees, consulting expenses, and other costs. Therefore, the gross return before any charges needs to be approximately 9% to deliver a net return of 8%. If the other investments return 11%, and the bonds return 4%, then the stock market would need to return 11.2% in order for the composite gross return to be 9%. Some plans develop their assumptions based upon estimates for each category, while others simply compare the overall return assumption to historical returns or to surveys of similar institutions. Regardless of the methodology used, a discount rate of 8% generally means that the implicit or explicit assumption for stock market returns, after considering fees and expenses, is well more than 8% and more likely 11% to 12%.

In reality, some pension plans have specific estimates for returns from individual asset classes over the next five to ten years that do not add up to their aggregate return assumption. In those instances, the pensions assume that longer-term returns over many decades will somehow achieve the assumed return. Again, hope springs eternal.

The GAO report dedicates many pages to discuss the issues of public pension plan governance, transparency, and investment oversight. It further highlights the importance of investments as the primary funding source for benefits. According to the report, investment returns from 1982–2005 contributed nearly two-thirds of the total funding to pension plans, while state and local government employers contributed about a quarter and employees contributed about an eighth. The report, though subtitled "Government Practices and Long-term Investment Strategies Have Evolved Gradually as Plans Take On Increased Investment Risk," dedicates little discussion to the return assumptions that relate to the increased risk. The report highlights the current shortfalls in funding status and the shifting risk profile of public pension plans, but the report ignores the validity and appropriateness of the assumptions and their attendant risks. Similar to Modern Portfolio Theory (MPT), an analysis of public pensions requires a reasonable assumption for future returns.

Other reports have begun to assess the potential magnitude of public pension plan shortfalls, especially since the plans ultimately obligate taxpayers. Some analysts believe that the liabilities of public pension plans should be discounted more conservatively based upon government bond yields, currently near 3.5%. Other analysts express concern that public pension plans have such large exposure to the stock market and alternative categories of investments.

In 2009, Robert Novy-Marx and Joshua D. Rauh presented a paper titled "The Liabilities and Risks of State-Sponsored Pension Plans." Novy-Marx is a professor at the University of Chicago, and Rauh is a professor at Northwestern University. Conducting an extensive analysis of the 116 largest state pension plans, the authors reported that the assets across those plans totaled $1.94 trillion at the end of 2008. The present value of liabilities, based upon reports prepared by the pension plans, was estimated to be $2.98 trillion at the end of 2008, a funding status of 63%. Losses suffered during the 2008 stock market decline significantly lowered the funding status of most plans. The recovery in the stock market during 2009 partially offset the losses and has somewhat improved the funding status. Nonetheless, the public pension plans remain far short of meeting their obligations even using aggressive assumptions.

Novy-Marx and Rauh went further and assessed the impact of using a lower discount rate to calculate the present value of the liabilities. Using interest rates from the U.S. Treasury yield curve in January 2009, the present value of the obligations increases to $5.17 trillion—a shortfall of $3.23 trillion. Keep in mind that many secular bear market scenarios generate returns that are well below the yield curve assumptions, and none of the secular bear scenarios is even close to the pension plans' current assumptions.

Some pension plans are internally discussing changes to their assumptions for expected investment returns. They are starting to conclude that their plans should lower the assumed rate of return. In many of those instances, the reductions are modest and the new rate would still be at or above 7%. Based upon the principles of stock market returns, bond market returns, and secular stock market cycles, such a small change would represent action without the potential for much result.

Though Novy-Marx and Rauh use the Treasury yield curve as the discount rate for liabilities, the authors do not assert that future investment returns might be limited to their assumed discount rates. Their research relates to discount rates for liabilities without regard to asset holdings. Ironically, Novy-Marx and Rauh may be unintentionally presenting a realistic, and possibly optimistic, assumption for returns from existing investments. The public pension funds are unlikely to fully fund their plans; rather, they are more likely to choose to meet the shortfalls with current tax revenues. The pension plans may therefore need to use both techniques for discounting liabilities. The first approach would require realistic return assumptions for liabilities funded by investments. The second one would apply to unfunded liabilities based upon liability discount rates.

The Novy-Marx and Rauh calculation of shortfalls uses a rate that is well below the current pension plan assumptions as well as the plan's likely revised assumptions. Nonetheless, even the authors' rate may be optimistic for composite portfolio returns under many of the probable outcomes for stock market returns over this decade and beyond.

To put the underfunding in perspective using the Novy-Marx and Rauh assumptions, the authors calculated that the state shortfalls represent 24% of the states' gross economic product and 431% of their current tax revenues. The shortfall of $3.23 trillion is more than three times the states' publicly traded debt of $0.94 trillion.

A subsequent paper by Novy-Marx and Rauh titled "The Crisis in Local Government Pensions in the United States" estimated that the aggregate unfunded pension liability for local government plans is $0.57 trillion. The local pension obligations were not included in their earlier report about the state pension plan shortfalls. As a result, the total state and local unfunded pension liability is $3.8 trillion.

Trillion is a number that has lost its perspective in recent years. For example, the debt of state governments is almost $1 trillion, representing over $3,300 per person in today's dollars. That debt is an existing burden that comes with further obligations. The interest payments on those debts create an even greater drain on the ability to use taxes for future government services.

The unfunded pension liabilities, which are much larger than the outstanding debts of state and local governments, represent over $12,000 per person in today's dollars. To put the magnitude of this amount into further perspective, note that the shortfall from state and local pension plans is about a third as much as the total federal debt, and over 70% as much as the deficit from the Social Security program. According to the 2009 report from the Board of Trustees for the Social Security program, the present value of unfunded liabilities over the next 75 years for the program's 162 million participants is $5.3 trillion. Given the heightened national concern about the magnitude of burden from the federal debt and the unfunded Social Security deficit, the unfunded state and local pension liabilities are equally worrisome. The shortfall will require either significant increases in taxes or dramatic reductions in services.

Alternatively, the unfunded portion of the pension liability represents more than $140,000 in today's dollars per covered employee or retiree. Over decades of benefit payouts, the cumulative amounts are substantial and will significantly exceed the present value of $140,000. As a result, taxpayers may seek to have beneficiaries participate in the solution by accepting benefit reductions. Though it may seem contrary to intuition, beneficiaries have a vested interest in encouraging pension plans to quickly adopt more realistic return assumptions. It will better enable the plans to address funding shortfalls with a broader range of solutions, rather than being limited during crisis with alternatives that could more heavily impact beneficiaries.

Lower stock market returns will increase pension shortfalls and thereby increase the pressure to reduce benefits. Ironically, the public pension beneficiaries with defined benefits may have a greater stake in stock market returns than they initially realized.

Clean Up Your ROOM

Many of these public pension plans have promised generous benefits that increase at 2%–5% per year. The benefits have been rationalized with assumptions for returns of 7.5%–8.5% or more on the existing assets. The justification generally relates to the use of historical returns over the past two decades or longer, ignoring that current valuations and fundamental principles are the actual driver of returns from financial assets. Pension boards and consultants ignored the warning label of investments, especially the stock market: "Past performance is not an indication of future returns."

The likely return shortfall is compounded by the fact that the average public pension fund has insufficient assets to meet its obligations. If the contributions required to fund the plans are delayed and paid over time, then they will not generate a return in the interim. The cumulative contributions will need to increase by the required return. As a result, the ultimate shortfall is much bigger than even the $1 trillion to $4 trillion estimated by the plans or the more conservative researchers.

How could it be that bad? The original model provides the framework to evaluate the situation. For these plans, the values for distributions and the inflation adjustment are generally known—by definition, defined benefits are defined. Likewise, the actuaries and accountants can count the beans in savings, so to speak, and therefore know how much money they currently have in the portfolio and how much they can expect to be contributed additionally. As a result, the amount of savings is known unless there are future contributions beyond the planned amounts. The only variable missing is an assumption for the percentage return related to investment income. With that single number, the computers can compute a present value for the future obligations (i.e., distributions increasing by the rate of the inflation adjustment).

As a result of the assumptions and computations, the model tells them how much they should have in savings to meet the obligations. If the current amount of savings is less than the calculated requirement, the actuaries report that the plan is underfunded (currently by 25%–50%+), and the plan sponsors promise to make up the difference. The source of the makeup is either more money from the active employees, more money from taxes, less money toward other programs, or any allowable changes to the annual inflation adjustment or distributions (i.e., benefit cuts).

Note that the typical approach is to discount the liabilities at the rate of investment return. In effect, this is the same as projecting forward the investment returns, and analyzing whether the income and principal will be sufficient to cover the liabilities. The advantage of the current approach is that it produces a single number (the funding status) that is understandable and quantifies the magnitude of shortfall or excess assets.

Since the public pension plans are playing a game of hope by using such optimistic assumptions for returns, it will probably not surprise you that some of these pension funds are creating opportunities to double down their bets. The double down is a play in the card game blackjack in which the player uses two cards and effectively doubles the opportunity to bet. When the cards are right, this is a high-probability strategy for the player. The pension funds, carrying the analogy forward, think that they are reading cards that say returns of 8% or more are highly likely.

Some plans have created side accounts or investment structures using Pension Obligation Bonds (POBs) that allow them to borrow money at relatively low interest rates and add the funds to savings. Double down! The funded status of public pension funds that use the double-down strategy reflects a higher percentage funded status. The gap between paying low interest rates and hypothetically receiving 8% is hugely positive. If returns are less than 8%, but more than the interest cost, they receive some benefit, but not the full amounts expected. If, however, the returns are less than the cost of borrowing, the ultimate effect is a decrease in the funding status. The borrow-and-invest strategy of leverage can quickly become a multiplied liability rather than a sneaky gain.

The typical public pension is well into the ROOM of shortfalls. The partial recovery in the stock market during 2009 has provided false hope to pension managers that the funding status will improve sufficiently over the upcoming years. As reflected in figures 9.8 and 9.9, secular bear market periods are filled with short-term bull market

surges and bear market falls. Mediocre returns in secular bear periods result from offsetting surges and falls. Too often, the falls are
ignored as anomalies and the surges are extrapolated into the future. While the overall impact of the secular bear market will result
in shortfalls for the pension plans over this decade, the most significant implication is that the plans will experience a grueling cycle of
hope and crisis.

If the funding status for public pensions improves over the early
2010s from a market rally, just as it did during the mid-2000s, there
will be optimism that the plans will become fully funded without
changes to contributions, return assumptions, or benefit reductions. Then, suddenly, a cyclical bear downdraft could again shock
the funded status. This would likely create a minor crisis, met with
slightly lower return assumptions, benefit reductions, and contribution increases. Each time there is a market pullback, the crisis cycle
will repeat. Each time, the package of solutions will likely be modest in relation to the full implications of a secular bear market. Ultimately, it will become apparent that time cannot make up for the
shortfalls, and that a complete solution is needed. Hope springs eternal, but not forever.

Pre-retirees have all of the retirement model variables at their disposal. Their ultimate decision about the probable outcomes for this
decade and longer will drive many decisions, and pre-retirees have
time and ability to compensate for early mistakes. Retirees have fewer
variables at their disposal, yet their decisions will return to be their
consequences. Public pension funds will continue to burden taxpayers, government workers, and plan retirees as the issues from this
secular bear market evolve. Hard decisions are best made early as
they have less adverse impact when spread out over longer periods
of consequence.

Points of Emphasis

- Secular bear markets have significant implications for investing constituencies, including pre-retirees, retirees, and institutions.

- Pre-retirees should build retirement assets through the accumulation of savings to have assets available for the next secular bull market.

- Retirees need realistic expectations with which to adjust their financial plans and investment portfolios far in advance; this can reduce the future risk of abrupt changes or employment.

- Safe Withdrawal Rate (SWR) analyses rarely take into account the significantly reduced return outlook that is driven by market valuation.

- Institutions, despite their long-term horizons, are confronting the reality of the current secular bear market. Public pension plans, in particular, can expect dramatic consequences due to their unrealistic expectations, massive liabilities, and continuing deferral of addressing both liabilities and return assumptions.

CHAPTER 12

THE FOUR BEARS

This decade starts with trepidation in the financial markets and economy, yet the lessons of history suggest that the ultimate outcome will be different than expected by either the pessimists or the optimists. The course of the stock market, as well as the economy, rarely descends to the feared gloom or achieves the loftiest hopes. The mid-range, however, is fairly wide. There may be a broad range of alternative endings to this story, but the most probable outcomes are grounded in the principles that drive the stock market and the economy.

Earlier chapters explored the interconnectedness of the economy and finance through the Financial Physics model. Economic growth, promoted by increases in real production plus the effects of inflation, drives earnings growth. Inflation, in addition to affecting economic growth and earnings growth, is a major driver of the stock market's price/earnings ratio (P/E). As a result, the combination of earnings growth and the P/E cycle explain the variability of stock market returns over time.

The prior discussions about the overall drivers of the economy highlighted some of the issues that could affect economic growth over the current decade. Most importantly, the perceived excesses of consumption and leverage during the 2000s did not result in above-average economic growth. Ironically, the past decade delivered economic growth of only 1.9%, well below the historical average. Economic growth was therefore identified as Major Uncertainty #1.

Inflation, or its negative state deflation, was subsequently identified as Major Uncertainty #2. The topics explored how and why the inflation rate has such a significant effect on P/E. Higher inflation and worsening deflation cause P/E to decline, while periods of low inflation drive P/E higher. Therefore, the inflation rate cycle drives secular stock market cycles, which presents periods of above-average and below-average returns.

The two major uncertainties have a wide range of potential outcomes. For this analysis, the outcomes can be simplified into sets of three assumptions. To illustrate, the inflation rate could be any number or fraction from zero to infinity. Once the inflation rate goes below zero into deflation, there are numerous additional possibilities. Granted that an inflation rate of 5%, for example, would have a different effect than inflation of 10%, both of these scenarios represent the concept of significantly higher inflation. Likewise, deflation of 5% and 10% are certainly different, yet both reflect a condition of significant deflation. Finally, if the inflation rate remains relatively low and stable near either side of 1%, then it is generally accepted to be near price stability.

For 2009, the inflation rate was –0.4% compared to the full year 2008. Though the inflation rate was slightly negative when comparing those two years, the direction during 2009 reflects a slightly upward trend of low inflation. Nonetheless, the tectonic plates of deflation and inflation are tightly bound and there are strong cases for either condition. As the decade of the 2010s begins, the inflation rate appears to be near zero. While the inflation rate could endure the decade near price stability, there is also a significant risk that it could trend in either direction.

There could be a wide range of courses for the inflation rate over the next ten years. To facilitate the analysis, three simplified assumptions will be used for the probable outcomes from the current secular stock market cycle. The first scenario is deflation, with the inflation rate starting at 0% and ending at –5%. The second scenario is price stability, with the inflation rate staying constant at +1%. The third scenario is inflation, which starts at +1% and ends at +5%.

Economic growth, which was a fairly constant factor for many decades, has now become a major uncertainty. When the economic growth rate declined during the 2000s, it cast doubt on the validity of using the long-term average rate as an assumption.

During the last century, with some now-explainable periods of variation, real economic growth as measured by GDP averaged near 3%. The prior three completed decades of the 1970s, '80s, and '90s delivered 3.2%, 3.0%, and 3.2% respectively. The most recently completed decade of the 2000s, however, crossed the finish line at 1.9%. Was it an aberration, or is it a new trend? The implications are significant and extend beyond a percentage point of earnings growth each year.

Though the range of outcomes for future economic growth is wide, the assumptions can concentrate the more likely scenarios into a set of three probable ones. As with the uncertainty of the inflation rate, there will be gray areas between the scenarios. Each investor will have his or her own opinion about where to place the bands of gray and lines of black. Nonetheless, the debate over precision should not become the enemy of insight, especially if acceptable simplification can illustrate the magnitude of the implications.

Trend is the first of the three scenarios. It assumes that the economy fundamentally shifted to a lower level of growth early in the recent decade, before the recession and financial crisis of the late 2000s. Even before the economic recession during the last two years of the decade, the first eight years compounded at only 2.6% annually. Further, cumulative economic growth throughout the decade did not exceed 2.7%. It would have required an unusual surge, near 4.5% annually, in the final two years for the full decade to reach the historically average annual growth rate of near 3%.

Since 1950, recessions have occurred about every seven to ten years as a normal part of the economic cycle. Some have been mild, while others have been severe. The prior two recessions, 1991 and 2001 for example, were mild by historical standards. In any case, a recession was probably due. Though 2008 (technically December 2007) might be considered a year or two early, and though the recession was deeper and longer than average, that period is not the only cause for the slower average growth during the decade of the 2000s.

The lower level of economic growth during the 2000s is not widely recognized, and thus far generally unexplained. Economists may someday determine that something significant occurred early in the 2000s to indefinitely shift the economy to a new, lower level of growth. For the Trend scenario, the assumption is a growth rate of 2% for the 2010s and beyond, very close to the actual trend of the 2000s at 1.9%.

Aberration is the second scenario for economic growth. This scenario assumes that the prior decade was an outlier along the long-term trend. At this point, there do not appear to be generally recognized reasons that explain the sudden shift in real economic growth during the 2000s to near two-thirds of both the historical average and the prior three decades. The most reasonable explanation is that the decade of 2000s includes two recessions that coincidentally book-end the period. Thus, the decade of 2000–2009 could be an anomaly period. For the Aberration scenario, the assumption is a growth rate of 3% annually for this decade, conservatively below both the long-term real growth rate of 3.3% and the prior three decades' average growth rate of 3.1%.

Reversion is the third and final scenario. Maybe the long-term trend is not lost. This scenario assumes that the fundamental factors of economic growth have and will continue at the historically average rate; the decade of the 2000s may have been a normal variation driven by unexplained causes. Reversion, unlike Aberration, assumes that the underperformance of the 2000s is offset by equally above-average gains over this decade (the 2010s). Both Reversion and Aberration, however, assume that the long-term trend remains near 3% annually. As a result, the Reversion scenario assumes a growth rate of 4% from 2010 through 2019, conservatively below the 4.1% annual rate that would deliver an average of 3% annually across the decades of the 2000s and 2010s.

This scenario is not unprecedented; it would be similar to the reversion in economic growth that occurred after the decade of the Great Depression. The shortfall in economic growth during the 1930s was offset with a surge in the 1940s. Though some of the economic surge can be attributed to World War II, the fact that the level of economic activity was sustained after the war ended and over subsequent decades reflects the fundamentals of economic growth. The population continued to grow during the 1930s. Underlying productivity progressed during that decade as education continued and technology advanced, yet it was not fully manifested until the 1940s as the economy recovered from depression. The level of economic output continued to grow in the 1950s and '60s, sustaining the prior productivity trend and increasing population.

The Reversion scenario assumes that growth continues at 3% once the average long-term economic growth rate has been restored to that level. The increased rate of economic growth to 4% for this decade is temporary; it is not a permanent shift upward.

Relevant to all three economic growth scenarios, some economists expect that the working population may decline as baby boomers retire over this decade. The effect is estimated to be a drag of almost 0.5% annually to GDP. Economists' forecasts, however, might not fully consider the impact of the current secular bear market on retirement savings and income. Low returns from the continuation of the current secular bear market may defer retirement for a significant number of the most economically productive boomers. As a result, the ultimate effect of boomers on economic growth is unclear.

In addition, the decade starts with the unemployment rate at 10%. If the decade ends with unemployment below 5%, as it was for almost half of the months during the 2000s, the effect of deploying those workers could increase average annual economic growth across the decade by almost 0.5%. Neither the effect of retiring boomers nor the reduction of high unemployment is specifically incorporated into the scenarios, though either one or both could certainly be implicitly incorporated into a scenario depending upon your other assumptions.

In summary, there are three scenarios for real economic growth (excluding the inflation rate): (1) Trend of 2%, (2) Aberration of 3%, and (3) Reversion of 4%. Keep in mind that the Trend scenario of 2% is a shift indefinitely to a lower rate of economic growth. The two other scenarios, Aberration and Reversion, assume that economic growth in subsequent decades continues at the historical average near 3%.

Effects

To explore the implications of these scenarios, it may be helpful to reiterate or identify the effect that the inflation rate and economic growth have on the outcomes. At the conclusion of this chapter, the information will be consolidated and the results explored to provide estimations for stock market returns over this decade.

As presented in the Financial Physics model, the combination of estimated values for earnings (EPS) and the price/earnings ratio (P/E) provide an outlook for the stock market index in the future. EPS, driven by economic growth over the longer term, can be estimated based upon the three scenarios for the economy. P/E, driven by the inflation rate, is determined according to the inflation rate scenarios.

The effects of the inflation rate scenarios on P/E are fairly straightforward. Two of them, inflation and deflation, drive P/E lower. Historically, secular bear markets did not end until P/E fell below 10. Some people will emphasize that some secular bear markets drove P/E to 8 or lower. Others, the optimists, will say that 12 could be the new low for secular stock market cycles. Rather than contemplate the potential for a 20% variance either direction from 10, P/E of 10 will be assumed as a reasonable midpoint for the inflation and deflation scenarios. While 20% could mean a lot to someone in ten years, the compounded effect on returns is less than 2% per year and pales in comparison to the implications of P/E going to 10.

The third inflation rate scenario, price stability, generally drives P/E into the low 20s. Again, there are good arguments for values closer to 20, and some secular bulls, even without a bubble, slightly topped 25. P/E of 22 is assumed to be representative of price stability, and thus will serve as the third scenario.

Historically, before economic growth became Major Uncertainty #1, real economic growth (GDP-R) was not a significant driver in the variability of P/E. The long-term consistency of GDP-R made it a constant assumption for the future. The recent history of economic growth, however, challenges that assumption. Therefore, there are three scenarios for GDP-R (2%, 3%, and 4%) toward the probable outcomes, and one of the three has an effect on P/E.

Two of the scenarios do not affect the normal range for P/E. The Aberration scenario for economic growth treats the prior decade as an anomaly and assumes that historically average 3% growth returns in the 2010s and continues indefinitely. Since the long-term growth rate for GDP-R is the same as the historical long-term average, there is no effect on the range for P/E. Similarly, under the Reversion scenario, once 4% growth in this decade compensates for the 1.9% growth of the last decade, the long-term trend of 3% economic growth continues thereafter. For this scenario too, GDP-R is consistent with the long-term average growth rate and has no effect on the range for P/E.

Trend in this case is not a friend. Real economic growth of 2% annually has significant implications that extend beyond the lower growth for GDP-R, and thus GDP-N and EPS, from 2009 to 2019. Slower trend growth adversely impacts P/E. As previously discussed, this occurs because slower growth reduces perpetually the stream of future cash flows.

P/E is a multiplier that gives credit for the long-term growth rate. If the growth rate slows, P/E shifts downward across all inflation-rate scenarios. In effect, P/E must decline to provide an increase in the dividend yield in order to offset the lower contribution of EPS growth to returns.

If, for example, the future growth rate for earnings and dividends from a stock market portfolio is 3% annually, then the portfolio will have a particular value. For another stock market portfolio with a growth rate of 2% annually, the value of the second portfolio will be less than the first. Investors in the second portfolio will not be willing to pay as much for the lower stream of future cash flows. As discussed at the end of chapter 7, the reduction in value due to changes in growth occurs at all levels of the inflation rate; the reduction in P/E occurs in addition to the declines caused by inflation and deflation. As a result, the Trend scenario of 2% economic growth will cause a shift downward in P/E across the spectrum of inflation rate scenarios.

The Trend scenario is therefore impacted by three factors: (a) lower GDP and EPS at the end of the decade; (b) declines in P/E under deflation and inflation; and (c) an additional overall decrease in P/E from slower future growth. The effect from slower earnings growth is significant. The downward shift is less at a lower P/E and greater at a higher P/E. A decline in growth from 3% to 2% decreases the high-inflation P/E from 10 to 8, an average P/E from 15.5 to 11.5, and the low-inflation P/E from 22 to 15. Keep in mind that a decline in growth reduces P/E in addition to the typical effect that the inflation rate has on P/E.

Implications

The two uncertainties of economic growth and the inflation rate represent independent events; the outcome of one does not necessarily cause or limit the other. When the three scenarios for economic growth are coupled with the three scenarios for the inflation rate, there are nine combinations. Some of them reflect similar outcomes in real terms, despite differences in nominal terms that are significant. For example, the scenarios that include inflation and deflation have similar assumptions for P/E (i.e., 10) and, therefore a similar multiplier effect on valuation. Inflation and deflation, however, impact nominal economic growth quite differently, and thereby generate quite different forecasts for EPS.

Under the deflation scenario, real economic growth is suppressed in nominal terms. On the contrary, in the inflation scenario, real economic growth is increased in nominal terms. As a result, EPS is much lower in nominal terms with deflation than it is with inflation.

In addition, the actual (nominal) level of the stock market is significantly higher with inflation than with deflation; yet, the results in real (inflation-adjusted) terms are relatively similar. To emphasize this point, the overall level of the economy and the stock market would be quite different following an extended period of inflation versus deflation, yet the inflation-adjusted results eliminate much of the difference. This is important because it affects the results of the analyses, which determines the application of bear labels.

Deflation suppresses not only the nominal value of EPS and the stock market but also the cost of living and, potentially, pension obligations.[1] Deflation therefore causes the nominal value of both assets and liabilities to be lower. Similarly, yet in the opposite direction, inflation increases the price level for both assets and liabilities. The upcoming analysis presents the results in both real and nominal terms.

For this discussion, it is important to have a common basis of comparison across the scenarios to put their effects into perspective. For example, consider two of the scenarios with 3% real economic growth. The nominal total return including dividends is a loss of −36% with deflation, but a gain of +15% with inflation. Which would you prefer?

Not so fast. When both are adjusted for the impact of the inflation rate, thereby better aligning the investment results with lifestyle and pension obligations, the real returns reflect a loss of –18% with deflation and a loss of –15% with inflation. Though there is a slight edge to the inflation scenario, the results are substantially similar in terms of ultimate purchasing power.

For the discussion and analyses that follows, the following is a summary of the assumptions and conventions. They are simplified into sets of three scenarios to provide perspective and an understanding of the concepts without compromising the general ideas and principles. Though the range for each assumption is broad, the sets illustrate the implications of the probable outcomes.

For real economic growth, there are three scenarios: 2%, 3%, and 4%. The growth rate is constant across the current decade from 2010 through 2019.

For the inflation rate, there are three scenarios for the end of this decade: –5% deflation, +1% price stability, and +5% inflation. The three series begin in 2010, after an inflation rate of –0.4% in 2009. For 2010, the deflation scenario starts at 0%, while the price stability and inflation scenarios start at +1%. All series progress ratably over this decade from the starting inflation rate to the values presented previously for the end of 2019.

To illustrate, in the deflation scenario, the inflation rate starts at 0% and ends at –5% over the ten years (averaging –2.5%). Under price stability, inflation remains at +1%. Finally, in the inflation scenario, inflation starts at +1% and ratchets upward to +5% in year 2019 (averaging 3%). Keep in mind that the annual values for the inflation rate affect nominal economic growth (GDP-N) and EPS, thereby impacting the level of EPS in 2019. Though the trend in the inflation rate would impact P/E across the decade, the ten-year results are driven by the level of the inflation rate and P/E in 2019.

Under the economic growth assumptions of Aberration and Reversion, P/E is assumed to be 10 in 2019 for both of the deflation and inflation scenarios, and 22 under price stability. For the Trend scenario, due to the downward shift in earnings growth, P/E is assumed to be 8 under deflation and inflation, and 15 under price stability. For all scenarios, the starting value for P/E is the normalized value of 19.9 at year-end 2009.

In addition, all scenarios include an initial dividend yield of 2.5% (the approximate normalized dividend yield in 2009). It is adjusted annually across the decade based upon the inflation-adjusted growth rate for earnings under each scenario.

EPS for each scenario is determined using its respective economic growth rate. First, the assumed real growth rate for each scenario is increased by the inflation rate assumptions to forecast values for nominal GDP. Second, as described in chapter 5, Crestmont Research's reference series methodology is used to produce future estimates for EPS. This is accomplished by using the nominal GDP values for the nine scenario sets to generate estimates for normalized EPS in 2019.

**Figure 12.1. Normalized S&P 500 EPS Outlook
Across All Scenarios: 2019**

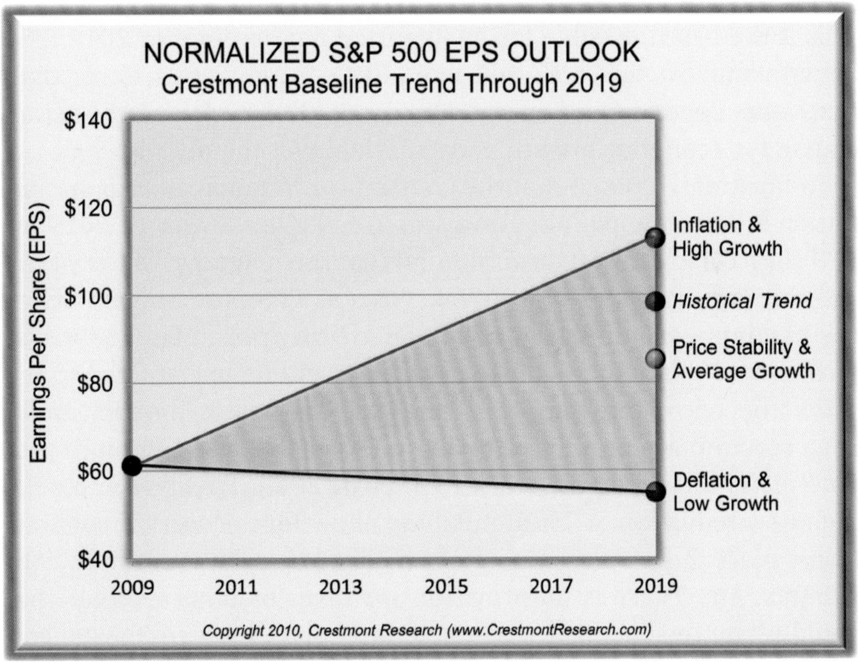

NORMALIZED S&P 500 EPS OUTLOOK
Crestmont Baseline Trend Through 2019

Copyright 2010, Crestmont Research (www.CrestmontResearch.com)

For perspective about the range of baseline EPS values in 2019, figure 12.1 provides a graphical representation of the range of outcomes. The upper and lower boundaries are baseline trend values under two of the more extreme scenarios. Keep in mind that over the decade, the normal and highly variable EPS cycle will likely deliver reported net earnings that extend beyond the range. Nonetheless, the baseline trend is expected to remain in the range depending upon economic conditions. The lowest earnings growth scenario includes 2% real economic growth and deflation. The result would be a nominal decline in EPS in 2019 from the start of the decade. The highest earnings growth rate occurs with 4% real economic growth and inflation. The result would be a baseline level of EPS in 2019 near $113.

Two other values for EPS are presented. The first one results from the combination of average economic growth and price stability. It is near the midpoint between the two outer scenarios. The second EPS value, titled Historical Trend, reflects a continuation of the long-term economic growth trend and slightly higher inflation than price stability. The result is baseline EPS in 2019 of slightly less than $100. This is the baseline value for As Reported net earnings in 2019. The actual value for that year will most likely be higher or lower than that value depending upon the point in the EPS cycle and the actual course for economic growth and inflation over the decade.

To illustrate, assume that the course for economic growth and inflation follows the path of Historical Trend. On the way to 2019, as EPS surges above $100, bear in mind that the magnetic center of the net earnings baseline is lower. Likewise, as EPS plunges well below the baseline, recognize that a balloon is being pulled below the waterline, and the natural course ultimately will be upward.

For the upcoming composite analysis, the values for EPS under each scenario are multiplied by the relevant P/E assumption to provide an estimate for the stock market in 2019. Finally, the results include a reduction of 1% annually to allow for the costs of commissions, bid/ask spreads, investment management, account fees, consultants, etc. There is no provision for taxes or other charges that could relate to some investors depending upon their circumstances. As a result, taxpayers and/or investors with other costs should adjust the results accordingly.

Figure 12.2 summarizes the probable outcomes for stock market returns over the decade of the 2010s in real terms. The values presented for each scenario reflect the total cumulative return [in

brackets] and the annualized compounded return {in braces}. In figure 12.2, denoted as real in the upper-left corner, the total and cumulative returns have been adjusted for the inflation rate by excluding
the effects of inflation or deflation. The matrix combines the three
scenarios for the inflation rate across the top with the three scenarios for the economic growth down the side.

Some of the outcomes have relatively similar results. They are
designated with categories of bears as an illustration of magnitude.
To facilitate the discussion, the categories of bears are conveniently
assigned according to the story of the three bears. The fourth set of
outcomes, when P/E remains high under price stability, reflects a bear
in hibernation. If this decade ends with P/E still high, then there will
not have been progress through the secular bear market, so it will
have remained in hibernation.

Figure 12.3 summarizes the probable outcomes for stock market
returns over the decade of the 2010s in nominal terms. Similar to the
previous figure, the values for each scenario reflect the total cumulative return [in brackets] and the annualized compounded return {in
braces}. In figure 12.3, denoted as nominal in the upper-left corner,
the total and cumulative returns reflect the actual results for investors.

When comparing scenarios across the matrix, figure 12.2 reflects
a better indication of the ultimate purchasing power of the investment portfolio. A low nominal return during deflation can produce
more purchasing power than a higher return during periods of high
inflation if the return is insufficient to overcome inflation. Thus the
real returns in figure 12.2 are comparable across the different inflation rate scenarios in the matrix.

Figure 12.3 provides the cumulative and annualized returns over
the decade in nominal terms, which reflect results as they would be
reported. While real returns represent purchasing power, nominal
returns relate to values that would appear on an account statement.
Though some scenarios provide positive returns over the decade,
higher inflation degrades purchasing power and causes a loss of real
value. This is similar to the period of the 1970s when slightly positive returns at times were insufficient to overcome rising inflation.

The magnitudes of the outcomes on a real basis determine the bear
designations on both figures. In addition, under the scenario in which

Figure 12.2. Probable Outcome Matrix (2010–2019): The Four Bears (REAL)

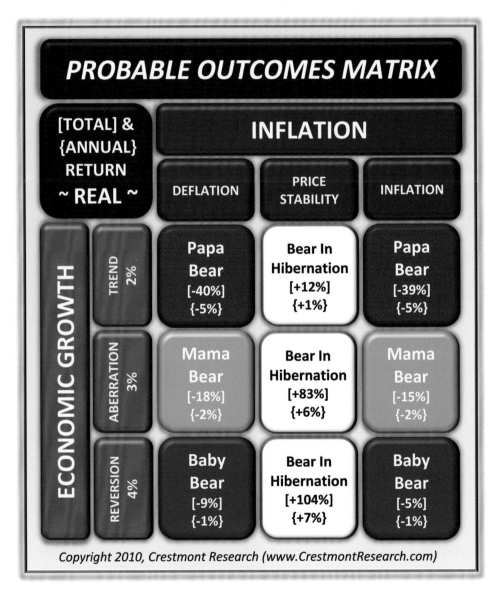

Figure 12.3. Probable Outcome Matrix (2010–2019):
The Four Bears (NOMINAL)

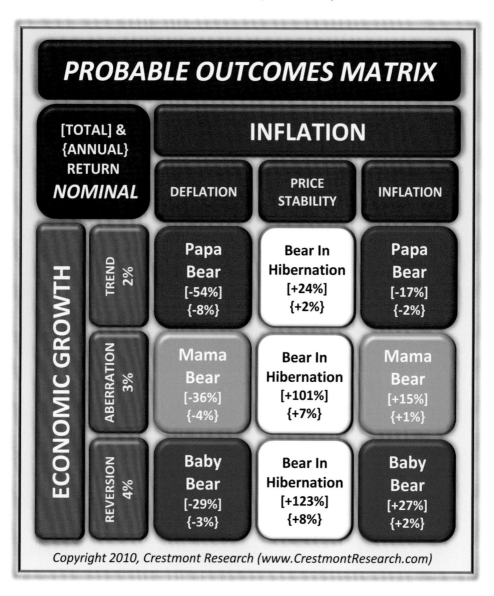

PROBABLE OUTCOMES MATRIX

[TOTAL] & {ANNUAL} RETURN NOMINAL		INFLATION		
ECONOMIC GROWTH		DEFLATION	PRICE STABILITY	INFLATION
	TREND 2%	Papa Bear [-54%] {-8%}	Bear In Hibernation [+24%] {+2%}	Papa Bear [-17%] {-2%}
	ABERRATION 3%	Mama Bear [-36%] {-4%}	Bear In Hibernation [+101%] {+7%}	Mama Bear [+15%] {+1%}
	REVERSION 4%	Baby Bear [-29%] {-3%}	Bear In Hibernation [+123%] {+8%}	Baby Bear [+27%] {+2%}

the inflation rate remains near price stability and P/E remains relatively high, the bear market will not have progressed. Upon reaching 2019, stock market returns over the two decades of this secular bear market will have been mediocre. Nonetheless, the stock market will be in a secular bear period; it's just that the bear will have remained in hibernation, as P/E will still be at a high level.

Papa Bear is the designation for two probable outcomes. The most significant driver of returns over decades and secular market cycles is the change in P/E. From the relatively high levels of 2009, the scenarios make P/E necessarily vulnerable to decline (and not positioned for potential increase). Therefore the two scenarios of inflation and deflation drive significant declines in P/E and attendant declines in valuation. Beyond the normal impact of deflation and inflation on P/E, the slower economic growth from the Trend scenario packs an additional two-fisted punch to the results: first, EPS is lower due to slower economic growth; second, P/E shifts downward under all inflation-rate scenarios due to the impact of reduced economic growth on the discount rate.

Papa Bear is a gruesome grizzly. Under deflation, the nominal loss is –54%. Even the inflation scenario leaves the portfolio down –17%. In real terms, after compensating for deflation and inflation, both scenarios effectively provide losses near –40% of the portfolio's value. This represents a compounded annual loss of –5%.

Mama Bear, while less bad than the ol' grizzly, captures two places as well. She prowls on the ground of slightly faster economic growth, but is still burdened with adverse inflation-rate conditions. Economic growth increases to 3% annually, which gets rid of the two-fisted punch. Not only does EPS grow a bit faster but also P/E is not discounted below 10 due to slower growth. Nonetheless, Mama Bear delivers real losses of –18% and –15% for the deflation and inflation scenarios respectively.

Baby Bear follows in the deflation and inflation footsteps of its two predecessors, yet receives a boost from higher economic and EPS growth. Though Baby Bear may appear cuddly and cute, this critter is cruel, with a snarl just as bad as its bite. An investor's stock market portfolio does not escape the claw marks, and ends down slightly in real terms at the end of the decade.

Bear in Hibernation signifies that the stock market does not make progress in the secular bear cycle. At the end of the decade, all three scenarios still have a relatively high P/E due to low inflation under the condition of price stability. As a result, investment returns will not have met most expectations. Investors could receive compounded annual returns of 1%–7% in real terms. In nominal terms, returns of 2%–8% will be somewhere between somewhat disappointing and reasonably acceptable, albeit below average and below many expectations.

The outlook from that point, however, is that the Bear will still need to run its course before a bull can take the lead. If this scenario occurs, be aware that investors will likely become complacently comfortable with the modest returns and their reasonable gains in purchasing power. They will likely begin to hope for the next secular bull, as the secular bear of the 2000s will appear to have been tamed. But, P/E will not be positioned to expand—it will still be at high levels. High P/E is bear territory, and cannot be bull ground. Secular bears must reach the point of low P/E due to inflation or deflation before the cycle can transition to the secular bull.

There are many other scenarios that are around and between the ones just explored, but these are the most probable outcomes for this decade. If any of the active Bear scenarios occur more quickly, it would cause a significant secular decline in the stock market. The magnitude of total losses would be worse without the benefit of a full decade of real earnings growth. More so than the cumulative results, the annualized losses could be shocking. Such a period more likely relates to the deflation scenarios rather than the inflation scenarios.

Across the past century, there have not been extended periods of deflation. When there was deflation, it typically occurred in series of two to four years. The scenarios in the matrix that assume a decade of progressive deflation are unprecedented, yet the scenarios presented should be representative of a decade of deflation. Nonetheless, the more likely scenario that includes deflation would be a shorter and more dramatic period. Due to the accelerated course through the secular bear, the losses would equal or exceed the cumulative results in the matrix and would reflect a commensurately higher annual rate.

Though the deteriorated conditions and related low valuation would position the stock market for a secular bull, the cumulative effect for the decade would still be disappointing. Even if the secular bull ran its full course in the second half of the decade, the full decade would reflect results similar to the Bears in Hibernation. In effect, such a scenario of plunge and surge would recreate a course similar to the secular cycles of the 1930s. The magnitude of decline would mean that the stock market would be near 600 for the S&P 500 and less than 6000 for the Dow Jones Industrial Average in four or five years. Since the driver of the decline would likely be a significant shift away from low inflation, this would end the current secular bear and start a secular bull market.

This significant point is worth emphasizing again: A secular bull market cannot start within the current decade without a dramatic decline in the market and P/E. The decline would need to be driven by a period of significant inflation or deflation, rather than by a short-term financial crisis.

Should a rapid secular bull market follow a near-term dramatic end to the current secular bear, the great gains and benefits of the secular bull will only serve to recover damage. It does not catapult the values of traditional portfolios beyond previous levels. Retirees, public pension plans, and many other institutions will have no or relatively limited additional contributions to begin working to off-set portfolio losses. Without additions of new capital to a traditional stock portfolio, the recovery in the market only provides recovery to principal. The situation does not provide new investments at lower prices that can generate profits from the bull market. A quick end to the current secular bear would make way for a secular bull, but that is not desirable for existing investments, as it could result in significant losses to stock portfolios.

A rapid bear and bull trough does create opportunity for new capital, from the Accumulators, for example. Contributions to a portfolio after or during the decline represent additional funds that can participate in a recovery. Further, investors who have successfully limited their losses during the decline will be better positioned to capitalize on the market's ascent.

Finally, when considering a dramatic ending to the secular bear, it is worth mentioning one additional scenario that is less dramatic. The current secular bear could extend into a third decade (the 2020s).

This would entail any of the active Bear scenarios extending beyond 2019. Though the total returns would improve from additional earnings growth, none of the outcomes would be satisfying to investors. Breaking even over twenty years is hardly a reason to celebrate avoiding a loss of money over this decade.

Rainbows

Investors are confronting the reality of the current secular bear market. It is both the consequence of the previous secular bull market and the precursor to the next secular bull. The duration of the current secular bear period is uncertain. Should inflation or deflation overcome the economic environment in the near term, this secular bear could end sooner. That reality, however, would cause significant losses to stock market portfolios. If inflation or deflation slowly creeps into the economy, over the next decade for example, then this secular bear will have been one of the longer ones. However, if this decade repeats the relatively low inflation of the past decade, then the secular bear should remain in hibernation.

Beyond the inflation rate, economic growth also will have an impact on the future of this secular bear. Following last decade's below-average economic growth, this decade could generate above-average growth to offset the recent shortfall. The result would be a solid boost to earnings in this decade. Economic growth, however, also could have downshifted during the last decade to a lower level for the foreseeable future. The result would be a significantly lower range of P/Es, but not necessarily a progression through the secular bear market. The economic growth rate can shift P/E upward or downward, but only inflation or deflation can end a secular bear market.

Whether this secular bear cycle ends in five years, ten years, or beyond, the result will be the start of the next secular bull market, which will bring an extended period of above-average returns. Spring finally will have sprung. This longer-term view of secular stock market cycles is the reason to look out across this secular bear to the next secular bull. The operative word is "across" this secular bear and not "past" it.

"Across" recognizes the reality of the risks and opportunities presented by secular bear markets. "Past" is the ostrich-like approach of ignoring reality with blind hope for an unrealistic outcome. "Across" is enabling, while "past" is disabling.

For investors who are accumulating for the future, secular bear markets are times to build savings for later investment. This is done not only through contributions but also through prudent investing with an absolute return approach to investment returns. The absolute return approach uses the dual strategy of risk management and investment selection.

Investment portfolios should be diversified across a range of investments that are diligently selected and actively managed, especially ones that control risk and enhance return. In particular, investors should not avoid the stock market or bond market. Instead, their objective should be to seek in both markets investments that incorporate elements of skill to enhance returns. Secular bear markets are not periods during which to avoid investing; they are periods that demand an adjustment to investment strategy.

For investors who are more dependent on their current assets, including pension funds and retirees, investment strategy should be paired with early recognition. The principles of absolute return investing are important for preserving capital and generating much-needed returns. But potentially more important than managing the investment portfolio, pension funds and retirees would be well served in this environment to manage their assumptions and expectations. Earlier recognition of secular bear market conditions enables potentially painful adjustments to be smaller. Delaying action until crisis has onset generally brings greater adverse consequences. It is not prudent to hope for the next secular bull market to arrive sooner as a way to address shortfalls. The longer expectations take to adjust, the greater the gap to fill with an increasingly short time to fill it.

Wrap-up

Earlier chapters explored economic and financial principles to foster an understanding of the fundamental drivers behind secular stock market cycles. The mere concept of these secular cycles contradicts many of the mainstream and modern theories about the stock market. However, it does not contradict the original concepts of valuation that drove the investment decisions of recognized sages for decades.

Secular stock market cycles are driven by changes in P/E, which is driven by the cycle of inflation and deflation. These long-term cycles do not lapse by the passage of time; a change in the cycle requires that P/E reach an extreme level and then reverse as the inflation rate cycle changes. Inflation cycles have historically varied significantly in length; thus P/E cycles have varied considerably. The average duration of the P/E cycle in years is a statistic of coincidence, rather than a timer. The current cycle has endured for a decade, but it has hardly made progress along the course of secular bear cycles.

Many individual and institutional investors still expect investment returns to revert to more historically average levels. Some even hope that the stock market will make up its lost ground. This places expectations on a slow collision course with reality. The Major Uncertainty duo of economic growth and the inflation rate portend scenarios that range from extended modest returns to more rapid negative returns. Economic growth, a stable trend for more than a century, declined significantly last decade despite burgeoning leverage and aggressive consumers. Its outlook remains uncertain, with the consequences determined by each of the likely outcomes. The inflation rate, always an uncertainty, is precariously perched near zero, with significant pressures pulling it in both directions. Though its outlook is uncertain, a significant move in either direction holds negative consequences. Only through an enduring stay on the tightrope of price stability can the inflation rate defer its impact on this secular bear cycle.

There are investment alternatives and portfolio approaches that can serve investors during these secular bear periods better than passive exposure to the stock and bond markets. The absolute return approach seeks to bring businesslike discipline and diversification to investment portfolios. It drives returns not only by incorporating multiple sources of return but also from managing and controlling risk. Whereas the traditional measures of performance highlighted prior returns, investors are increasingly expecting measures of risk.

Pre-retirees, retirees, and institutions are recognizing that risk is not limited to the concept of losses; risk is also the shortfall to expectations and obligations. Within the community of institutional investors, public pension funds have slid down the slippery slope of long-term denial. Creative accounting rules and unchecked assumptions led to increasingly generous benefits at the expense of taxpayers. A program that covers almost 10% of Americans is slowly ripening as a burden on all Americans. For all investor constituents, an early recognition of the probable environment can help to avoid bad consequences. There is no reason for the ultimate response to be "who knew?"

The previous chapters have sought to help you develop (1) a deeper and richer understanding of secular stock market cycles; (2) a more realistic and objective outlook for stock market returns over the decade of the 2010s; and (3) a confident recognition that the traditional investment approach of buy-and-hold for the long term should give way to a more active, skill-based, and diversified way of investing. Hopefully, the insights from history will lead to more successful investment results.

POINTS OF EMPHASIS

- Three outcomes for economic growth are assumed: 2% as the new trend, 3% consistent with long-term history, and 4% to make up for the recent decade — Major Uncertainty #1.

- Three outcomes for inflation are assumed: deflation, price stability, and inflation — Major Uncertainty #2.

- Four major scenarios can be built from the nine combinations across the two Major Uncertainties. Three scenario sets drive the secular bear to conclusion over this decade with limited or negative returns. One scenario set defers the conclusion of the secular bear and provides modest, albeit below-average, returns from the stock market.

- Recognition of the current secular bear market enables investors to skillfully invest through this period with greater success than those who ignore the environment and openly expose their portfolios to market risk.

Appendix A

Unexpected Returns – Ten Key Concepts

Unexpected Returns: Understanding Secular Stock Market Cycles developed the thesis of ten key concepts that impact investors in the stock market and in the financial markets in general. As background, here are the original ten key concepts and brief commentary about each. In the journey through *Probable Outcomes* these principles will be revisited as they become applicable.

1. *Valuation matters. Over periods of decades, the average rarely happens; above-average returns occur when P/E ratios start low and rise, and below-average returns occur when P/E ratios start high and decline.*

   The most significant factor in the variability of stock market returns over time is the starting level of valuation. Since P/E is effectively bounded with upper and lower limits, the ultimate change in P/E over time is skewed by the starting point. Further, the absolute level of P/E impacts other components of return, including the dividend yield.

2. *The financial markets are much more volatile than most investors realize! Volatility matters. Two gremlins can devastate the returns that are actually realized: negative numbers and the dispersion of returns.*

   Investors' experiences in the last secular bull market of the 1980s and '90s distorted perceptions about the concept of normal returns, especially as it relates to volatility. Further, human nature and psychology are more sensitive to volatility associated with losses than to volatility associated with gains.

3. *The stock market experiences extended periods of secular bull markets and secular bear markets based on the trend in P/E ratios, which is driven by the trend in inflation.*

   A common misunderstanding is that returns from the stock market converge toward some average rate over a decade or less. The historical reality, based upon readily accepted principles of finance and economics, is that the stock market alternates through extended periods of above-average and below-average returns.

4. *The Y-Curve Effect reflects the strong relationship between P/E ratios and inflation or deflation.*

   The level of P/E is often associated with the level of interest rates. The Y-Curve Effect reflects, however, that inflation actually is the driver of P/E. Further, interest rates are also associated with the inflation rate, which is likely the reason why interest rates became a simplifying proxy for inflation as the driver of P/E. In periods of deflation, however, the trends of interest rates and P/E diverge. This distinction has significant implications for periods of uncertainty across low inflation, high inflation, and deflation, especially when the potential for deflation is heightened.

5. *The current financial conditions indicate either low or negative returns from stocks and bonds.*

   Periods that begin with high valuations end with below-average returns. In 2004, when *Unexpected Returns* was written, P/E was well above average. Likewise, at the start of 2010, P/E remains above average. A movement toward lower P/E will result in low or negative returns.

6. *Crestmont's Financial Physics model aligns the interconnected relationships between the economy and the financial markets, which determine the stock market's overall direction.*

   The Financial Physics model is a simple graphic representation of the connections and interactions between the elements of economics and finance that drive long-term stock market cycles.

7. *P/E ratios for the market have a sustainable peak or limit in the range of 20–25 when inflation is near price stability—very close to where P/Es were in 2004.*

   P/E cannot go below zero, and generally has tended to trough in the mid to upper single digits. The relationship between bond yields and equity returns generally sets the upper limit for P/E.

8. *The progressive strategies of absolute return investing rely on skill for seeking consistent returns, and the traditional strategies of relative return investing rely on taking a long-term view of market risk for return.*

   The traditional view of investment return is that it is driven by the level of risk assumed. Further, the traditional approach to investing (i.e., buy-and-hold) expects returns from the passive allocation to the market and market risk. More recent investment alternatives include an element of skill to extract returns in excess of passive market returns.

9. *During secular bull markets, the investment strategy of "sailing" by buying and holding stocks and bonds can be very effective; during secular bear markets, the investment strategy of "rowing" with absolute return strategies can be very effective.*

   An investor's approach can and should change with the market environment. Rowing and sailing is a boatman's analogy to differentiate between the more active rowing and the more passive sailing as means to manage an investment portfolio.

10. *Evolution in the financial markets and investment management is expanding the concept of risk management from use in absolute return strategies to use in traditional portfolio management.*

   As the current secular bear market progresses, investors will need the techniques of risk management to complement the continued search for investment returns.

GLOSSARY

Absolute Returns: investment returns that are driven by the skill of investment selection and investment management rather than passive exposure to market risk. For example, the use of alternative investments, active return management, active risk management, and skill-based investing are based upon absolute returns.

CPI: consumer price index; a measure of the inflation rate based upon a basket of goods and services.

Discount Rate: the factor used to calculate the current value of a future stream of cash flows.

Dividend Yield: the percentage represented by the amount of dividends received annually divided by the price of the market or an individual stock.

GDP-D: gross domestic product deflator; a measure of inflation derived by subtracting real GDP from nominal GDP.

GDP-N: nominal gross domestic product; a measure of economic production that includes the effect of inflation in prices.

GDP-R: real gross domestic product; a measure of economic production that determines the value of production units, excluding the effect of inflation in prices.

Inflation Rate: the rate of change in prices throughout the economy, rather than specific changes in price due to supply and demand. Inflation is the positive increase in the overall price level. Deflation is decline in the overall price level.

Nominal GDP (GDP-N): nominal gross domestic product, a measure of economic production that includes the effect of inflation in prices.

Price/Earnings Ratio (P/E): the price of a market index divided by the aggregate earnings of a market index or stock, respectively. P/E is a measure of market valuation. See also: P/E10, P/E (Crestmont), and P/E (Unadjusted).

P/E10: the price/earnings ratio of the stock market based upon the methodology popularized by Robert Shiller at Yale University in his book *Irrational Exuberance.* Price can represent either the stock market index for a day or the average index across a period (often a year). Earnings represents the average of reported net earnings across the trailing ten years adjusted to current dollars using the CPI. The long-term average annual P/E10 is 15.5, when adjusted for extreme values. This measure of P/E is used in figures 2.1, 2.3, 7.1, 7.2, 7.4, 9.6, 9.7, 11.2, and 11.3.

P/E (Crestmont): the price/earnings ratio of the stock market based upon the methodology developed by Crestmont Research and presented in Ed Easterling's book *Unexpected Returns.* Price can represent either the stock market index for a day or the average index across a period (often a year). Earnings represents the measure of adjusted net earnings based upon the historical relationship and regression of earnings to nominal economic growth. The long-term average Crestmont P/E is 14 when adjusted for extreme values. This measure of P/E is used in figures 7.2 and 7.4.

P/E (Operating Earnings): the price/earnings ratio of the stock market based upon the stock market index for a day and estimated operating earnings for either the most recent four quarters or the forward four quarters or year. This measure of P/E is highly susceptible to the distortions of the earnings cycle, subjective add-backs to actual reported earnings, and subjective forecasts of earnings.

P/E (Unadjusted): the price/earnings ratio of the stock market based upon the stock market index for a day and reported net earnings for the most recent four quarters. This measure of P/E is highly susceptible to distortion from the earnings cycle. The long-term average Unadjusted P/E is 14 when adjusted for extreme values.

Present Value: the value currently of a future stream of cash flows based upon an assumed discount rate.

Price Stability: an inflation rate that is near zero, generally accepted to be near 1%.

Real GDP (GDP-R): real gross domestic product, a measure of economic production that primarily measures additional units of production and excludes the effect of inflation in prices.

Relative Returns: investment returns that are driven by passive exposure to market risk rather than the skill of investment selection and investment management. For example, the buy-and-hold approach of investing and Modern Portfolio Theory-based approach of investing are based upon relative returns.

Secular: a term meaning an era or extended period of time.

NOTES

Probable Outcomes is intended to educate investors, and should not be construed as investment advice or as a recommendation or solicitation to purchase or sell any security or investment.

Chapter 3

1. Reprinted from "Integrated GDP-Productivity Accounts," courtesy of Steven Rosenthal and Michael Harper.

Chapter 5

1. The 15% rule of thumb is based upon the conceptual variance using historical average growth rates. The earnings cycle and dynamics of the 10-year methodology cause the actual adjustments to vary significantly at times. The Crestmont methodology for normalizing EPS can be used as a proxy for the baseline trend since it does not include the real growth rate lag. The historical difference between the 10-year approach and the Crestmont approach has been near 15%. When the average EPS under both methodologies is compared for 1900 to 2009 and 1960 to 2009, the variances between the averages are 15.4% and 15.6% respectively. Nonetheless, the range for individual years during the later period, which reflects actual data for the S&P 500, extends from –12% to 37% with sixty percent of the years between 5% and 20%.

Chapter 7

1. Three formulas can be used to approximate the effect of slower growth on P/E. First, estimate the initial normalized dividend yield by multiplying the dividend payout ratio (i.e., 45%) times one

divided by the starting P/E [Div 1 = 0.45 * (1 / P/E 1)]. Second, subtract the estimated reduction (or increase) in the growth rate [Div 2 = Div 1 – g; where g equals the change in growth]. Third, divide the dividend payout ratio by the newly required dividend yield [P/E 2 = 0.45 / Div 2]. P/E 2 represents the P/E ratio that provides the same expected return following a change in the growth rate. For an example of 1% lower growth, the change in the average P/E of 15.5 is: 2.9% = 0.45 * (1 / 15.5), 3.9% = 2.9% minus – 1.0%, and 11.5% = 0.45 / 3.9%. Similar results are returned from multi-hundred year models of future earnings and dividend growth as well as other methodologies of stock market valuation. This footnote includes simplifying assumptions for illustration: (a) the expected rate of return from the stock market remains constant as the growth rate changes; (b) the change in growth rate relates to the change in earnings growth which is generally slightly less than the change in overall economic growth; and (c) the dividend payout ratio remains similar as retained earnings beyond depreciation are needed to cover the effects of inflation, industry and technology obsolescence, company turnover, etc.

Chapter 9

1. Some people compare the earnings yield to U.S. Treasury debt yields. The so-called Fed Model is based upon this relationship. The basic concept behind the comparison of the earnings yield and Treasury yield is that both measures of return are impacted similarly, which is generally true due to the effect of present value. Though the Fed model is a reasonable rule of thumb for mid-range conditions, it does not signal as well in higher inflation conditions and breaks down completely in deflation.

Chapter 11

1. Some pension plans (and other investors) will assert that their long-term investment horizon enables them to view assumptions for bond returns based upon multiple turnover cycles. They contend that even though bond yields currently are well below the assumed rate of return, future yields are more likely to be near or above their assumption, which is often based upon the long-term

average return for bonds. Once the current low-return bond portfolio matures, they expect to reinvest in higher yielding bonds.

Some pension plans include a long-term return assumption for their bond portfolio of 6% or more expecting to replace current bonds maturing in 5 to 10 years with higher yielding bonds. The implicit assumption is that higher yields are normal and that the current yield has minimal effect on cumulative long-term returns. First, contrary to the assumption, near-term yields have a significant impact on cumulative returns due to the power of compounding. Second, and most important, this position ignores the reality of bond yields and the related effects on the stock portfolio.

If bond yields are significantly higher in 5 to 10 years, then inflation will also be higher. Bonds yields and interest rates are primarily driven by inflation over time. If inflation is higher, it will adversely affect returns from the stock market portfolio as P/E declines. At this time, it is irrationally inconsistent for an existing portfolio to assume long-term average bond yields and solid stock market returns. From the current period of low inflation, with its low bond yields and high stock market valuation, the only way to get higher bond yields after the current bonds mature is to suffer significant declines in P/E and stock market returns. Pension plans and other investors are not only injecting irrational hope into their assumption for stock market returns but also magnifying the error with an inconsistent assumption for bond portfolio returns.

Chapter 12

1. Pension obligations would decline under deflation if the obligations freely change with the inflation rate. If the pension obligations are determined based upon specified cost of living increases, or precluded from decreasing when inflation turns negative, then the pension obligation would not commensurately decline in deflation.

BIBLIOGRAPHY

Balke, Nathan S., and Robert J. Gordon. "The Estimation of Prewar Gross National Product: Methodology and New Evidence." *Journal of Political Economy,* 1989, vol. 97, no. 1.

Burton, Jonathan. "Revisiting the Capital Asset Pricing Model." Reprinted with permission from *Dow Jones Asset Manager.* May/June 1998. www.stanford.edu/~wfsharpe/art/djam/djam.htm.

Covey, Stephen. *7 Habits of Highly Effective People,* Free Press, revised edition, 2004.

Easterling, Ed. Crestmont Research. www.CrestmontResearch.com, 2004–2010.

Easterling, Ed. *Unexpected Returns: Understanding Secular Stock Market Cycles.* Fort Bragg, CA: Cypress House, 2005.

Friedman, Milton. "The Role of Monetary Policy." *The American Economic Review,* Vol. LVIII(1). March 1968.

Friedman, Milton, and Anna Schwartz. *A Monetary History of the United States, 1867–1960.* Princeton, NJ: Princeton University Press, 1971.

Friedman, Milton, and Rose D. Friedman. *Free to Choose: A Personal Statement.* San Diego, CA: Harcourt, Inc. 1990.

Graham, Benjamin, and David Dodd. *Security Analysis* (the 1934 edition). New York: McGraw-Hill Trade, 1996.

Heilbrunn Center for Graham and Dodd. Value Investing History. Columbia Business School. 2003. www.1.gsb.columbia.edu/valueinvesting/about/history.html.

Homer, Sidney, and Richard Eugene Sylla. *A History of Interest Rates,* 3rd rev. edition, Rutgers University Press, 1996.

Keynes, John Maynard. *The General Theory of Employment, Interest and Money.* New York: Harcourt, Brace, and World, 1936.

Krugman, Paul. *The Conscience of a Liberal.* New York: W. W. Norton & Company, Inc., 2009.

Lefevre, Edwin. *Reminiscences of a Stock Operator.* Originally published 1922. New York: John Wiley & Sons, Inc., 1994.

Markowitz, Harry. "Portfolio Selection." *Journal of Finance,* 1952.

Mauldin, John. *Bull's Eye Investing: Targeting Real Returns in a Smoke and Mirrors Market.* New York: John Wiley & Sons, Inc., 2004.

Mauldin, John. *Just One Thing: Twelve of the World's Best Investors Reveal the One Strategy You Can't Overlook.* New York: John Wiley & Sons, Inc., 2005.

Novy-Marx, Robert, and Joshua D. Rauh, 2009, "The Risks and Liabilities of State Sponsored Pension Plans," *Journal of Economic Perspectives,* 23(4): 191–210.

Novy-Marx, Robert, and Joshua D. Rauh, 2010, "Public Pension Promises: How Big Are They and What Are They Worth?," *Journal of Finance,* forthcoming.

Novy-Marx, Robert, and Joshua D. Rauh, 2010, "The Crisis in Local Government Pensions in the United States."

Rosenblum, Harvey. *Business Economics,* January 2003.

Shiller, Robert J. *Irrational Exuberance.* New York: Broadway Books, 2000.

INDEX

Note: Page numbers in *italics* indicate graphs and charts.